KUNDALINI MUSINGS

JJ SEMPLE

A Life Force Books Publication

Disclaimer: The information in this book is for educational purposes only and is not intended
as medical advice. Neither the author nor the publisher of this work will be held accountable
for any use or misuse of the information contained in this book. The author, the publisher,
and/or the distributors of this book are not responsible for any effects or consequences from
the use of any suggestions, recommendations, or procedures described hereafter.

The author made all reasonable efforts to contact all literature sources quoted in the text.

Life Force Books
PO Box 302
Bayside, CA 95524
www.lifeforcebooks.com

ISBN: 978-0-9962386-5-6

Contents

The Cosmology of Kundalini

Enlightenment

The Polemics Surrounding Kundalini

Converging Paths

Other Life Force Books Titles

Introduction

This book consists of essays written over the past seven years. Each essay has been edited and updated to reflect the latest findings across a broad spectrum of kundalini research — a wide assortment of kundalini-related topics and writings under one cover, all my 40 plus years of kundalini experience contained in this one book, that is… until my kundalini guides me to new experiences — which it will inevitably do — and I shall be compelled to write new essays, new books. The point is, kundalini doesn't stop; we're only beginning to understand it.

Even though the subject matter ranges far and wide, there's a single unifying factor — kundalini. It's my hope that the efforts I've put into experiencing these aspects of kundalini over the last half century — the knowledge and experience I've gained — will help you avoid some of the pitfalls and challenges of arousing and living with this evolutionary energy.

First Things

"In the beginner's mind there are many possibilities; in the expert's mind there are few."

~ Shunryu Suzuki Roshi

Situating Kundalini

People don't think about tax audits or natural disasters until they find themselves being audited or a mudslide heading towards their house. Many fewer people show interest in life force-kundalini energy arousal until they experience an awakening. Once awakened, they spend hours scouring the Internet for books and searching websites in an attempt to understand and validate their experience.

It's quite a predicament: being thrown into a new state of being, in many instances without warning. Sadly, available information is often contradictory, does not apply to a specific experience, or is even harmful because it's incomplete or inaccurate.

This, coupled with the tendency to attribute the awakening experience to some sort of religious or ecstatic context, may end up leading the initiate astray. This is normal; kundalini was first discovered by the ancients during religious or ceremonial practices — before science existed. It has retained its religious origins or roots and is still part of religious practices. For example, meditation — an integral part of some religions — can activate kundalini safely and permanently.

Nevertheless, more and more people now acknowledge kundalini as a science with its own physiological subsystem. Why? People now realize that kundalini is a biological process, not a belief system.

If you're a Buddhist, you can be converted to another belief system. You can change your mind and become a Christian or a Jew, for example. You cannot be converted to kundalini any more than you can be converted to an orgasm or a heart attack. They are biological processes, not cults or belief systems. You don't "believe in" the physiological channels, chakras, nadis, meridians, or energy centers known to Eastern medicine and yoga adepts. They are fact. Someday, science will acknowledge them, just as a growing number of people who've experienced kundalini now do.

"Although the intellect has been tremendously successful in dealing with the physical Creation, its dependence on sensory input has made it highly ineffectual in dealing with consciousness, which has no physical component. Although the intellect's primary tool for exploration of the phenomenal universe—mathematics—is a construct of our consciousness, its scope of operation seems to be limited to the physical realm, and cannot be applied to consciousness itself.

"If consciousness is the primary reality, and if the trend in evolution towards more complex mental faculties continues, then the next logical step in evolution would be a new faculty of perception that allows us to apprehend reality directly in its ultimate form as consciousness. The possibility of such an evolutionary leap is quite consistent with this trend, but it has not even been remotely considered by science. As far as it is concerned, the intellect is the only possible faculty of mind for the apprehension of reality. But there is no logical or scientific reason to suppose that our evolution is finished, and that no other faculties of mind will ever evolve to augment the intellect in its ability to apprehend Creation."[1]

Moreover, because it's science, kundalini is not merely about bliss states, even though a kundalini awakening often induces behavioral states, not dissimilar to religious ecstasy. I believe this is due to the fact that kundalini opens up vistas of higher consciousness that most people never experience — states that are so breathtaking and so different from "normal" consciousness that people tend to believe they've been catapulted into a kind of wonderland or Oz.

However, if you make kundalini about bliss states or ecstasy,

---

1 Bradford, Michael. *Consciousness: The New Paradigm* (pp. 13-14). Institute for Consciousness Research. Kindle Edition.

you're missing the point. Even if you're able to hover five feet off the ground, you're still missing the point: you won't be able to live the rest of your life in a blissful state. Bliss states are a kind of escape. At some point, you'll have to start relating to the physical world. This is not to diminish your experience, only to put it into perspective. I've lived with kundalini now for over forty years. I've weathered its vicissitudes.

What Exactly is Kundalini

Kundalini is the formative, biological life force energy in your body. In its creative state, it's known as *Kundalini Shakti* — creative in the sense that it shapes your very substance in the womb. After birth, it works in the background as *Prana Shakti*, the maintenance form of kundalini. And unless it reactivates involuntarily or you reactivate it intentionally through the practice of a reliable method like Golden Flower Meditation (GFM), it remains in the background throughout your life. Think of it as a racing car that's idling; the motor's turning, but it's not going anywhere. It manages your body's autonomic functions: cell division, breathing, blood flow, digestion — without you're being aware of it or appreciating it. Like a computer routine that works in the background, it's there. If it stopped working altogether, you'd be dead.

Contrary to conventional wisdom, kundalini is never dormant, never completely inactive. It's either in a maintenance state (*Prana Shakti*) or a creative state (*Kundalini Shakti*) during your lifetime:

- During gestation, it's *Kundalini Shakti*, the creative force, responsible for your incarnation,
- During so-called "normal" life, it's *Prana Shakti*, maintaining your autonomic functions, until,
- Upon reactivating, it takes over once again as *Kundalini Shakti*, the super-conscious creative life force.

Most people don't realize that kundalini resides within them; they are simply unaware of its actuality and its potential. Which means, of course, that they may never "re-activate" it either spontaneously or otherwise, not unless they learn how to induce a Kundalini awakening through meditation practice. Even then, the outcome is never certain. There's a quantum or karmic aspect to the process.

At birth, Kundalini sort of hibernates. Why? Because the wonders of the material world ignite our senses and we start to process and explore its delights. We let the thrall of the material world take over our thoughts and emotions. We become Ego driven, seeking mastery over all. Only the spiritually motivated become curious about the metaphysical aspects of Creation. Only a few seek to discover their hibernating birthright — *Kundalini Shakti*. And it's a shame, because...

We are all perfect at the split-second moment before conception, a magic, quantum moment when consciousness becomes flesh, a process the Bible expresses thusly: *And the Word became flesh*. Of course at that moment, like a building before the foundation is laid, our beings are only blueprints, i.e., *the Word*. These blueprints — the numinous plans for our incarnation — are perfect. At the moment of conception — the moment the egg is fertilized by the sperm — the body begins to take shape, i.e., *becomes flesh*.

It's the moment when, were you able to stand over your perfectly drawn blueprint, you'd wonder if it will be executed faithfully. That's the job of *Kundalini Shakti*, the creative agent responsible for not only providing the raw energy for your incarnation — not a simple task when you think about it — but also for creating the blueprint, the master plan for your embodiment and your ultimate Being.

Until the moment of birth, *Kundalini Shakti* controls your growth. The moment you are born, you become conscious and kundalini — your natural life force — hibernates. Heredity, environment, and those aspects unique to your DNA take over the direction of your life and the formation of your physical body while in the background, *Prana Shakti* manages your body's day-to-day, minute-by-minute maintenance functions.

Nevertheless, even though *Kundalini Shakti* toils away in the background, it's waiting for you to activate it. A popular explanation, really a misconception, says that if kundalini is not awakened, it is dormant, completely inactive. If that were true, we'd have stopped evolving. Kundalini has a maintenance state, *Prana Shakti*, which is always functioning. It's actively at work on you now, maintaining your autonomic functions. The life force has two aspects: *Prana Shakti* maintains your basic functions such as blood flow, digestion, and breathing. *Kundalini Shakti* creates and ultimately changes your Being.

Once reawakened in a later life, *Kundalini Shakti* starts to effect changes to your nervous system, somatic structure, your metabolism, your genetic profile, and sometimes to your anatomy. It doesn't stop there. Some changes occur gradually — deep psychological, cognitive, emotional changes, for example, take years to assimilate. Abilities and talents surface on their own; suddenly you're speaking a foreign language, playing an instrument, or manipulating large numbers in your head.

As kundalini opens the metaphysical breadth of human cosmology and consciousness, you feel the urge to describe your experience to friends, family, and even to strangers. I've spoken with many individuals who do this. What they're not aware of — especially in the first rush of kundalini ecstasy — is that their descriptions are usually incoherent. This is normal; everyday language is rarely up to the task of describing the phenomenon. In these instances, however, not only does the individual lose credibility, the whole topic of kundalini attracts scorn, skepticism, and ridicule. Kundalini doesn't need this; there are enough outsiders who already doubt its actuality.

The metamorphosis kundalini imposes — whether immediate or gradual — can be difficult to accept and integrate into your life, making you easy prey to impulse, instability, or inertia. What kind of effects am I talking about?

• Be prepared for an across-the-board increase in sensitivity. A kundalini awakening accentuates the senses: smell, taste, hearing, touch, and even sight. It's very possible that loud noises, noxious odors, bright lights, and other sensory activity will do more than annoy you and you may become agitated to the point of wanting to renounce kundalini altogether. This is the nervous system adjusting to the additional energy kundalini introduces into your system. You may not be able to support waiting, much less any of the above, including electromagnetic energy. I once had to leave a factory because of the noxious electromagnetic energy I felt. Another time, I had to jump out a friend's car to escape a traffic jam and its hovering carbon monoxide fumes. Over time the nervous system adjusts. Nevertheless, there are instances when your body may become overwhelmed with too much energy to the point of discomfort and even pain. This is an acknowledged side effect. At the moment, I don't know any way of mitigating it.

- Amplified emotions, such as anger and fear, may sweep over you in the beginning.
- Involuntary movements are also a product of kundalini. Observing these occurrences without panicking is the best way of dealing with involuntary movements. Stressed emotional states are more difficult to manage. I advise mindfulness training.
- Many people feel the urge to "do good," not just volunteer for all sorts of spiritual missions and duties, but to do good on a monumental scale. This is unrealistic, not only because it's too much, too early, but also because you're not really suited for this type of work. Don't let something you've never done become an all-consuming crusade. Better to work on adjusting to kundalini energy and then, after waiting five years or so, see if you still feel motivated.
- Undergoing a change of being. This is difficult to grasp before kundalini awakens. I do however address the topic in later chapters.
- So what's an initiate to do? Do not resist kundalini energy. It is benign and intelligent. It knows what to do; it has a plan. There are modifying circumstances, for example:
  - How your experience was triggered;
  - Physiological, psychological blockages. It may take time to clear a blockage, so have patience;
  - Karma.

- Quell the desire to understand everything immediately. Kundalini, though everything seems to happen all at once, actually works gradually. It takes years for the full effects to be made manifest
- Be scientific. If you can't talk about it coherently, don't talk at all. Document everything that happens in writing. Writing, if you take it seriously, demands practice and coherence. You owe it to kundalini to be coherent.
- Resist the impulse to join groups, especially belief system-based cults run by self-styled authorities.
- Listen more; talk less. On the one hand, people with no spiritual inclinations will not be receptive to the accounts of your experience. On the other, self-styled experts on spiritual matters — evangelists for other practices/doctrines — will also be hostile to any discussion you may initiate.
- Develop situational awareness.
- Be mindful. Observe your reactions when you get carried away. Step back from the fray. Emotional control is the secret to success for life on earth.
- Talk to people who've lived with kundalini for many years; the more the better.
- Verify everything you see, hear, or feel.
- Watch out for people who try to limit kundalini to a given belief system, cult, or method, people who tell you there's only one way of experiencing it. Kundalini has no boundaries — national, religious, geographic, educational, social, language, or cultural.

Two types of people will mislead you. Be wary of:

- A supernumerary appointed by a well-heeled cult or religion bent on attacking those outside their own belief system, especially individuals who dare to go it alone or who dare to point out empirical fallacies in conventional wisdom.
- A self-appointed arbiter of doctrinal purity who takes it upon himself to pepper you with generalizations, launch ad hominem attacks, and denigrate your experience or your method without knowing anything about it.

These people refuse to face the fact that every kundalini experience is different, has its own specific triggers and effects.

When I encounter doubters, they often base their disapproving remarks on second-hand information. Under questioning they admit they know nothing about kundalini and have never experienced an awakening. It's as if the biological aspect of kundalini poses a threat to their conventional belief systems, which is absurd. Why should an evolutionary mechanism such as kundalini threaten anyone?

Neuroplasticity and Kundalini

When I was seven-years old, I suffered an accident; a long splinter became lodged in my foot, shutting down vital growth energy to various parts of my body. This accident changed me, physically. I imploded. Literally. For reasons known only to that seven-year-old boy, I hid its presence from everyone. I was taken to Doctor's Hospital in NYC, given penicillin and blood. I drifted into a coma-like state for three months. Then when the wound healed over, I was shipped off to Florida to live with my father. After a while the doctor there noticed the splinter starting to work its way to the surface and he removed it.

I had been a child prodigy in math and an excellent singer, the soloist in the choir. When I started school the next year, I noticed that my abilities at math and singing had vanished. I had also been an excellent tennis player. No longer. All my talents had disappeared. No one around me connected the loss of my talents with the accident. They told me the loss was due to the school time I'd missed by being in the hospital. Because they sloughed it off, I let it slide. I was only seven, so I buried it away in the lower depths of my consciousness. Twenty something, I began to wonder why I had limitations others didn't have, why there was nothing I excelled at, because in the past I knew I had excelled at math and music. Poof! My talents had evaporated. I didn't know where to find the answer, but some impulse kept me trying to find a way to transform myself back into the person I once was and pushed me to transcend the self-destructive, negative person I had become.

When I was thirty, I started meditating using the method in

The Secret of the Golden Flower. At first, I was restless; I didn't seem to be "getting it" or getting anywhere. Nevertheless, I continued to practice. About 100 days in, I noticed a sensation at the base of the spine that felt like the cracking of a small egg and the spilling out of its contents, which began to climb my spine. In one month it reached the top of my head and energy poured into my brain, lit it up. I could see inside my brain, see the third eye, taste the sweet elixir it sprayed on parts of the brain, which, once it touched a certain region of my brain had an immediate effect on a corresponding part of my body.

One particular part of the process involved the opening up of the solar plexus and the release of a forcefield of energy that shot out from the solar plexus in an arced trajectory to the third eye, which opened like a castanet to receive this energy. Once received, the third eye sprayed this energy on various sections of my brain, energizing and revitalizing various parts and organs.

Thanks to my accident I discovered why my being had changed. This accident turned out to be a kind of neuroplasticity experiment in reverse, in that a part of my brain actually deteriorated due to the lack of normal growth energy, a direct effect of my accident. How is this possible? The splinter shut down a vital nexus in my nervous system, denying growth energy to that whole synaptic neural circuit. You see, each part of the body is governed by a specific area of the brain. If either the part of the brain or its corresponding body part is damaged, the related part also suffers. The answer lies in the way the two are connected. How are they connected? By the nervous system. That's right, when one node — the brain or the limb it governs — is damaged, the other atrophies either because it's deprived of vital growth energy or it no longer has any work to do. In the case of brain damage, it is no longer able to govern the related body part because the neurons themselves are damaged. In the case of a damaged limb, the brain simply shuts down that part of itself because it no longer has to use the particular neurons to control a limb that no longer functions.

What's more, damage to a part of the brain affects size and shape of overall gray and white matter, and consequently affects the shape of the head and the symmetry of the entire body. Normally, human growth is accomplished in a relatively linear pattern. In my case, because the splinter affected my development, my growth started to deteriorate quite rapidly, shown by the curve in the following graph:

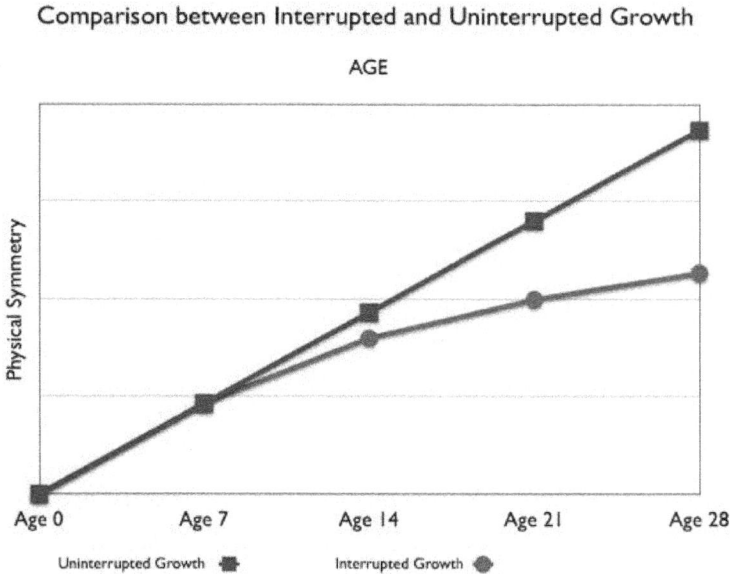

Comparison between Interrupted and Uninterrupted Growth

AGE

Physical Symmetry

Age 0   Age 7   Age 14   Age 21   Age 28

Uninterrupted Growth   Interrupted Growth

My brain developed asymmetrically, which affected the size, shape, and symmetry of my head, which changed my bodily symmetry, which also affected my behavior, sexual prowess, self-image, personality, and outlook. *Deciphering the Golden Flower One Secret at a Time* chronicles how I started to regain my symmetry at the age of 35, and how regaining it altered my abilities and personality once again:

Comparison between Interrupted and Uninterrupted Growth

AGE

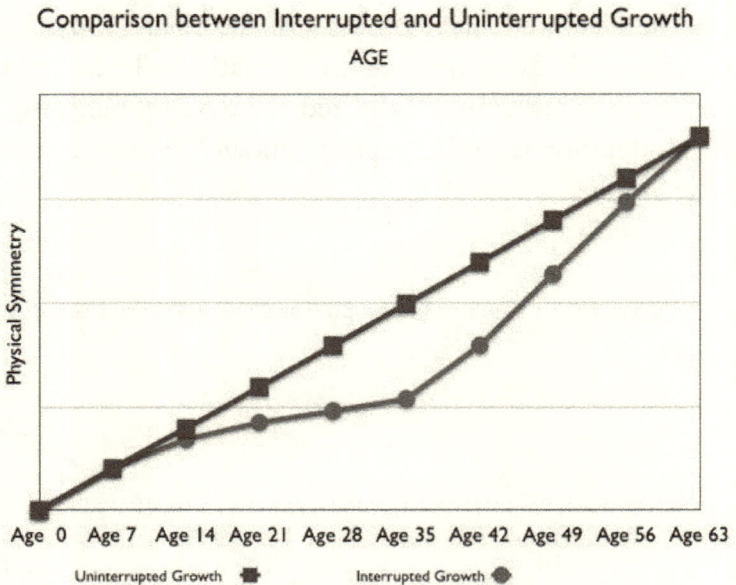

Age 0 Age 7 Age 14 Age 21 Age 28 Age 35 Age 42 Age 49 Age 56 Age 63

Uninterrupted Growth ■   Interrupted Growth ●

According to neuroplasticity theory, it is possible to transfer control of a limb to another part of the brain. But, if that occurred in my case, it wasn't enough. The conductor of vital growth energy to both the body and the brain is our central nervous system. This network — the conduits that contain the nerve fibers — can also be damaged and interrupt the process. How do I know this? Because I proved it in the laboratory of the body. My own body. I had to find a way to revitalize the affected body parts. Of course, after my accident I didn't think about regenerating brain cells or neuroplasticity. I was too busy stumbling through life with a damaged, deformed body. In fact, I stumbled for many years. I looked in all the wrong places. *Deciphering the Golden Flower One Secret at a Time* is a testament to my follies. It is also a testament to overcoming the obstacles to self-realization.

Eventually, I found a system that revitalized my brain from the inside-out: a kundalini meditation system for triggering the autonomic self-healing and restorative mechanisms of the body. For 40 years, I have practiced the method in that masterpiece of Chinese alchemy, *The Secret of the Golden Flower*, the book many adepts now recognize is not unlike the Buddha's own meditation system.

Kundalini energy is responsible for slowly reshaping my head and body to their original symmetrical proportions. If this is true, when were these plans conceived? Where did the plans/blueprints for my embodiment reside from the age of seven (my accident) to thirty (activated kundalini)? In some ethereal computer memory-like storage? In some inaccessible partition of DNA? In some metaphysical compartment associated with my being? In the metaphysical Akashic records? I am not alone in examining this:

> "This control and guidance is also evident in the experiments done with developing animal embryos in which the removal or substitution of tissue, if done at an early enough stage, does not result in a totally deformed final form but rather in a smaller or modified, but still complete form. If the process of development were strictly a mechanical one, this would certainly not be the result. One logical explanation for this phenomenon is the existence of a controlling field, such as the Pranic spectrum, which has a predetermined form towards which it is guiding the development of the organism via the growth processes."
>
> ~ Institute for Consciousness Research – Michael Bradford

The word incarnation means "the act of being made flesh," as in the biblical expression, "The Word became flesh." Same goes for the words *embodiment* and *substantiation*, they mean the same thing: the act of being made flesh. Take it a step further and you begin to realize that the incarnation process, the taking on of a bodily form, must include working from some sort of plan.

Shouldn't science explore this, wonder if plans for our incarnation really do exist? And if so, how these plans remain associated with us? At what moment they come into existence? Do they play a part in healing deformation or illness? Can an active kundalini access these blueprints and then use the nervous system to convey healing energy to affected areas? Does this work continue until completed? Do our bodies hold extraordinary energies, little known, little appreciated by science? Do the millions of anecdotal accounts like mine carry weight even though scientific methods cannot verify them at this time? Can permanent kundalini stave off the effects of neurological degeneration better than cognitive drills (Lumosity-type exercises) or affective therapies? Is it true that Lumosity type, "cognitive exercise" companies — and there are many of them — are only for profit? Is it true that kundalini meditation — safely and reliably undertaken — is free of charge, requiring only commitment and diligence to practice it.

If kundalini unlocks concealed DNA information, isn't it reasonable to assume it is able to use this information to recondition the physical, cognitive, and emotional properties of our bodies over time?

Kundalini Changes Your Perspective

"The truly wise know they can teach themselves for what you speak of is within and requires no teacher, just use of the heart to feel and the mind to observe."

~ Ginga Paul Gladman

Day One

Day One is the day you begin your spiritual search. For some it's a literal Day One accompanied by fireworks and drumrolls; for others, it's a gradual process, not marked by a special happening. It's whatever sets you on your pilgrimage of self-discovery.

In my case, although I didn't plan it that way, sometime around 1965 I found myself on a solitary path, gradually intensifying my efforts as serendipitous happenstance propelled me forward and narrowed down the search for me.

I was in my mid-twenties then. Within seven years I would upend my mostly conventional life, and undergo a complete metamorphosis, culminating in a permanent kundalini awakening. It's been over 40 years since that day. Now approaching my 81st year, I believe it's fitting to expand on my experience at the same time I try to make sense of the effects kundalini has visited on me over the decades.

With Farad, my guide, at Dal Lake, Kashmir (1977)

I didn't plan to go it alone, but after sampling a few practices, I found I had an extrasensory knack of knowing whether a method or path was suitable or not for my particular condition at the time. Not knowing much to begin with, I learned to feel my way as I got more and more into the process. On-the-job learning was at once, difficult and easy. Difficult, in that there wasn't much information in the late 1960s — certainly no Google or Internet. Easy, because there was so little information I was able to proceed without getting caught up in the hype surrounding the flavor-of-the-month cult. There was something in the core of my being that was antithetical to my becoming a follower. I knew I didn't know anything, but by finding my own way, I was more likely to retain what I'd learned and be certain that it had worked for me.

Was there really one specific day when it all started? Or did a series of events get me looking?

I remember lying in bed at a young age, ruminating about life. Do most five-year olds think about the purpose of life, I wondered? Whatever other five year olds were dreaming about was surely colored by their circumstances; mine were sufficiently agreeable. I had lots of time to ponder the unknowns. And yet, there were various touchstones:

- My father — his spiritual investigation with Bill W. and Alcoholics Anonymous influenced me. He had a large collection of books on spiritual subjects. Got me wondering about other things besides baseball and girls.
- Intuition — that life had a greater purpose.
- Feelings — that I had lost some of the abilities I'd had at a younger age.

George Washington Hospital appendix removal — given morphine for two nights after the operation, I'd floated to the ceiling of my room, turned around and looked at my physical body in the bed below. This out-of-body experience got me thinking there must be something else.

In Pursuit Of Self-Realization - Then and Now

In olden days, spiritual pursuit was more of a trial-by-fire that required proving yourself before being admitted to the ultimate truths, as per the following example:

"Knowing that his revenge was wrong, Milarepa (then known by his boyhood name 'Fortuitous') set out to find a lama and was led to Marpa the Translator. Marpa proved a hard taskmaster. Before

Marpa would teach Milarepa (c. 1052 – c. 1135 CE) he had him build and then demolish three towers in turn. Milarepa was asked to build one final multi-story tower by Marpa at Lhodrag: this 11th century tower still stands. When Marpa still refused to teach Milarepa, he went to Marpa's wife, who took pity on him. She forged a letter of introduction to another teacher, Lama Ngogdun Chudor, under whose tutelage he practiced meditation. However, as he was making no progress, he confessed the forgery and Ngogdun Chudor said that it was vain to hope for spiritual growth without the guru Marpa's approval.

"Milarepa returned to Marpa, and was finally shown the spiritual teachings. Milarepa then left on his own, and after protracted diligence for 12 years he attained the state of Vajradhara (complete enlightenment). He then became known as Milarepa. 'Mila' is Tibetan for; 'great man', and 'repa' means; 'cotton clad one.' At the age of 45, he started to practice at Drakar Taso (White Rock Horse Tooth) cave — "Milarepa's Cave," as well as becoming a wandering teacher. Here, he subsisted on nettle tea, leading his skin to turn green with a waxy covering, hence the greenish color he is often depicted as having, in paintings and sculpture."

Marpa said to Milarepa, 'I was very hard on you, but do not be distressed. Be patient. Teaching is very slow work. You have the energy to work, so build a tower of Sutra. When you have done that, I will instruct you and I will supply your food and clothing.'"

~ *The Magic Life of Milarepa*

Contemporary seekers of enlightenment, truth, self-realization would chuckle at the prospect of building and tearing down towers and would quickly move on to the nearest strip mall offering kundalini yoga, a tee shirt, a yoga mat at a 10% discount. Not so in yesteryear.

Western civilization is not cut out for "slow work". We want answers, shortcuts, formulae, handholding, and all manner of emotional sustenance — especially the "high-maintenance" among us. After all, compared to the life of an eleventh century Tibetan monk, all modern Americans are fairly high maintenance.

Back then, the student stayed with the teacher/guide/guru 24-7, living in his house or boarding with a group of like-minded seekers — however long it took. Today, it's fitting in an hour of Tai Chi here and there, then back to the rat race.

So what kind of effect does the difference between the two paradigms have on the initiate?

Whether it's a weekend workshop or a Thursday night yoga class, there's an immediate dissipation once the practitioner is back on the street, in the subway or on a bus, a dissolution of energy. The student begins to question the process: "After all, what's the point? I won't be able to go next week because my daughter has a recital."

Motivation is eroded. It's normal. There are a lot of demands in modern life, and so little training in school on how to manage it. We might look around, pick a role model and follow it, but this is often hit or miss. So we end up wondering: "I sit, I meditate, but nothing happens. How did I ever get involved with this stuff? Where does it all lead? How can it solve my problems?"

And instead of being in the now, we let our minds bask on past glories, such as they were, often sugar coating memories, turning them into triumphs, as these two popular songs attest to:

"Yesterday, all my troubles seemed so far away.
Now it looks as though they're here to stay.
Oh, I believe in yesterday."
~ *Yesterday* – The Beatles (1965)

"Yesterdays
Days I knew as happy sweet
Sequestered days
Olden days
Golden days
Days of mad romance and love
Then gay youth was mine
And truth was mine
Joyous free and flaming life
Forsooth was mine

Sad am I
Glad am I
For today I'm dreaming of
Of yesterdays"
~ *Yesterdays* – Jerome Kern (1933)

Without the harsh discipline imposed by the teachers of yore, our minds are bombarded with doubts and longings; we can't stay focused on the present. No towers to build and tear down, no sure source to turn to for advice. And yet the towers are still there, in other forms: bills to pay, dishes to wash, jobs to go to, meals to cook, beds to make, dogs to walk, intimate conversations to have. These are our towers. All we have to do is recognize them and change the ways we think about the various intrusions in our personal space and daily lives.

Once we're able to change perspective, the task is no longer drudgery but an exercise in mindfulness. And once mindful, our deep breathing kicks in to lower stress, making us even more mindful, and we whisk through menial tasks joyfully.

Mindful, we no longer waste time questioning things that must be done and we see our daily life as an extension of the weekend workshop or the Thursday yoga class. The paradigm is turned around; the restlessness vanishes. It begins to make sense: that it's not so much about teaching as it is about learning to remember yourself.

I Find Kundalini
Or did It find me?

Like many seeking knowledge, I started as a novice, looking for something that didn't exist in the material world. Religion hadn't worked for me. Neither had higher education, nor specializations such as law, medicine, or business. I wanted to take an active part in my development, to probe for truth beyond the confines of my narrow world. I wanted to be the creator of my own Being.

Bailing Hay – Normandy, France (1980)

As far as career paths go, I felt that everyone around me had already figured things out. All they had to do was learn the ropes, keep their mouths shut, and the doors of riches and success were open to them. I wanted something else, something that would allow me to figure out who I was. At the time, I didn't know much about spirituality. I wasn't attracted to it, per se. In fact, the first self-realization technique I came across was self-hypnosis.

As a result of inducing altered states through hypnosis, I sensed there were other forms of consciousness. I picked up a few books, listened in on a few conversations about yoga and meditation. Pretty soon I found myself on the spiritual bandwagon — yoga magazines and studios, spiritual bookstores, so-called highly evolved friends, etc. I began to investigate the concepts and employ the vocabulary. Initially I was a dabbler, I practiced hatha and kundalini yoga off and on, but something pushed me toward a deeper exploration.

I advanced from dabbler to practitioner. A few months into my meditation practice something unexpected happened. I started getting feedback from my body.

I could feel energy buildups, energy looking for somewhere to go, but finding no direction. I felt that my body was changing. Profound psychological and cognitive changes occurred as well, but the bulk of the transformations occurred in my physical body. Moreover, once the transformations began, my body took over on its own. How does a body take over and effectively transform itself? Very simply, I had aroused a power within myself known as kundalini, our natural life force, the power that shapes our bodies in the womb. I began to think yoga and meditation were merely means of physical restoration. Little did I know that the Golden Flower Meditation I was practicing would lead me to metaphysical discoveries.

If it wasn't for a childhood injury that deformed me. I might never have discovered the amazing transformative power of kundalini. The extraordinary factor in my case was that my injury occurred when I was very young, so young I actually suppressed all memory of the accident that caused my injury.

Years later, when I was thirty-four, a stranger handed me a book entitled *The Secret of the Golden Flower*. It was a serendipitous moment, the beginning of my recovery process. I didn't realize it at the time. In fact, I put the book away for over a year. Sometime later however, I picked it up and began practicing the method of meditation in the text. At first I thought I was wasting my time.

The method in *The Secret of the Golden Flower* was for real. Not only was it for real, this ancient method turned out to be the safest and most complete kundalini method I've come across in my forty years of practice and research. Why? Because it advocates using the backward-flowing method.

Upon awakening, kundalini recognized my deformity and immediately began to restore my body to its original state, a pristine state of perfect symmetry that existed before my accident. If that hadn't happened, my focus on kundalini — like the focus of so many others — would probably have centered only on consciousness. As it was, I realized the practical healing benefits of kundalini are as important and as wondrous as the metanormal effects that occur later on.

The fact that my childhood injury allowed me to discover the amazing transformative power of kundalini has led me to frame kundalini in entirely different terms from many other practitioners and researchers. I believe that the most important aspect of kundalini — aside from its amazing curative power — is that kundalini is actually an ancient scientific tradition, one that might be called Life Force Science. I didn't get this from reading books like Wholeness and the Implicate Order or Mysticism and the New Physics, books written by scientists who, for one reason or another, hit a dead end in their interpretation of the universe, thus turning to mystical explanations. I came to a realization that kundalini was a key to exploring a new science — the science of consciousness. The act of raising my kundalini turned my body into a laboratory — one whose processes I could observe and document in a scientific manner. A process for others to explore...the same way I've explored it.

First, I observed that the diaphragmatic deep breathing I practiced created an energy buildup in my lower belly. I realized this was Prana, the life force energy, and it had a purpose. During meditation, I was able to slow down my heart rate, which seemed to create a vortex of all-encompassing consciousness with my puny being at the center. I noticed this energy in the belly had the property of direction and, if it had direction, I realized I might be able to guide it. But how and where? The words "backward-flowing method" came to mind. Quickly, I looked up the term in *The Secret of the Golden Flower*. And there it was — almost taunting me to order the energy to change direction. Which I did — the rest is kundalini lore, experiences, and wonders so many others have

shared. The energy:
- Worked its way up my spine to the brain,
- Opened the chakras along the way,
- Re-engineered my body,
- Plunged me into the energy continuum.

All of which should not be thought of as only metaphysical phenomena, but should be treated as scientific actualities, albeit ones the science of today has not yet discovered. Gopi Krishna knew that kundalini was science; he wrote about it eloquently in his many books. Kundalini is part of the science of consciousness, just as the heart attack is part of medical science or the orgasm is part of reproductive science and biology.

Not only did I learn about the self-healing potential of kundalini, I realized the method I used to arouse my kundalini was more related to science than to mysticism, religion, or spirituality. Why? Because Golden Flower Meditation (GFM) is capable of producing results with the consistency and predictability of a scientific experiment. So even though I started out as a spiritual seeker, I have become a Life Force Scientist. And as I scientist, I suggest researching all aspects of kundalini awakening, from documenting the most reliable methods of activating it to examining the metanormal effects it induces. What is the best way of documenting kundalini experiences? Tried and tested peer reviews!

The reason I pursue this is because I have firsthand observational experience of metaphysical activity in my own body, along with millions of others. Trouble is, even though our experiences are very similar, and occur irrespective of culture, language, geography, or physical characteristics, without any intimate contact between subjects, material scientists still label these experiences as anecdotal. But every scientific breakthrough starts out as a hypothesis, based on some combination of intuition and anecdote. The reason that biology is important is that, unlike divine inspiration, which must be seen as God randomly choosing candidates for inspiration, kundalini, induced by the body's biological triggers, becomes an evolutionary mutation capable of modifying DNA within the span of a single lifetime and, even more important, an evolutionary improvement capable of being passed through DNA to future generations.

The Secret of the Golden Flower - Revisited

For over 40 years, I've practiced Golden Flower Meditation (GFM), the method in *The Secret of the Golden Flower* (SGF) that many adepts recognize as derived from the Buddha's own meditation system. When I first started, I had no idea it was a manual for activating kundalini.

Perhaps it was because the Wilhelm translation of the SGF has a poetic quality that inhibits unambiguous execution of the meditation techniques embedded in the text. Metaphor rather than easy-to-follow, step-by-step explanation is the norm. A modern How-To it is not. The text often sidesteps the underlying process, hints at it, describes the end result in lyrical prose, meandering into discussion of ontological terms, all of which leaves you wondering if you are doing it correctly. Some terms overlap in meaning; some techniques are referred to by more than one term. Only by obstinate practice are the techniques understandable.

Nevertheless, I kept at it. I'm not sure why. Part intuition, I suppose. Part distrust of mass movements: I was turned off by Scientology and similar movements that herded initiates toward obedience as dictated by a single leader. Buddha and Milarepa had done it on their own. Why couldn't I?

Life in 1970 — when I started — was quite different from today. No Internet, not many books on yoga or meditation. It took me over a year to understand the method and practice it in a systematic manner. The one thing that kept me motivated was that, once I caught onto the breathing techniques, I began to detect sensations of energy stirring and flowing throughout my body.

I became a skilled observer, applying techniques in a manner best suited to my particular morphology and anatomy. I created a step-by-step order for my practice, which turned out to be important because it's not possible to jump over or skip a step; each one has to be mastered before moving on to the next one.

I stress the point about becoming a skilled observer as much as I stress learning to meditate on your own. Groupthink rarely gets it done; you can only learn so much from others. The real work is done in the laboratory of your own body. You must become your own best "spiritual" detective.

'Smart' and 'Stupid' are perhaps too severe, too divisive. I only use the image to underline one reason so many people get sidetracked — they join groups/movements/cults without due diligence. They turn their power over to persons not fit to wield it, much less propose a path to self-realization.

Better words than 'Smart' for helping an individual find the right path are: single-minded, committed, unswerving, unwavering, resolute, purposeful, dedicated, uncompromising, tireless, tenacious, persistent, indefatigable, dogged, relentless.

Better words than 'Stupid' that apply to indiscriminate joiners of groups are: tractable, pliable, acquiescent, yielding, complaisant, acquiescent, easily influenced, persuadable, pliable, responsive, susceptible. For example... Milarepa (a person that could not be deterred) as opposed to Jonestown (people who let themselves be influenced to the point of a meaningless death).

We can't all have vision and perspicuity. I'm not sure I do, but you can still ask questions. And if you seek enlightenment, it's your duty to question everything you see, hear, or feel. Before you join something, try the solitary path. See if you're not up to finding your own way. Become single-minded and relentless.

Golden Flower Meditation

GFM has entirely reengineered my nervous system, body, and brain. The method is composed of three techniques, each of which must be mastered in turn before beginning the next:
- Diaphragmatic Deep Breathing (DDB)
- Control of Heart Rate
- The Backward-Flowing Method (BFM)

The Backward-Flowing Method

It's a system that Gopi Krishna, the 20th century's great elucidator of kundalini, described as "containing unmistakable hints about the sublimation process."

He's referring, of course, to sexual sublimation, a process that uses distilled sexual energy to wake up the nervous system, revitalize the brain and the body, and ultimately arouse kundalini. Although sublimation sounds mystical, it's an actual biological process, entailing the diversion of sexual energy to the brain. Instead of flowing out, as it does during normal sexual intercourse, the seminal fluid, or cervical fluid in a woman, is diverted to the brain in a distilled form known as Prana, which is the key to enhanced neuroplastic activity in the brain.

"There is no doubt that there is nothing in the world so enchanting, so alluring, so inspiring as sexual love. It has inspired some of the greatest thinkers. It is the women whom they loved who inspired some of the greatest writers, thinkers, politicians, conquerors of the world. There is nothing comparable to love for the happiness, health and evolution of humanity. But it has not to be abused, as this energy is designed by Nature both for evolution and procreation. And evolution must have its share. It would be saner to conserve the energy, even to be a celibate, than it would be to overspend it. This is the reason why celibacy has been recommended in religions. Otherwise there is no reason. Why should religion in some way insist that you have to be celibate unless the energy is used in some way? But we need not go to those extremes. The rational, normal and natural course is to adjust our life so that we allow that part, which is meant for our evolution, to go for our evolution, to be used for our evolution.

"There are some facts that Nature also is always giving us warnings. Many people, after the climax, after the expenditure of the energy, feel a sense of disgust or coldness, or antipathy, or great tiredness. That is a warning from Nature that you have overdone it. After the sexual climax, [a person] should feel as energetic as before. That means that [s]he has not used from the amount that is needed for evolution."[2]

Sexual sublimation is the physiological driver in activating kundalini in whatever form it takes. I say this because the kundalini experience takes many forms, probably because the sublimation process takes so many forms. Hidden channels can open in dissimilar ways, triggering an upward flow of distilled sexual energy that varies according to individual's metabolism and soma. Here's a first-hand account of my observations during awakening:

"For a week I observe my breath circulate in the opposite direction

2   "Gopi Krishna Talks about Sex and Love" – Gopi Krishna, http://www.koausa.org/Kundalini/sex.html

without noticing any effect. The mind goes on autopilot and I go back to my uninspired routine: walking, cooking, meditating. Then, two weeks later, about the length of time it takes the backward-flowing process to become permanent, there's something new. On the day in question, I feel a sensation at the base of my spine like the cracking of a small egg and the spilling out of its contents. For the next month, I observe the fluid-like contents of the egg trickle out of its reservoir and slowly begin to climb my spine. What is this fluid? I can't describe it exactly. It seems to emanate from the base of the spine and press upward. Each time I sit to meditate, it has risen a half an inch higher."

~ *Deciphering the Golden Flower One Secret at a Time*, JJ Semple, Life Force Books, 2007

It took about three months for this process to complete. I never felt sexual arousal; I felt a benign hydraulic sensation, as if a liquid was slowly climbing up my back. Contrast my experience, which could be described as "verging on the machine-like," with Dale Pond's account:

"With that, my eyes rolled upwards and began to flutter and I became very sexually aroused but there were no thoughts of sex involved. I began to feel a rising sensation from my genital area and as the sensation neared my heart, it began to beat incredibly fast. I thought if it beat any faster it would leave my body. Then it was as if my mind was being pulled into the tiniest black hole and all of a sudden with a burst it was as if I had expanded and entered the universe. I felt as if I were one of the stars. They were everywhere glittering beside me and then I saw the moon in all its brilliance hovering in the distance. However, not having the discipline that is needed to stay with this experience, my attention went to the sexual feelings below and I felt what was once the rising sensation, begin to descend downward where it had originated. I then opened my eyes and everything was vibrating in and around me. I closed my eyes again and the experience started all over. When it was finished or should I say when I was exhausted, I opened my eyes to find my body in a state of vibration. I just sat there for a moment full of awe and wonder at what had just taken place in my interior."

Meditating is easy for some, but not for others. It took me a long time to get comfortable with the process, to learn the posture and to concentrate. I was alternately bored and restless, fidgety and impatient, sleepy and indolent. Sitting in the lotus position, my mind used the time to review the events, impulses, and relationships in my life. I was powerless to stop this inner dialogue, to clear my mind of chatter. I knew it could be done; others had written about it. To succeed in meditation, it had to be done; all the teachings said so.

> "Nor must a man be led astray by the ten thousand ensnarements.
> This happens if, after the quiet state has begun, one after another,
> all sorts of ties suddenly appear. One wants to break through
> them and cannot; one follows them, and feels as if relieved by
> this. This means the master has become the servant. If a man
> tarries in this stage long he enters world of illusory desires."[3]

I dropped everything and concentrated on meditation in the hope it would improve my breathing, allowing me to become a better musician. However, sitting in the lotus position, I couldn't get the breathing right. One day while walking, I decided to sync my breathing to each step, counting my breath over a series of strides. Exhale four counts, hold four counts, inhale four counts, hold four counts. Start over. I practiced a lot, walking great distances until my breathing became regular. The process of counting obscured the chatter, and it gradually disappeared. Eventually, I stopped counting; my mind had emptied. I returned to sitting meditation, which then kicked into high gear. It had taken me over a year to get my mind under control, but once I was able to, the meditation advanced quickly.

As a result, my kundalini activated at the age of thirty-five. Energy I didn't know existed started flowing through the neural channels of my body. I could feel and observe it. It took about three

3   *The Secret of the Golden Flower* – Routledge & Kegan
    Paul, Wilhelm Translation, 1931, p. 46.

months for this process to complete.

> "When one begins to carry out one's decision, care must be taken so that everything can proceed in a comfortable, relaxed manner. Too much must not be demanded of the heart. One must be careful that, quite automatically, heart and energy are coordinated. Only then can a state of quietness be attained. During this quiet state the right conditions and the right space must be provided. One must not sit down [to meditate] in the midst of frivolous affairs. That is to say, the mind must be free of vain preoccupations. All entanglements must be put aside; one must be detached and independent. Nor must the thoughts be concentrated upon the right procedure. This danger arises if too much trouble is taken. I do not mean that no trouble is to be taken, but the correct way lies in keeping equal distance between being and not being. If one can attain purposelessness through purpose, then the thing has been grasped. Now one can let oneself go, detached and without confusion, in an independent way."[4]

After awakening kundalini, I was able to visualize my body as a real time, transparent, 3-D model, much like a life-size version of a child's human anatomy toy model. I could see the defective parts; they lit up and vibrated at a different frequency. I could see how certain parts my body had torqued as a result of their being denied vital life force growth energy. I could see how the physical work of meditation and yoga had given birth to the metaphysical phenomena I was now witnessing. How do I know this to be true? I know it firsthand; it happened to me. I felt and observed the energy rising along my spine, felt and observed it entering my brain. But don't take my word alone. Test it in the laboratory of your body.

Almost immediately, I realized that this Pranic, super-conscious energy was the Primal Spirit (another label for kundalini), a term I'd come across many times in *The Secret of the Golden Flower* without really understanding what it meant. According to SGF, the Primal Spirit is the formative energy responsible for our physical

4   Ibid p.46

embodiment in the womb from embryo to fetus to fully formed being. The Conscious Spirit is the ego and its agents, the senses. The senses feed us an endless flow of information. Society (our parents, teachers, friends, and family) tell us what this information means, and we are bound by these cultural patterns until we're able to break free. What we perceive with our senses becomes reality. What we are taught to believe in and hold as values determines our opinions and beliefs. We think we are free, but we are slaves to the cultural, familial, and educational patterns bequeathed to us. Living under the various illusions we are conditioned to, it is very difficult to extract (de-condition) ourselves without recourse to the primordial super-conscious Primal Spirit.

To the uninformed and self-satisfied this sounds like crazy talk. I know, it's how I felt and reasoned at one time. One day, however, it clicked. I thought about the time it had taken for conventional wisdom to catch up with the discoveries of pioneers such as Galileo, William Harvey, Gregor Mendel, Dr. Barry Marshall, Francis Peyton Rous, for instance. There are always persons out in front of conventional wisdom, as well as persons blocking the process of catching up.

When I first read the SGF over 50 years ago, I realized my interpretation was not clearly stated on the page; I had to read between the lines for the meaning of its teachings. And it wasn't easy to decipher. I had to live the lines to get the hidden, between-the-lines meaning; I had to practice.

Living the lines meant accepting there was substance to them, even though I wasn't sure what that substance was. It meant practicing the meditation — more like feeling my way through it because, once again, I wasn't sure I was following the instructions correctly, much less understanding their exact meaning. Nevertheless, somewhat to my surprise, I succeeded. My kundalini became aroused and ultimately active.

I realize some readers may get lost trying to relate the details of my kundalini awakening to the distinct terminologies used in the various Eastern traditions — Indian, Tibetan, and Chinese. They're different, one from the other, but there are many similarities. The problem is: Kundalini has become an all-encompassing term, too big for one language or tradition alone. So let's forget terminology and look at kundalini as a two-step biological process that:

- Distills sexual fluids into a powerful essence, a process known as sexual sublimation,
- Releases super-conscious life force energy throughout the body, once the sublimated sexual energy rises to the brain.

However, while kundalini is a biological process, it is also a rebirth/maturation process, which most seekers tend to ignore until faced with the prospects of living the rest of their lives with this awakened energy. How does the rebirth process work? Firstly, you must accept kundalini energy and not struggle against it. Unfortunately, many have trouble with acceptance — to their ultimate chagrin. But let's say an individual accepts this energy, what next? Kundalini doesn't only reengineer your body; it remakes your cognitive and emotional essences. Talk about seeing things differently, growing up quickly. Overtime, kundalini removes conditioning, steers you towards selflessness, and has you doing things you never thought possible, not because you suddenly became smarter and thought them up, but because you were driven to do them. You become an instrument, not in a mindless or robotic way. You are an eddy in the pool of super-consciousness, a part of the evolutionary master plan. At the same time, your rational powers become enhanced, you are able to solve problems and make better decisions. You learn not to choose or support things against nature.

What was it that so captured my attention that I spent two years deciphering and practicing the meditation?

At first, it was the text, the poetic ways it was phrased:

"The great One is the term given to that which has nothing above it. The secret of the magic of life consists in using action in order to attain non-action. One must not wish to leap over everything and penetrate directly."[5]

What's so startling about the above? For me, it was cryptic and at the same time cosmological. More than the Bible or any other explanation I had run across. Intuitively, I understood the notion of the great One and the goal of attaining non-action — great power resides in stillness.

And that's only the first page!

"The work on the circulation of the light depends entirely on the backward-flowing movement, so that the thoughts (the place of heavenly consciousness, the heavenly heart) are gathered together. The heavenly heart lies between sun and moon (the two eyes).

"The Book of the Yellow Castle says: 'In the square inch field of the square foot house, life can be regulated.' The square foot house is the face. The square inch field in the face: what could that be other than the heavenly heart? In the middle of the square inch dwells the splendor."[6]

The phrase "circulation of the light" is used right from the beginning. I understood it to mean an energy phenomenon, something that would occur if I practiced correctly. The designations referred to in The Book of the Yellow Castle were probably related to chakras. I wasn't sure, but I allowed myself to skip over them and proceed with the meditation.

"At the time of birth the conscious spirit inhales the energy and thus becomes the dwelling of the newborn. It lives in the heart. From that time on the heart is master, and the primal spirit loses its place while the conscious spirit has the power.

"The primal spirit loves stillness, and the conscious spirit loves movement. In its movement it remains bound to feelings and desires. Day and night it wastes the primal seed till the energy of the primal spirit is entirely used up. Then the conscious spirit leaves the shell and goes away."[7]

5   Ibid p. 21
6   Ibid p. 22
7   Ibid p. 29

Understanding the meaning of the Primal and Conscious Spirits was gradual. I really didn't get it until kundalini took effect and I witnessed the changes in myself, observed that a new entity had taken control of my being and was leading me in new directions. Along with the physical changes — the rebuilding of my body, which I freely accepted — came changes in attitude and life style. None of these originated from my cognitive processes. All came from the newly reawakened Primal Spirit. I realize this sounds esoteric, but it's very palpable and real once kundalini rises.

Most important for the meditator are the passages on posture, attention, and breathing:

> "One looks with both eyes at the tip of the nose, sits upright and in a comfortable position, and holds the heart to the center in the midst of conditions. In Taoism it is called the yellow middle, in Buddhism the center of the midst of conditions. The two are the same. It does not necessarily mean the middle of the head. It is only a matter of fixing one's thinking on the point which lies exactly between two eyes. Then all is well. The light is something extremely mobile. When one fixes the thought on the mid-point between the two eyes, the light streams in of its own accord."

> "In sitting down, after lowering the lids, one uses the eyes to establish a plumb-line and then shifts the light downward. But if the transposition downward is not successful, then the heart is directed towards listening to the breathing. One should not be able to hear with the ear the outgoing and intaking of the breath."[8]

Learning these techniques took experimentation. I still don't know if I got everything exactly right. I have to work backwards from the results of my meditation. The fact that they matched the description of the results in the book means my practice must have been nearly, if not completely, satisfactory.

> "The light is not in the body alone, nor is it only outside the body. Mountains and rivers and the great earth are lit by sun and moon; all that is this light. Therefore it is not only within the body.

8   Ibid p. 35

> Understanding and clarity, perception and enlightenment, and all movements (of the spirit) are likewise this light; therefore it is not just something outside the body. The light-flower of heaven and earth fills all the thousand spaces. But also the light-flower of the individual body passes through heaven and covers the earth. Therefore, as soon as the light is circulating, heaven and earth, mountains and rivers, are all circulating with it at the same time. To concentrate the seed-flower of the human body above the eyes, that is the great key of the human body."[9]

Not only is *The Secret of the Golden Flower* a how-to manual on meditation, it also offers descriptions of human ontology/cosmological reality — how, once the meditation successfully takes its course, once the light starts to circulate, the practitioner is catapulted out of the limiting duality of the physical world into the metaphysical actuality of the "great One which has nothing above it."

Today's seeker is impatient, keen on quick results. The SGF advises us not to try to "leap over everything and penetrate directly." Are its teachings still valid in the 21st. Century? I believe they are and I refer you to my continually updated info about the method on the Golden Flower Meditation web page. Should you succeed in activating "the circulation of the light," the outcome will probably differ from mine, or from the next person's. Don't worry about it. You'll find your way.

Sexual Sublimation

Sexual sublimation, the process of distilling sexual energy and drawing it up into the brain, is the basis of kundalini activity, which, in one way or another, is the basis of self-realization. I say this because the kundalini experience takes many forms, probably because the sublimation process takes so many forms. Hidden channels can open in various ways, triggering a flow of conditioned sexual energy to the brain. If you read, *Deciphering the Golden Flower One Secret at a Time*, you are aware that I took the backward-flowing path

---

9   Ibid p. 33

— a relatively structured, formal path — that consists of drawing distilled seminal fluid up the spinal column to the brain.

Sexual Sublimation Powers Kundalini

Here's how kundalini, and by extension, sexual sublimation, works. At least, this is how it worked for me. How do I know? I observed the kundalini mechanism (its biological characteristics) in the laboratory of my body.

I'll skip over my meditation experience — its techniques are explained on these pages and in greater depth on the Golden Flower Meditation website — and pick up where the meditation method leaves off. And that is with the sudden ability to detect an energy buildup in the lower belly region. I use the word "region" because the exact location is difficult to pinpoint. Others, who've succeeded with the meditation confirm the energy buildup event, but also report having difficulty pinpointing the exact location. No matter. Kundalini activity begins with the energy buildup — a result of the breathing exercises in GFM. What is this energy comprised of?

The composition of this energy for both males and females is sexual in nature and substance. Semen and cervical fluids are distilled into psychic fuel, often described as an essence or an elixir.

Once the energy buildup is detected, you can observe psychic fuel starting to climb the spine, using as yet unrecognized-by-medical-science channels along the spine (consult your favorite esoteric source for detailed channel information). This is the sexual sublimation phase, that is, the distillation and redirection of sexual energy — normally used for procreation — being diverted up the spine to the brain.

Once this psychic fuel reaches the brain, it's like a coup d'etat. Acting as a command and communications epicenter, kundalini takes over certain biological and metabolic functions. Via the nervous system, kundalini sends feelers throughout the body for the purpose of inventory, diagnosing the status of cells, tissue, and organs — the complete anatomy, physiology, histology, and embryology.

Kundalini compares the information received from each and every part, system, and subsystem of the body with the master plan for your embodiment, the blueprint for your being that came into existence just prior to your birth. It then releases healing energy to those parts that need it. Some of this healing work is accomplished immediately; some takes a lot longer. The healing energy is also composed of sexual energy and is summoned, as needed, by kundalini from the sexual apparatus.

After my activation, I watched as my brain received information from my body. How did this work? A particular node was touched, and like a switch being thrown, I felt a click in the brain. Immediately after the click, a corresponding body part received an influx of energy that either healed it or made it expand. Every event was part of kundalini's effort to synchronize my actual body and being with the master blueprint. I say "effort" because kundalini is intelligent; it knows what it's doing. It has a plan and carries it out. If it doesn't accomplish all that it sets out to do, it's either because:

- The body is too far gone, overtaken, most likely, by degenerative disease. If it's a neural impairment, kundalini is usually able to heal it.
- The kundalini awakening is not complete and permanent.
- The activation method was involuntary — all the kundalini components were not "installed" correctly.

In permanent awakenings, when all the components are correctly installed, the command and communications epicenter not only has an inventory component, it is able to dispense and release life force healing energy, it also includes a governor that controls the precise amount of energy to release in a given circumstance, and it expands consciousness over time.

In temporary or involuntary cases, the governor is not completely operational and therefore it releases either too much or too little energy. Too much energy may lead to situations of pain, discomfort, or other suffering. No one likes to see a person in agony, unhappy that kundalini ever came into his or her life. At this stage, however, techniques to relieve the suffering due to neural pain or discomfort are not readily available.

In most cases, kundalini gradually expands consciousness and fosters anatomical, somatic, and metabolic improvements. It is even capable of modifying an individual's genetic profile and passing these beneficial mutations along to future generations through DNA.

Sexual Energy Is Always Present When Kundalini Rises

Although it is experienced in many different ways, the sexual energy is always involved as kundalini rises. Is awakening always accompanied by sexual arousal? Is there a link between kundalini and sexual awakening? All legitimate questions. One thing is certain: it must be summoned, whether by intent, such as meditation, or by accident, and it must get to the brain. How do I know this? What else accounts for the spontaneous eruption of neuroplastic energy that revitalized and reengineered my physical body? What other phenomenon could regenerate a degenerating body? What other power could quick start a non-existent creativity?

Many persons, including Gopi Krishna and myself, have written about a lessening of desire once the sexual sublimation process kicks into high gear. Is this a physiological or a psychological effect? Does it last or does it dissipate? That, like every other effect of kundalini, depends on the metabolic, somatic, psychic structure of the individual. As for me, I can confirm that desire fluctuates, depending on how much sexual and psychic fuel the kundalini process needs at any given time. Remember, it's not up to you. Once kundalini becomes active, you no longer DO it; it DOES you! However, if you've activated kundalini in a safe, permanent fashion, it is benign.

So how do we really know the effect sublimation has on the bodies of those who trigger it? An article in Current Biology, Volume

22, Issue 18, R792-R793, 25 September 2012 gives us a hint of this:
"Male sex hormones are responsible for shortening the lives of
men, a new study has suggested. The evidence comes after careful
study of genealogy records of noble members of the Imperial court
of the Korean Chosun dynasty (AD 1392-1910)."

What is this article really saying and how do its findings relate to
kundalini? The article tells us sexual hormones that remain in the
prostate region can turn against the body. It stumbled on a rather
drastic solution — castration. Now this wasn't determined by an
experiment set up in the Chosun dynasty: people were castrated
back then for political and social reasons. But the records left by this
practice — comparing castrated men to intact men — yielded data
for a modern day study that tells us about effects of hormones on
men's bodies as they age.

So, is there another solution to avoiding "shortening the lives
of men" besides castration? Ancient adepts learned that sublimation,
the practice of redirecting sexual hormones to the brain, was a
powerful factor in longevity, in effect, a substitute for castration.
People frequently ask me about the optimal time in life to begin
kundalini meditation. I tell them at the end of useful child-bearing
might be a time. This study sets another criteria: a reasonable period
before prostate damage occurs — at a time in a man's life when
family responsibilities are lessening and the "rest-of-life" challenges
begin to surface. In fact, the two might work together as a kind of
life plan for better senior living. We certainly don't think castration
will make a comeback, in spite of this study! But years of creative
fulfillment? That's worth considering.

Imagine that you came home one day to find the cat sitting at
your computer sending emails. That's the same kind of change that
occurred the moment man used the first tool. An outside witness —
say an interplanetary observer — would have been astonished. This
bestial creature all of a sudden using a club to fight off invaders? What
caused it? How did the brain suddenly make the connection? What

made the synapses fire? What made the hand suddenly reach down and pick up a club at the very instant the brain realized its deadly purpose? The leap from using tools such as fire or clubs to creating art is a short one — once consciousness kicks in. Sexual energy has two purposes: reproduction and neuroplastic brain development, aka, kundalini activation. There must be a balance between these two ends. Imagine if everyone took to raising kundalini to the exclusion of reproduction, civil society would collapse. But think about evolution for a moment. Where is it headed? Look at the millions who are striving for spiritual release.

Are Evolution and those attempting to raise kundalini not headed in the same direction? Google the term kundalini. There are thousands of websites with their own interpretations. Why, all of a sudden? To what evolutionary purpose?

You only need to look at the world around us for the answer. How long can we go on this way? Exhausting our resources, killing and fighting, shouting and screaming, overcrowding and wasting. Look at how evolution is responding to this turmoil. It's sending millions to yoga, kundalini, and the like. Imagine, then, that the ultimate in neuroplastic brain development might be the bodiless brain or the ethereal brain or the bodiless being? If we were to exist in bodiless form, what happens to all our problems? Suddenly, they don't exist. Suddenly, we are free. Will it happen tomorrow? Don't confuse evolution with history; the two are not synonymous. It took us millions of years to evolve into our present form. It may take another million to get to the next stage, but evolution is trying to adjust, trying to keep us alive.

One of the big differences among realized practitioners is permanency of kundalini energy. In some, the energy keeps pumping slowly and continually, like the dependable oil well that never seems to dry up. In others, it comes and goes. Regardless of how the energy acts upon the individual, regardless of the metanormal gifts it bestows, sexual energy is the driving force. The wonder of it: that our bodies are able to repurpose our reproductive energy into something sublime! No wonder Gopi Krishna writes about kundalini as being the source of genius and religion!

One thing is certain: because kundalini is related to sexuality, it is difficult to talk about in an everyday social context. A friend of mine says those who don't succeed in raising kundalini are blocked at the second chakra. "I was just supposing that MAYBE people were blocked at the second chakra because they gave away their power... Dunno if it's a fact. Seems possible if not probable however, considering the way we treat sexuality in most places across the planet. We don't even use the proper names for our genitals when talking to little kids, and we hate disclosing our bedroom practices in front of others, sometimes even to our partner. We're sort of encouraged to be simultaneously ashamed of our sexuality while at the same time we are bombarded with imagery that uses sex to sell... It's a strange world."

SO, would being more open about sexuality help us to achieve spiritual release? Are two such seemingly unrelated subjects intimately tied together? Most meaningful kundalini literature says they are. And isn't there a price to pay for seminal retention? Good question, because kundalini doesn't like sharing the Life Force energy.

Nevertheless, if there's one chance in a hundred that something is stuck or blocked because of sexual repression, you need to rethink your sexuality. The last thing you want to do is give away your power instead of using it yourself.

What about those who attempt to raise kundalini, who work diligently and sincerely at it, but can't seem to get there? I'm not talking about dabblers; I'm talking about those who work hard, follow every step of the method, yet ultimately fail — for whatever reason.

I can only conclude that, no matter how fervently they strived, the distilled sexual elixir was not disposed to climb or to be drawn up the spine into their brains. For more on the conditions for activating kundalini, reread So how can you tell if your kundalini is really awakened.

But is not activating kundalini really a failure? Should not making the Olympic team after putting forth the requisite effort be considered a failure? Failure is part of life.

Whether for anatomical, biological, or Karmic reasons, some make it and some don't. Is it because some little valve at the base of the spine got stuck? I don't know. Whatever the reason, the inability to activate kundalini shouldn't be considered a failure. Many principles are involved: method, state of mind and body, age, health, discipline, Karma. Sure, it means a realignment of goals, but I never intended to activate kundalini and yet I did. Why did it happen to me — a person who kind of backed into it — and not to others? I don't know.

It turned my life around, both physically and psychically. Yet it has made me wholly abnormal and different. Perhaps, it happened because the Karmic rulers knew I could withstand the psychological stress of abnormality, but others who strove more ardently than I did, couldn't. Again I don't know.

I do know everyone is meant to follow a specific path. But it's only a single lifetime, after all. There are many more to come. Don't be impatient.

Triggers and Effects

I use the notions of triggers and effects to denote causes and results in describing kundalini arousals, triggers being the cause of an arousal, and effects being the results, which include changes of being as well as the appearance of new abilities.

How you activate it? (Triggers)

In my 40 years of listening to kundalini awakening stories, I have heard so many trigger variations it is nearly impossible to categorize them. Everything from meditation to drugs, physical exertion to sexual ecstasy to Shaktipat to minding one's own business. For me, the trigger was meditation.

But my activation method only applies to me and to those who have practiced the Golden Flower Meditation method. Once you practice a given method and get to a point where the sublimation process becomes active, it is difficult to change course and begin all over again with a new method.

This is especially true with those for whom kundalini is permanent. I could no more undo my permanently active kundalini, go back to a time before it was active, and start over with a new method than I could reinsert myself into my mother's womb and be born again.

So what does this tell us? Simply that there is no one size-fits-all trigger for arousing kundalini and no guarantee that a given trigger will actually work in a specific case. So if you're looking for one, you may not find it in books, conversations, or retreats. It may up and hit you when you least expect it...or not. However, once the experience is triggered, accept it as the ultimate experiment in the laboratory of your body.

And while we're at it, the triggers I referred to are really only different kinds of detonators. The actual explosion occurs when a quantity of stored-up, distilled sexual energy pollinates certain nodes in the brain.

No matter the detonator — be it drugs, meditation, or sexual rapture — each detonation causes a release of life force energy. The initiate may not feel sexual activity during the release — kundalini works at a deep neurological level, — but the sensations/effects/symptoms the individual does feel when kundalini activates are related to the release and upward climb of sexual energy to the brain. For example, you may feel tired, enthralled, frightened, or depressed without any erotic undercurrents. Nevertheless, sexual energy is present. The reason you may not feel sexually aroused is because the energy kundalini releases to the brain initiates a rewiring of neural and cerebral circuits, which once fired, can cause behavioral irregularities, up to and including bliss, psychosis, and depression. If the initiate realizes what he/she is undergoing is benign, any aberrant cognitive and psychic states can be stabilized by accepting kundalini, not fighting it. So be patient. Let the rewiring and the restorative work begin.

There's another element that must be accounted for, a deterministic element I call the Field. Not every person seeking to activate kundalini is able to do so. At the same time, not every person in whom kundalini becomes active wants it to happen. This is especially important at the present time when so many people are striving to arouse it by so many different methods. Most of these individuals have no idea what awaits them if they succeed. What's more, if and when they do succeed, they are often ill prepared to deal with the aftermath.

So how is the determination made on who's going to succeed? This is important because forcing kundalini activation is beside the point in evolutionary terms. We're going to achieve higher states of consciousness anyway over time. Evolution will see to it.

For the trigger and the explosive charge to collide, the Field must move them into alignment; that's its deterministic nature. This Field could be called The Energy Continuum or Consciousness or even a Quantum or a Karmic event, one whose moment has come to pass: the collision in time and space of Detonator (sexual energy), Explosive charge (brain matter), brought together by the Field (quantum event) whose purpose is to escort an individual's destiny through an evolutionary leap.

Today, there's so much buzz and crosstalk about kundalini, but so little sharing of kundalini knowledge and experience. Everyone's off in his or her corner, trying to protect his or her itzy bit of kundalini turf, scared someone else will steal it or, at the least, somehow diminish its gainfulness. Trying to convince the world that one trigger is better than another is counterproductive. I could tell you that my method is the one true and only method, but I've found that promoting exclusivity leads to a compartmentalization of knowledge. Kundalini doesn't need insider bickering among adepts; there's enough hostility, doubt, and prejudice directed at it from outside sources. Better to spend time sharing information on triggers and testing them under laboratory conditions.

As far as I know, there are no statistics on the success rate of any given trigger, so although there's a lot of information out there, it's muddled. How do you choose a method or a trigger? In my case, my method chose me. Someone gave me a copy of *The Secret of the Golden Flower* and I practiced the method in the book. One factor that helped me succeed was sticking with a single method once *It* found me. Doers complete the journey; dabblers tend to end up back where they started. Recognize the difference.

What it does for/to you (Effects)

The foregoing applies to the activation method (the trigger). When we speak of the effects and aftermath of kundalini, we find many effects are shared. However, each case is different. It would be great if that wasn't the case, but it is. Until there is a trigger that produces the same effects time after time over a given population, and a critical mass of practitioners who share a comparable set of effects, we won't achieve unanimous acceptance from researchers. So even though I'd like to consider my method as capable of producing uniform results, the sample group of practitioners is as yet too small.

The general question "What does kundalini do for you?" must be rephrased as "What did it do for me?" This I can answer. For me, the effects included, but were not limited to:

- Triggering autonomic self-healing mechanisms capable of correcting defects due to neural degeneration;
- Rejuvenating the brain and the body as a result of intense neuro-plastic activity;
- Retarding the aging process;
- Reversing self-destructive and addictive behavior;

- Heightening and enhancing consciousness through the awakening of various metanormal effects and powers;
- Cleansing the ego by removing the effects of conditioning and programming: self-realization;
- Clearly demonstrating that the spirit persists after death;
- Helping to end dependency on ineffective health-care models; and
- Facilitating the transition into the next state of being.

And it didn't necessarily stop there. Not all of the effects come "Online" as soon as activation takes place. Kundalini is still DOING me — forty years after I activated it! And it doesn't operate randomly. Kundalini is intelligent.

What's more, these are not the only effects I will ever experience; new effects are happening all the time, without warning. Kundalini doesn't stand still. And that's part of the challenge. Don't try to contend with the power of kundalini, don't try to control it because you won't be able to. Once permanently activated, it's best to submit to whatever kundalini has in store for you.

So how can you tell if your kundalini is permanently awakened?

For Gopi Krishna and myself, two persons who practiced kundalini meditation, we were able to observe somatic and metabolic changes in the body as the sexual sublimation process engaged and as it ultimately reached a dramatic crescendo, ushering waves of Pranic energy into the brain, igniting all chakras. In these cases, the proof is incremental. The trigger induces the effects and you can follow the process as you would follow a laboratory experiment. One sure way that Gopi Krishna and I knew with certainty whether kundalini was actually awakened was when after sexual intercourse — or ejaculation — there was an immediate debilitating effect. Others, however, react differently. Some get extremely energized after sex. It floods their entire bodes and brain with energetic rushes that are by no means debilitating.

"Many years ago when I occasionally served as a front man for some Kundalini gurus, an issue would come up among couples where one of them would be going into what I call Kundalini samadhi and every cell in their brain would be bursting with orgasmic bliss and they'd be having profound mystical insights. A 'normal' sexual relationship would drain this bliss and bring them down. The other partner would want a 'normal' sexual physical relationship and usually didn't understand what was happening. So they'd say their partner was in a cult and we were influencing them. Which wasn't true. The most likely truth is they'd discovered a more evolved expression of sexual energy which they preferred. By a lot. Anyway, a lot of couples and marriages split because of this. Probably for the better."

~ Tom Thompson, The Awakened Heart Center for Conscious Living[10]

What about those whose kundalini has been ignited surreptitiously? In these cases, you have to work inductively, from the effects back to the cause. If you can identify a number of acknowledged kundalini effects/symptoms, you can conclude that kundalini has somehow been aroused. Nevertheless, this is tricky. There is a tendency to attribute kundalini symptoms to various abnormal psychological states, persuading yourself that kundalini has actually awakened when it hasn't. In such cases, you must verify everything you see, hear, or feel.

For me, the effects have been benign. Whether this holds true in your case, I can't say. And whether you're able to withstand the effects depends on your physical stamina as well as your ability to accept kundalini and adapt yourself to its dictates. I've talked with many people who have shared some, if not all, of the effects included in the list above, and, in doing so, have thrived. Nevertheless, since effects vary from subject to subject, but are also shared in many instances, I believe it would be useful to classify effects by triggers and then rate each effect by impact from negative to positive. That way we might learn which triggers to avoid, if possible, and which ones produce positive effects.

10 http://www.theawakenedheartcenter.com/

What about ecstatic states of bliss? Yes, they are common, especially at the beginning. But don't get caught up in them; they take you away from the real world. I'm not saying you should discourage them, only that you need to keep them in perspective. I still have them, but once they pass, I return to the Now. For as long as we inhabit bodies, the real world makes demands on us, and we must balance these demands with the thrall that an awakening experience casts over us as we learn to put the layers of past conditioning into proper perspective.

The True Teachings

From a Tweet I came across recently: "@XXXxxxxxxxxx good to see Yogi Bhajan's familiar face, some are misdirecting away from the true teachings"

Sorry, what are the true teachings again? Are they like the US Constitution that some say can NEVER be amended no matter what? Do true teachings mean that certain ideas and principles are frozen in perpetuity like the insects ancient Romans found in blobs of crystallized amber? Can we not discover new ways — sometimes, even better ways — of doing things?

Resistance is to be expected, even in science. Yet, aren't pioneering, innovation, and trailblazing accepted features of the scientific method? A better way, or a more complete way, a new way, a way we never thought of, lateral thinking, new and improved, fresh, unusual, unprecedented, inventive; advanced, state-of-the-art, revolutionary, radical; important, noteworthy.

Some people are always experimenting with new ways; others are dedicated to protecting the old ways. Experimenting with new ways doesn't necessarily mean that the old ways are obsolete. It usually means that the subject matter was larger than we believed at first and there is more to learn, more to uncover, new hurdles or conditions to overcome. If we only held to the old ways, we'd still be sitting in saber-tooth tiger skins rubbing sticks together to make fires.

The human being is evolving right before our eyes. In spite of all the issues that grab at our attention — pro football, rampant terror, hacked celebrity nude photos — our collective and individual consciousness is evolving at this very minute. Ideas and new notions are popping into people's heads at an amazing rate — not only in science and self-development, but in every walk of life. It's natural that there be a clash between the old and the new. But to become a dedicated fan of only one way — refusing to acknowledge or examine new data — is tantamount to wishing the clock would run backwards or evolution would reverse its course. That's not going to happen! Not in science, spiritual exploration, finance, cooking, sports, fashion, literature, or art.

You may say there's nothing new under the sun. In one sense, that's true. Fashions repeat themselves; fads and fancies run in circles. But I'm not talking about under the sun; I'm talking about beyond it — universal truth — of which we know so little, in which so many are engaged, in one way or another. Puttering around with it, burning the midnight oil to understand it, coming face-to-face with it in the laboratories of their bodies, accidentally brushing up against it in the night — like meeting a wolf in the dark and standing up to it.

Finally, new ways, like new ideas, are traded in the marketplace, so to speak — like the handy cleaning device that makes washing the dishes easier. If it's better, people will support it, most of the time.

Gopi Krishna hit the nail on the head when he coined the term, evolutionary impulse:

> "The aim of the evolutionary impulse that is active in the race is to mold the human brain and nervous system to a state of perception where the invisible world of intelligent cosmic forces can be cognizable to every human being."

When he made that statement, he realized this would not

happen over night. Even if thousands discovered and started to experiment with kundalini, it would take eons before our beings develop the faculties he describes. In the time it takes to get to that point, the true teachings will be added to and revised many times, just as evolution continues to revise every species over time. Nevertheless, inherent in his statement is the notion of inevitability. That much is clear: that we don't know exactly HOW it will happen, only that it WILL happen.

Finding Balance in the Effort to Integrate Kundalini

One day there was a Me, the next day there wasn't. One day I was practicing meditation, breathing in and out in a rhythmic manner; the next I was transported to another dimension I'll never be completely able to explain or describe. That doesn't mean I'm going to stop trying. After all, I have one advantage: I never really returned from that other dimension; I live with a foot in both — the physical world we know as the "real world" and that other dimension. To describe it, I use terms from science as well as those from various spiritual traditions, not because I like arcana or confusion, but because when I say kundalini, you'll say chi, someone else will say orgone; and we'll be talking about the same thing without knowing it.

Nevertheless, once it happens to you, you'll understand how unimportant terminology is. Each awakening experience is manifestation of the same energy. Sure, it involves struggling with terminology and understanding the same notions phrased in slightly different ways. The closest we get to clarity is a series of approximations of an actual awakening experience. And that's perfectly understandable because it's not easy to express or describe. But there is a constant: everyone who experiences kundalini has one foot permanently in that other dimension.

There's a corollary to that constant, one we learn, not during the kundalini activation experience per se because during the experience we are floating in a no-mind state. Immediately after — when we "come back to our senses" — we know there is an all-pervading consciousness behind the universe and behind human evolution. It's not a hallucination or an abnormal psychological projection.

This consciousness is much greater than our bodies or the physical world we perceive. We are part of it, contained in it. In this consciousness, nothing is separate. All is Whole and Undivided. This cannot be learned in school or books, it can only be Known.

Very few of us progress straight from birth to self-realization. To perceive whole and undivided Oneness, we first serve an apprenticeship, as it were, in a world of duality, a world in which every aspect seems to be in opposition to every other. This is not reality; it is the world of the senses, one to which we are conditioned from birth. Once we recognize that we are conditioned to think in terms of duality, we are able to find ways and means of extracting ourselves from that conditioning; and we are offered an opportunity to do so.

Many individuals are so completely conditioned they remain that way for the rest of their lives. Some are able to recognize this conditioning. A few are able to work their way through it to the cosmological Oneness behind duality. Those who achieve this may attempt to integrate this knowledge with their real world lives; others are content to remain immersed in the bliss they've discovered. I chose a balance: remaining in the world, at the same time, realizing I am a part of an Energy Continuum. I didn't really choose It; It chose me. That's the kind of purposeful compulsion kundalini introduces into our lives. After awakening, we can't take credit for anything we do, say, or write. We are driven to it.

Yet, spurred on by an urge to understand my experience to the extent I can — how conventional science views evolution as opposed to how someone like myself, a person with a foot in two different worlds, perceives it — I concluded that kundalini is an evolutionary force with a guiding intelligence behind it, and I looked for an evidence-based paradigm for examining it.

Science recognizes "survival of the fittest" and "natural selection" as the operative mechanisms behind evolution. But is there not another mechanism working at a higher level, one Gopi Krishna called the evolutionary impulse? Not perceptible by everyone at this time, this mechanism drives certain beings toward super-consciousness, allowing them to recognize and access energy fields beyond the confines of the circumscribed physical universe, beyond the five senses. Those who do experience it say this super-consciousness manifests itself as vibrational energy. If so, could it become perceivable at some future time by all humans as a result of a rapid surge in the quality of human evolution? A revised layer at the top of Maslow's pyramid dedicated to higher consciousness? In other words, could all human beings eventually become conscious of consciousness at each and every moment of their lives? Human evolution has not reached its apogee; we may not even be halfway in terms of mental capabilities as well as our human form.

> "The reason that faith assumes that we are one small step removed from Divinity, and science assumes that almost all knowledge has been discovered and that the intellect is the only channel for acquiring this knowledge, is because they believe that the human species, in its current form, is the final limit to which evolution can proceed. Although there is no justification whatsoever for this assumption, it has dominated thinking in both faith and science to this day. The premise that our mental faculties are still evolving is so simple, so logical, and so consistent with evolutionary trends that in generations to come, it will be wondered why this discovery took so long to be known and accepted."[11]

Can we not apply an evidence-based approach to studying its role in evolution? The thousands of anecdotal accounts of kundalini and its relation to higher consciousness cry out for critical-mass evaluation.

Do I Need a Teacher?
Two of the most common immediate after-effects of a kundalini

11 Bradford, Michael. *Consciousness: The New Paradigm* (pp. 49-
50). Institute for Consciousness Research. Kindle Edition.

awakening — in the form of ideas that pop into the head — are:

- Intense feelings that "I" need to do something that improves the condition of all mankind,
- Overwhelming desire to meet someone in the form of a highly evolved teacher that knows much more about kundalini than "I" do.

Both of these usually lead nowhere and here's why. Gopi Krishna had these same feelings after his awakening in India in 1938. He searched the entire country without finding an authentic someone who knew more, or even as much, about kundalini as he did.

A newly awakened kundalini is like a sudden, violent storm. How long the storm lasts is only partially up to you. Kundalini has its own timetable.

What Gopi Krishna did discover is that it's up to the awakened one to fend for him/herself. Yes, I write books, host a blog, offer comment on a YouTube channel, and generally try to help people integrate this energy, but in the end, it's up to the individual. He/she does a much better job of managing his/her own kundalini energy than anyone else can. It's a long haul. It took me about one hundred days to awaken kundalini via GFM, a length of time that pales beside the 40 years I've spent getting used to its power.

I made up my mind early on that I would give into the kundalini energy and find a way to accommodate its every whim. Why? Very simple. I realized it had my best interests at heart. That it could do no wrong. It was out to help me forge an "I" out of the "me" of my ego.

For good measure here's an account (excerpted from *Deciphering the Golden Flower One Secret at a Time*) of my attempt to gather information about kundalini from Swami Muktananda at the moment of his leaving Paris for the US. This is not to denigrate his ability to confer Shaktipat, rather it is a parable on finding a guide. Thankfully the lesson I learned was I would have to become my own best teacher.

"I have ventured forth in my newly purchased Quatrelle to witness the departure of Swami Muktananda. I'm not keen on the shotgun approach to finding a teacher, especially a sensation like Muktananda, surrounded, as it were, by layers of handlers who seem little more than glorified bouncers. Anyway, someone told me about him. So I thought—what the hell.

"To enter the ashram, I have to stand in line and be screened. Waiting to enter the big room, I overhear his acolytes buzzing about who is going to ride with him in the car to the airport. That is the spiritual concern of the day. More like backroom political maneuvering—jockeying for votes, bargaining for influence.

"And the prize: proximity to the guru during the final trip to Charles de Gaulle Airport. The winners get to ride; the losers get to follow in a motorcade. Dressed in robes of saffron, white and red, they huddle by the door whispering and cajoling, earnestly vying to move up the ladder of distinction.

"Attended by still more acolytes who buzz around him, the guru is seated on a platform in the big room. I watch him while the bouncers quiz me. I picture Milarepa alone in his Himalayan cave. Somehow, the two don't jibe.

"I have a vague idea about the questions I want to ask, but when I'm finally admitted to the big room, I see it may be impossible. First, I am one of a large group of people seated on the floor. I may never be recognized to speak because of the on-going ritual. All this makes me impatient, for I am only interested in knowing if the illustrious guru has some answers to my specific condition. The ceremony, trappings and schmoozing make me uncomfortable. I'm sorry that I've driven through all that Parisian traffic. And now I have to sit through the chanting, which I guess would have its place if the context didn't resemble a White House press conference with its hubbub of kibitzers and white noise.

If any present are on a spiritual mission, personal or otherwise, I can't detect it. It seems more like the worship of a particular personality, whose followers take their status from proximity to the Master.

"I am probably missing the true meaning of the chanting, but the shuffling, the ritual mutterings of Muktananda, only underline the general impatience, as if everyone in the room is waiting for the mad scramble to the cars.

"I can't remember if he asks for questions, I just remember my hand being in the air at a particular moment and his pointing at me. The noise level drops to zero as I stammer forth. Can't remember my exact words, only a paraphrase: 'I recently spent one year in isolation, meditating. During this time hidden channels in my body were awakened…and eventually energy streamed into a place…a location in my head…that I can only call the third eye. Now, it continues on its own without my intervention, and my head cracks while it does…'

The Guru interrupts me. His acolytes turn their faces expectantly, as if ready to savor his reaction. My fellow floor sitters turn to stare at me.

"'It is not possible. The head does not crack. There are no muscles in the head…' replies Muktananda.

"Giggles and titters, as if the crowd were saying, 'You don't know that, stupid? Everyone knows that!'

"'Then something is cracking in every room I've occupied…'

"'It wasn't your head.'

"'It must have been the radiators then,' says someone in the crowd.

"More derisive laughter. I'm not so much annoyed by people laughing at me as by the complete refusal to accept the possibility of a head cracking. That's what growth is all about, from infancy to maturity—the head changing imperceptibly over time.

"'That is impossible; the skull cannot crack,' he continues.

"'But can it change its shape?'

"'That is another matter.'

"He whispers to someone behind him in a light green robe. Everybody rises. Question time is over.

"In his denial, is he saying that it didn't happen to him so therefore it couldn't happen, period? I don't put any limits on the power inside me. Obviously, once maturity is reached, cracking might be difficult, but not impossible. Being him, I would have wanted to hear more. Being me, I believed he could look at me and see my inner workings, and therefore know I was telling the truth.

"So, I am disappointed, but not much. It only reinforces what I've learned. I figure I need a few experiences like this to learn to ignore conventional wisdom. In the solitude of St. Jean, as a kind of empirical detective, I learned to keep my mouth shut, perhaps by virtue of having no one to talk to. And now, reintroduced into the world, I am flush with success, like I have accomplished something—even though, in my heart of hearts, I know I haven't. The road is never ending—for as long as I have the strength to push my body out of bed. It's the same for the ordinary person as it is for the enlightened.

"Good for you, I say to myself while walking into the bistro across the street from the ashram. You got laughed at and you deserved it. Now wake up, continue on your way, and forget conventional wisdom—even from the mouths of the so-called enlightened."

Activating Kundalini

"I am fully experienced in movement of energy as my grid is highly active and energetic movement is a way of life for me. Yet I can't stand religion or dogma attached to it, the truth does not come in print but rather through direct experience."

~ Ginga Paul Gladman"

Who Should I Listen To?

Whether it's expressed openly or whispered subvocally, *Who should I listen to in spiritual matters?* is the most important question one can ask. *Who should I ask? Where do I begin? Who can I trust?* are all the same question. What most people don't realize is the answer is actually quite simple. It's YOU yourself.

YOU are the only person you can fully rely on. You may deceive yourself, lie to yourself, but in the end if you learn to be honest with yourself and apply rigorous standards of evaluation, you will find what you're looking for and apply it in your life.

Believing in Yourself

Although the title of this section has become a cliché, shopworn and ubiquitous, it still has significance. So much so that, having heard it a thousand times before I was twenty-one, never understood the real meaning until after kundalini altered my metabolic and cognitive processes and changed my being. I was too busy flirting with the suffering artist paradigm, too busy feeling my pain and drowning it in alcohol, drugs, and women. Forty years ago — before kundalini — I had the feeling I was missing something that was happening somewhere, only not where I was. While the world was passing me by, I was standing still.

I learned to believe in myself when I discovered there was something out there, something beyond the material world, something beyond feeling sorry for myself.

Up to then I'd been influenced by my various preceptors'

sentiments on the great orthodoxies of life. Their takes on religion, education, goals, ambition, status, marriage, success, politics, accomplishment had been beaten into my brain. Yet, so much of what they taught me didn't jibe. If there was really something out there, it must reside beyond the limits of my indoctrination. And if it did, I wanted to find it. Trouble is, I didn't know where or how to start. In the meantime, I wallowed in *nothing to believe in, so why bother.*

Later, I was attracted to yoga and meditation, possibly because they were outside the traditional Western orthodoxies I'd been raised with — again without any idea that these practices might lead me to that something beyond the lifestyle I'd rejected. That was over forty years ago.

Once I knew the "metaphysical dimension" was real, my first impulse was "to spread the word." And I did. Once.

Thankfully, I paid attention to my listener's reactions; I watched her face. It wasn't that she blew me off; she had no idea what I was talking about, as if I had all of a sudden started a lecture on metallurgy at a baby shower. I didn't feel resentful. It wasn't her fault; it was mine. I had two choices: never mention my experiences again or wait until someone else brought up the subject. Realizing it's impossible to communicate the actuality of metaphysical experience, I became very selective. I never thought about self-realization as anything but a solitary exercise. From the beginning, I knew I had to go it alone, avoid groupthink and mass movements.

I chose another path — a way that's shown me:
- There is no death (death is only a change of state),
- We keep evolving,
- The phrase Circulation of the Light in *The Secret of the Golden Flower* has real meaning in the Chönyi bardo.[12]

12 The fifth bardo of the luminosity of the true nature which commences after the final 'inner breath' (Sanskrit: Prana, vayu; Tibetan: rlung). It is within this Bardo that visions and auditory phenomena occur. In the Dzogchen teachings, these are known as the spontaneously manifesting Thödgal (Tibetan: thod-rgyal) visions. Concomitant to these visions, there is a welling of profound peace and pristine awareness. Sentient beings who have not practiced during their lived

- We pass our kundalini-magnified consciousness through genetic mutations to future generations.

My path was a choice, my choice a path. One ordained by Karma. And now, looking around, there are more and more people acting spontaneously, less bowed by the weight of orthodoxy — interested in self-realization, whether it be dancing in the park at a street fair, meditation, yoga, mindfulness, study of the occult, energy healing, astral travel.

Can I say there are more people who believe in themselves, who think they can find their own way? Alas, even though a per capita increase in college attendance and graduate degrees has swept across the Western world, it seems that follower syndrome has also increased.

Now approaching elder status, I see old acquaintances who took that other path, frozen with looks of surprise on their faces, surprised that the end is near. That after retirement things wind down swiftly and there's nowhere to go, so book that Caribbean cruise, reserve that barge trip down the Rhine, plan the bicycle excursion through Thailand, pencil in the monuments of ancient Egypt. And once that's done, collapse into the waiting arms of death — without a thought to what lies beyond.

Permanent vs. Temporary Kundalini

Some people have the luxury of selecting a method; for others kundalini arrives involuntarily. The goal of a method is to permanently awaken kundalini. An involuntary or spontaneous kundalini activation may be temporary. Although some effects may endure, no one forgets a kundalini awakening.

The following is taken from my book, *The Backward-Flowing Method: The Secret of Life and Death*...

"According to Gopi Krishna's findings, 'There have been very

---

experience and/or who do not recognize the clear light (Tibetan: od gsal) at the moment of death are usually deluded throughout the fifth bardo of luminosity.
~ https://en.wikipedia.org/wiki/Bardo

few instances of individuals in whom the serpent fire burned ceaselessly from the day of its awakening until the last.' What does this have to do with 'kundalini meditation'? It establishes a criterion for qualifying a method of 'kundalini meditation': namely, that the results must be permanent, not temporary. What's more, we must realize that when we speak about method, we automatically exclude involuntary kundalini experiences. Why? Because, by definition, if we talk about involuntary, we are talking about a kundalini experience that can happen anytime, anywhere, in any set of circumstances, and cannot, therefore, be the result of any method. A method must be a systematic process with documented controls and predictable results. It must be a system that anyone with the proper training can apply in order to produce the same results over and over, time after time. Moreover, to be considered, it must be a method that is safe, repeatable, and standardized. So, what is the ideal 'kundalini meditation'? I would say it's a system that is:

- Voluntary. It doesn't happen on its own account. Its techniques are based on the documented experiences of others. The practitioner chooses to apply these techniques in order to achieve predictable results.
- Permanent. The results last a lifetime; the individual experiences daily Kundalini-Life Force activity that "burns ceaselessly from the day of its awakening until the last."
- Safe. It does no harm to the individual. In fact, it serves as 'an upgrade mechanism,' restoring proper health and stability to the body and the entire being.
- Repeatable. The method can be used over and over, time after time, in a scientifically controlled manner to produce the same set of predictable results.

"Does this mean that involuntary or impermanent kundalini experiences have no value or validity? No, it means that in order to advance this work, we must define what the work is. Can we not learn from involuntary or impermanent kundalini experiences? Yes, of course we can. But just as a material scientist, who accidentally mixes several chemicals together in his lab, must repeat the process under scientifically acceptable conditions for it to be considered valid, the person who experiences an involuntary kundalini awakening must be concerned with the repeatability of his process. If it isn't repeatable, what lasting validity can be attributed to the process? And if the effects do not last, isn't that sort of like taking off in a flying contraption only to have it crash to the ground after 150 yards?"

The biology behind kundalini is linked to evolutionary advancement. One way or another, it will ultimately be available to all persons, so we need to refine and vet available methods. Let the experiments with kundalini in the laboratory of individual bodies become an experiment on a mass scale across a vast number of willing and able bodies.

I'm glad I used a method; everything it claimed it would accomplish has been accomplished.

Kundalini Activations Take Many Forms

When I visited Gopi Krishna in 1977, we discussed the reasons behind this phenomenon. "Why," he asked me rhetorically, "do some people experience kundalini so fleetingly while others — a very select few — live it 24 hours a day from the time of awakening till the day they die? And why do awakenings take so many different forms?"

I stated that from my experience I'd gleaned that the difference must reside in the method, "In my case, once I penetrated the symbolic, poetic language of *The Secret of the Golden Flower*, it read like an instructional manual. It's hard to imagine that this method was the work of one person, that one person discovered the method and then wrote the book. I have trouble believing it worked only once, for the person who wrote the book, and then twelve centuries later, it worked once again for me. Since its discovery, this method must have worked for thousands in its initial oral form, handed down over many generations before it was eventually published in print form."

Permanent kundalini is like an electrical current that never stops. The individuals who experience it know it never stops. Permanent kundalini does not include cases where individuals felt a jolt of electricity over a given interval, followed by a complete cessation of same, even though, as a result of experiencing kundalini, they had their lives irrevocably changed. No one forgets a kundalini awakening. Although the lingering effects of a temporary awakening are unforgettable, all sentiments or memories — no matter how intensely felt — do not constitute permanent kundalini. Permanent kundalini is a condition under which kundalini energy circulates 24 hours a day. That is the difference between permanent and temporary.

Some areas of confusion between the two must be considered — what it is and what it isn't. It is not an afterthought, a longing to recapture an effervescent moment of clarity. Nor is it a Close-Encounters-of-a-Third-Kind feeling that something will, or has, happened. Permanent kundalini is happening now and will be happening twenty minutes from now, and for the rest of your life.

It is not a foreshadowing or a frisson, exhilaration or rush, a fleeting sensation, a bliss state, or a lasting memory. It is not an unbearable lightness of being. It is more like a medical condition, a very rare condition. A constant companion. Like high-blood pressure, you cannot shake it. Start with the earliest childhood memories of yourself, what you might call Condition Normal. Set aside the commotion in your head and concentrate on your physical being as you first apprehended it as a child. Add to that the element of energy constantly welling up from below, a newfound sensitivity to energy sources (food, beverages, natural, mechanical and electronic forces) and a heightened sensory awareness and you have permanent kundalini.

Welcome or not, it's invested you, and you can't shake it; you can only learn to live with it. Which brings us back to the question of why some experiences are temporary and others are permanent. Is it a question of method? Does the way the experience is triggered determine its permanency?

I have met and talked with many people about their kundalini experiences. Not as many as Gopi Krishna, but quite a few. Generally, they fall into three categories:

- Those who are not sure they have really experienced kundalini. Difficult to gauge.
- Those who experience kundalini temporarily and retain vivid memories of the experience. Quite common.
- Those whose kundalini, once activated, continues 24-hours a day. Very rare.

Those who are not sure they have really experienced Kundalini

In a perfect world this group should not exist — Kundalini Shakti is either active or it isn't. Nevertheless, the group does exist and its members exhibit various and sundry states of affect. In a perfect world there would be people trying to activate kundalini, people in whom it was active or who activated it at one time and in whom it has since returned to a *Prana Shakti* state, and people in whom it was awakened or who awakened it permanently. No one would be unsure. In our less than perfect world there is less surety.

People often think they are ill, yet they are perfectly well. It called hypochondria, and it's startlingly prevalent. Abnormal psychological states and predispositions often cloud what's really happening in the body and the mind. That's why Gopi Krishna came to the realization that kundalini was often mistaken for mental illness. While mental illness is an accepted phenomenon, until recently most people knew nothing about kundalini, so it's easy to understand how a kundalini experience that stirs up energy centers might be mistaken for mental illness, especially in a culture featuring offhand remarks like, "I must be going crazy" and "Are you nuts?" There's a lot of confusion out there, people confusing what's happening in the body with what's happening in the mind, and vice-versa. Nevertheless, as kundalini becomes more familiar and the term is used more frequently, people may begin to understand the differences, even though it is probable that some forms of mental illness and all forms of kundalini have a biological origin.

For those striving to awaken kundalini, yet never seeming to get there, the problem isn't mental illness; it's one part method and one part Karma. After working with kundalini for a long time, I have realized that some people are not destined to activate it, no matter how hard they try.

Those who experience Kundalini temporarily

A large part of this group activates kundalini accidentally. This is neither good nor bad; it is what it is. When it happens and the person knows nothing about kundalini, there's a temptation to fight it, to resist giving in to it, which is foolish because, once activated, kundalini takes control.

Kundalini can be triggered by yoga, by meditation, by ingesting drugs, or just plain not-doing. It can occur while walking down the street, driving a tractor, chewing your food, or making love. Just about any banal activity or non-activity can set it off. When it does occur, don't fight it. Why? Because you can't. So submit and learn. Perhaps, it will go away, perhaps it won't. If it does go away, it's probably because you did something to temporarily release sublimated sexual energy or the energy shook loose on its own. If the energy does cease for some reason, the conduits — between the base of the spine and the brain — have not been permanently opened; there is a blockage. Or, as Gopi Krishna put it, the "serpent fire is not burning ceaselessly."

How it burns is just as important as if it is actually burning. As Osho said:

> "Kundalini is not felt because it is rising; kundalini is only felt if you do not have a very clear passage. If the passage is completely clear-cut, then the energy flows, but you cannot feel it. You feel it when there is something there that resists the flow. If the energy flows upward and you have blocks in the passage, only then do you feel it. So the person who feels more kundalini is really

blocked: there are many blocks in the passage, so the kundalini cannot flow."

At this point, it's up to you whether you want to pursue raising kundalini. Read case studies like *Deciphering the Golden Flower One Secret at a Time*. Read the many other first hand accounts of kundalini awakenings. Do you want to move forward? Do you want to induce permanent kundalini? If so, use a reliable meditation method, one that you've vetted scrupulously. Do NOT attempt it if you're not absolutely sure and/or you don't have the time and the support system to follow through.

If you have experienced kundalini in any way, shape, or form, vivid memories of the experience will stay with you, even though the condition itself may have receded, even though the current may have ceased to flow. You will be able to use this experience in your ontological understanding of life.

Those whose Kundalini is permanently active

In *Kundalini: The Evolutionary Energy in Man* Gopi Krishna describes his search for individuals whose kundalini functioned 24-hours a day without respite. He did not find many. This in India — a country renowned for spiritual exploration and practices.

So if Gopi Krishna couldn't find them, and modern investigators can't find them, there can't be many. Why is this? There are as many reasons as there is diversity among individual experiences. Perhaps there should be a directory of case studies with gradations and classifications, especially given the interest in the subject and the various gurus and methods extant. But there is no directory.

The only testimony I can bring to bear is my own. That I've lived with kundalini for over forty years, that it's a biological transformation triggered by sexual energy, which produces intense neuroplastic activity which, in turn, leads to an extension of consciousness and in some cases, although it varies, the appearance of metaphysical phenomena.

I'd like to say that each permanent kundalini awakening is due to the successful application of a method but I can't. Even though I used Golden Flower Meditation (GFM), a time-tested method derived from *The Secret of the Golden Flower*. Even though I've been saying, "It worked for me. It ought to work for others."

So while the method should constitute a testimony to the ancient adepts who discovered it, I can't say with any certainty how many others have used my method successfully, even in cases where the individual insists he or she has. Is that a cop out? No, merely a scientific approach — the realization that each case is difficult to verify and document.

As with all historical information of this type, this method — the one I used — must be continually tested and improved. Why? Because if a serious line of study is ever to emerge around kundalini, methods must be tested and peer reviewed. After all, wouldn't you rather start your kundalini activation efforts with a reliable method than have kundalini strike you while riding the subway or watching a baseball game? I would.

For the moment, however, even with the extraordinary buzz surrounding kundalini and kundalini yoga at this time, there's no telling how, when, or where it will strike, and once it does strike, whether it will be permanent or temporary.

Since the death of Gopi Krishna in 1984, kundalini has fragmented into various and sundry groups, all believing they hold the answers to the mysteries of higher consciousness. Not that the focus was more acute while he was alive, it probably wasn't, but his voice — supported by his incisive writings — was practically the only consistently sensible voice out there. Since his death, a babel of voices has commanded the stage, and that disunity is responsible for the lack of focus and clarity.

Compare the research on kundalini to that on near death experience (NDE) and you see a disorganized set of rival tendencies compared to a phenomenon now being studied in Psychology

Departments at universities.

Why? NDEs have one trigger; kundalini has many. NDEs share the same effects while the effects of kundalini are varied and disparate. Yet, the effects of an NDE are a mere subset of those manifested after a permanent kundalini activation.

Why do I use the term activation, rather than awakening? While I don't use it exclusively, I do think it's appropriate because it shifts the discussion to a more scientific basis so we can begin to investigate the biological nature of this amazing phenomenon. If we are unable to do this, kundalini will remain a cult or sect with quasi-religious overtones in most people's minds. And we will keep spinning our wheels.

I don't rule out the divine in my investigation, but I have no a posteriori evidence to support it. Yes, I can hypothesize divine origins to certain aspects of kundalini, but, since I have no evidence of a divine origin, isn't that only the bias of cultural conditioning that's doing the hypothesizing? Rather than starting with assumptions about a divine connection, I want to start with a clean slate — tabula rasa, adding the only concrete bits of evidence I have, namely the sensations and phenomena I witnessed and experienced during my activation. These elements were biological in nature and they support the "biological basis" thesis that Gopi Krishna so ably pointed to forty years ago. If divine entities show up during this research, fine, but I'd rather work scientifically, with a clean slate than with assumptions that limit my research and may not turn out to be true.

Beyond the Relaxation Response

Until recently, meditation was considered a "spiritual" activity, a perception that caused many people to turn away from or avoid altogether. In the 1970s, however, research led to the development of the Relaxation Response, Dr. Herbert Benson's technique for promoting stress reduction and worker productivity. By borrowing techniques from Transcendental Meditation and other Eastern meditation methods and re-purposing them, Dr. Benson discovered a creative way of popularizing meditation.

My own research has uncovered benefits that go way beyond the Relaxation Response, and point to meditation as more than self-reflection. It's physical exercise, a less-is-more form of aerobics, which, by the way, if scrupulously practiced, removes the veil of duality.

By adding one simple step to the Relaxation Response, or any other serious meditation method, I have designed a system with tangible therapeutic and restorative health benefits. I call it Golden Flower Meditation[13] or (GFM), not for religious or spiritual affiliation reasons, but out of deference to the ancient Chinese who developed and practiced the method.

The key to GFM is "the backward-flowing method." Adding this one step to a meditation practice like the Relaxation Response opens the door to a safe, permanent kundalini awakening, after which self-healing, higher consciousness, stable life style, and emotional control are probable by-products.

After researching energy cultivation techniques for many years — and getting nowhere — I obtained a copy of *The Secret of the Golden Flower*, an ancient Taoist text from a stranger. I spent two years mastering the intricacies of the method, especially the arcane "backward-flowing method." Ultimately, success unleashed a powerful transformational force that rooted out all traces of illness and malformation in my body.

Through GFM my nervous system was stimulated such that the natural chemical substances of the body were recombined and used for healing. Is this remarkable meditation technique capable of bestowing similar therapeutic benefits on all those who master it? I believe it is. As long as the method is implemented correctly, many

---

13   For up-to-date information on the method, visit the Golden Flower
     Meditation website: https://www.goldenflowermeditation.com/the_method/

disabilities related to the nervous system are susceptible to treatment by this method. No, degenerative illness like heart disease, diabetes, and stroke cannot be cured by kundalini because, just as the term degenerative suggests, harm done to the body by poor diet, smoking, drinking, vaping, and other bad habits are difficult to reverse.

If the Relaxation Response establishes a healthy climate for combating stress, consider the extended benefits of GFM. GFM is not only about becoming a healthier person; it's also a useful ingredient in the pursuit of self-realization. Once the practitioner has mastered GFM, their ability to avoid addiction, to make well-reasoned decisions, to manage their health, and to live naturally improves dramatically. Who is suited for GFM? I believe it particularly interests doctors, trainers, researchers, scientists, nurses, students, laymen in all walks of life — in hospitals, businesses, universities, schools, progressive learning centers, and clinics.

Deciphering the Golden Flower One Secret at a Time is the story of my unearthing of the "backward-flowing method." It's not my technique; I didn't "invent" it. I came across it in *The Secret of the Golden Flower* during my practice of the method.

As for "the secrets," my book is not a laundry-list of techniques; it's an account of one individual's trial-and-error discovery and practice of GFM. Why take this approach? In teaching the GFM method, I've discovered that:

- People are impatient; they want get to the payoff without putting in the work. The method is a series of dependencies. You must master each step in turn; you cannot skip steps,
- In the past, even though I offered a meticulously prepared list of steps and how to apply them, many people either got lost, misunderstood, or misapplied the steps in practice,
- The book allows would-be practitioners to get a sense of what's involved, not only in the practice of the method, but also in what to expect afterwards. I've been living with kundalini for over forty years; that prospect is not something to be taken lightly.

Although some of Dr. Benson's acolytes have divided the

Relaxation Response into many sub-steps, Benson describes the critical steps as being:
- Breathe through your nose. Become aware of your breathing. As you breathe out, say the word, "ONE", silently to yourself. For example, breathe IN ... OUT, "ONE",- IN ... OUT, "ONE", etc. Breathe easily and naturally.
- Do not worry about whether you are successful in achieving a deep level of relaxation. Maintain a passive attitude and permit relaxation to occur at its own pace. When distracting thoughts occur, try to ignore them by not dwelling upon them and return to repeating "ONE." With practice, the response should come with little effort.

He sums up the two steps as follows:
- Focusing the mind on a word, phrase, or sound.
- Passively disregarding interfering thoughts.

According to the following republished in the Sun Sentinel:

"Herbert Benson, M.D. coined the phrase (Relaxation Response) after studying people who practiced Transcendental Meditation (TM). Benson took the principles of TM and removed them from their Eastern religious context in order to make them more accessible for westerners.

"The Relaxation Response represents a form of meditation which has been practiced for many years. The technique can be found in every major religious tradition. It is a simple technique, but it is not easy to practice or to incorporate into your life. You will find your mind wandering, and you will probably find it difficult to set aside the time to practice. It feels like setting aside twenty minutes a day to sit and do nothing.

"If you incorporate this or any relaxation technique into your life, you may notice at least the following four benefits:"
- "You will gain increased awareness of whether you are tense or relaxed. You will be more 'in touch with your body.'
- "You will be better able to relax when you become stressed-out.
- "You may even reduce the resting level of your autonomic nervous system — walking around more relaxed all the time.
- "Your concentration may improve. By repeatedly bringing yourself back to the meditation you are strengthening the part of

your mind that decides what to think about."[14]

That's a third party take on the Relaxation Response. The big news here is his discovery that meditation impacts health in a positive manner. This is no surprise to those already familiar with meditation, but the scope of Benson's project and its scientific methodology demonstrated the enormous potential of meditation.

What about Benson himself? What does he think? According to him, "The Relaxation Response seemed to cure or help any medical condition or illness to the extent that condition or illness was caused or exacerbated by stress. Because this physiological state was accessible to everyone, I became convinced that the Relaxation Response was the opposite of, and perhaps the antidote for, the stress-induced, fight-or-flight response. I found that anyone who employed the two steps could elicit the physical changes of the Relaxation Response."

More important than his health claims is Benson's insistence that meditation induces physiological changes or transformation.

First of all, whether a basic meditation method like the Relaxation Response contains two steps or two hundred, its immediate purpose is to produce the physiological change and transformation observed by Dr. Benson. So instead of judging a method by the number of steps, we need first to understand the physiological changes a basic two-step method hopes to induce and how efficient that method is in inducing them.

The physical changes produced by a basic two-step meditation method are:
- The development of systematic diaphragmatic deep breathing,
- The use of diaphragmatic breathing to control heart rate.

I propose a third, and even more powerful transformational step, but first I want to discuss the two steps mentioned above, both of which require intervention on the part of the practitioner.

14   "People Who Practice Transcendental Meditation Are Living Longer" – Alison Bass, The Boston Globe, March 12, 1990 http://articles.sun-sentinel.com/1990-03-12/features/9001290074_1_transcendental-meditation-tm-dr-herbert-benson

In Step One you encounter the notion of diaphragmatic deep breathing or the training of the diaphragm to regulate and improve your breathing. Unfortunately, since you cannot control or even isolate the muscles of the diaphragm directly, you must find a "handle" that allows you to do so indirectly. That handle is the belly or abdominal muscles.

If you push the belly out to pull in air on inhalation and pull the belly in to expel air, you are embarking on a regimen of abdominal and diaphragmatic calisthenics. Starting this activity for the first time — whether sitting, walking, or lying down — you may feel a burning sensation. This is the muscles of the abdomen and diaphragm telling you that you're breathing correctly. Using the belly muscles is like pump priming, i.e., using the handle of a pump (the belly) to activate the pump mechanism (the diaphragm).

Step Two uses the acquired diaphragmatic deep breathing skill as a means of slowing down the heart rate, which has the effect of relaxing the body, hence achieving the stated goal of the Relaxation Response. Again, since you cannot influence or control the heart rate directly, you must use a subterfuge or "handle" to accomplish it — in this instance, you use your mastery of Step One (diaphragmatic deep breathing capability) to make the breathing more profound and more regular. What do I mean by more regular? Regular means both rhythmic and deep.

Because you've acquired the diaphragmatic deep breathing skill, you can now take in more air during each breath cycle. How does this work? Shallow breathing merely fills the lungs. Deep breathing fills the lungs, the diaphragm, the belly, even pockets behind the kidneys. With diaphragmatic deep breathing you not only take in more air, you slow down the inhalation/exhalation cycle to the point where breathing is entirely silent. *The Secret of the Golden Flower* says, "Only the heart must be conscious of the flowing in and out of the breath; it must not be heard with the ears." Like the diaphragm, the heart is a muscle you cannot isolate or control directly. Once again you use a "handle" to control the heart (the source of emotion). As *The Secret of the Golden Flower* says, "The heart cannot be influenced directly. Therefore, the breath-energy is used as a handle."

The particular genius of Dr. Benson lies as much in his packaging and marketing approach as it does to the actual process. The first two steps in the Relaxation Response are common to most serious Western meditation methods imported from the East.

However, many teachers, including Dr. Benson, appear to gloss over or avoid one of the most challenging issues of all meditation methods and that is how to control wayward thought processes, the issue Dr. Benson identifies in his second step as "passively disregarding" interfering thoughts.

As opposed to the techniques in his method that he deems active, or "physical transformation processes," this process is defined by many, including Dr. Benson, as a passive process. He says so in the wording of his second step: "Passively disregarding interfering thoughts." Contrary to Dr. Benson, I believe the practitioner must take an active approach in quieting cognitive activity during meditation.

This uncontrolled cognitive activity has many names. One of the most colorful is the Taoist expression "the ten-thousand things." There are others, like "the inner dialogue," "monkey mind" — all our crazy secret thoughts and schemes. Dialogs with ourselves that not only interfere with meditation, but also stifle all efforts to realize one's full potential.

Nevertheless, it is difficult to control the mind directly, almost impossible to tell the mind to just "shut up" or try what Dr. Benson calls "passive disregarding." We need a kind of subterfuge or "handle" to stop the mind from running wild. Each teacher has his own approach. Yet frequently, the discussion over the best approach devolves into acrimony. I recommend two approaches to "handling" the 10,000 things. It's an attempt to "sidestep" the mind completely by giving it something banal to do.

And that is letting the little voice in your head — what psychologists call "inner speech" — count your breaths to yourself as you breathe. So, in a series of four beats, you would count: on inhale, one-two-three-four; on hold, one-two-three-four; on exhale, one-two-three-four; on hold, one-two-three-four. Start over. Inhale-four, hold-four, exhale-four, hold-four. Start over. This counting activity occupies the mind just enough to forestall the 10,000 things. Some practitioners have even found that the counting drops away of its own accord after a while, as diaphragmatic deep breathing becomes second nature.

A second approach to counting entails walking, that is, timing the breath cycle over a given number of strides, always breathing through the nose, of course. So you would time one breath cycle over a series of steps, for example, inhale one breath over four steps, hold that breath over four steps, exhale that breath over four steps, hold over four steps. Start over. In this way, the activity of walking and counting occupies the mind even more than inner speech alone does. It compounds its efficacy, especially if practitioners let themselves become mindful of the oneness of nature and being, the sights and sounds of nature come alive in him, thereby subduing the distractions of material life.

Now for the third transformational step and the physical changes it produces. Adding this next step takes the meditation process "Beyond the Relaxation Response." And it involves implementing "the backward-flowing method."

My familiarity with "the backward-flowing method" stems from extensive first-hand experience with Taoist meditation, detailed in *Deciphering the Golden Flower One Secret at a Time*. Written in narrative form, the book describes how I was given a copy of *The Secret of the Golden Flower* by a stranger in Paris during the early 1970s.

I was a bad actor at the time, so I put this book away for over a year. Then one day, as my life began to spin further out of control, I picked up the book and began reading it. Soon after, I started to meditate. At first, I didn't understand the text. Slowly, however, I began to "figure out" what to do.

I became so involved in the meditation that I left Paris to live in a small village in the south of France. The experience was one day, one page at a time. I didn't know what to expect, had no idea there would be such a dramatic outcome. I had never heard the word, kundalini. This was 1972. And Gopi Krishna's book wasn't available yet, not in my tiny French village.

The House I Lived in while Practicing GFM (1972)

Page by page I worked my way through *The Secret of the Golden Flower* until one day, while meditating, I noticed something different in my breathing. In *Deciphering the Golden Flower One Secret at a*

Time, I describe the moment thusly:

> "Observing my breath as I sit one morning, I am aware that it has the property of direction. At each inhalation the hitherto imperceptible wind in my belly appears to eddy slightly at the bottom of my abdomen as it descends before taking an upward circular course. Or so it appears to me. Down the back, then up the front, in a circular motion.

> "Something clicks. I remember the words 'backward-flowing method' in The Secret of the Golden Flower. Words I'd passed over a hundred times, never having a clue as to what they meant, never imagining they might be important. I break off to look for the passage. In two quick flips, I've located the text, 'At this time one works at the energy with the purpose of making it flow backward and rise, flow down to fall like the upward spinning of the sun-wheel…in this way one succeeds in bringing the true energy to its original place. This is the backward-flowing method.'"

Yes, diaphragmatic breathing is the key to stabilizing heart rate, but the key to causing the energy to flow upward to the brain is the 'backward-flowing method.' Again it works like pump-priming, that is, reversing the direction of the breath begins the process of drawing distilled seminal fluid (cervical fluid in the case of a woman) up the spinal column. This passage from my book describes what happened after I reversed my breath:

> "I visualize a plumb-line and close my eyes half-way. I command the breath to change direction and it obeys. I am elated at receiving confirmation from the book. What I don't yet realize is that this is the last time I will direct the meditation process. From now on I am on automatic pilot. I remember the words of Ram Dass: At first, you do it; later, it does you. Action to attain non-action.

> "For a week I observe my breath circulate in the opposite direction without noticing any effect. I go back to my uninspired routine: walking, cooking, meditating. Then, two weeks later, about the length of time it takes the backward-flowing process to become permanent, there's something new. On the day in question, I feel

a sensation at the base of my spine like the cracking of a small egg and the spilling out of its contents. For the next month, I observe the fluid-like contents of the egg trickle out of its reservoir and slowly begin to climb my spine. What is this fluid? I can't describe it exactly. It seems to emanate from the base of the spine and press upward. Each time I sit to meditate it has risen a half an inch higher."

I believe — and I discuss it in detail in my book — that *The Secret of the Golden Flower* contains the safest, most reliable method of taking one's meditation practice beyond the Relaxation Response, so much so that I have modernized it into a method for contemporary practitioners called Golden Flower Meditation or GFM. Of course, there are many methods, it's impossible to know them all. Some, it seems, like MCO, although more complex, are very close to GFM.

Although the 'backward-flowing method' is the key to arousing kundalini, it's a big step to consider because there's no turning back. I got confirmation of this fact first hand, for shortly after I willed my breath to change directions, the kundalini activation process began. Yes, there were glitches, but overall using *The Secret of the Golden Flower* to activate my kundalini has been a restorative process — physically, mentally, psychically, spiritually. And I believe it can be so for others.

When I met with him in Kashmir during the summer of 1977, Gopi Krishna termed my experience, "One of the most far-reaching, permanent kundalini awakenings I've encountered. Rare, very rare, indeed."

I ascribe the positive results I achieved in activating the restorative powers of kundalini to successful mastery of the "backward-flowing" technique in *The Secret of the Golden Flower* and, of course, to Karma, a concept Western science has little patience with.

Adding this one extra step to the two-step Relaxation Response process wakes up the hidden powers of kundalini and primes the body for restoration, renewal, and an explosion induced by a flood of psychic fuel into the nervous system. So I prescribe a three-step transformational process:

- The development of systematic diaphragmatic breathing,
- The use of diaphragmatic breathing to control heart rate,
- The moment you detect the property of movement, change the direction of your breath — the backward-flowing method.

The transformation that results from employing the "backward-flowing method," the secret techniques in ancient Taoist texts that I ultimately deciphered, were used by the ancients for reliable kundalini arousal.

Centering and Breathing

Nothing is More Important Than Proper Breathing — Diaphragmatic Deep Breathing[15].

Still, even if you breathe correctly, bad habits such as smoking, lack of exercise, overeating may negatively affect your overall breathing capacity. When you are a prisoner of habit, devotional practice and good intentions are to no avail. And that's where diaphragmatic deep breathing comes in. It can actually help you break bad habits.

So, is there a purpose to deep breathing, beyond its beneficial therapeutic effects? Diaphragmatic Deep Breathing allows you to slow down your metabolism, which in turn allows you to center yourself. What do I mean by centering?

It is hard to define centering because it is both a physical state (locus) and the awareness of being in that state. It's like being in the center of yourself and feeling and visualizing the confines of your being, watching it ebb and flow, and ultimately widen. Once you are able to center yourself, the very notion of confines drops away, and you exist in a state of undivided entirety.

Focusing on the tip of the nose with the eyes half-closed is

---

15   A web page dedicated to diaphragmatic deep breathing in the Kundalini Meditation context: https://www.goldenflowermeditation. com/the_method/making_preparations.html

helpful in learning to center yourself. In case the eyelids flutter, try to find just the right amount of "openness" until they stop. Once you find the optimal position for your eyes and are focused on the tip of your nose without straining, you might begin to feel a sensation of the "head expanding," as if some force is prying you apart from the center outward. If you can "lock in," so to speak, you're centered. Now hold it and breathe.

You can enter and exit this state (center yourself) at will. Moreover, knowing that this state exists and you are able to enter it allows you greater power in fending off the rigors and challenges of daily life. Not that the world around is shrinking; you become one with it and your being looms large in it. You feel yourself expanding, able to fend off any challenge. Breathing is the key to this state and needs to be mastered as a precondition to Golden Flower Meditation. I found a great description of the process, one that parallels and broadens mine. Check it out:

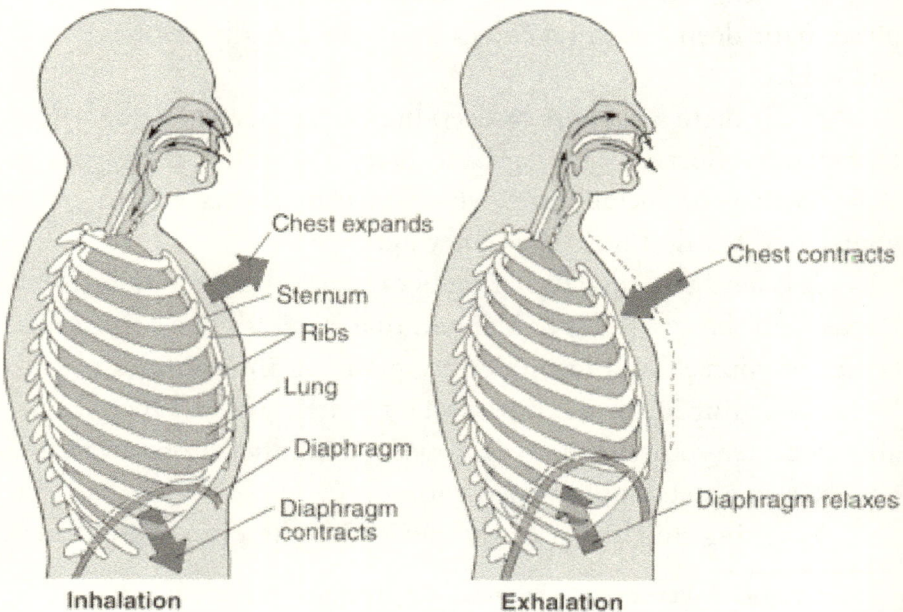

Chest expands
Sternum
Ribs
Lung
Diaphragm
Diaphragm contracts

Inhalation

Chest contracts
Diaphragm relaxes

Exhalation

"In the image above, the action of the diaphragm is shown. The diaphragm is located towards the bottom of the rib cage, and its job is to bellow down to draw breath into the lungs. This is much like squeezing a turkey baster. When you release the bulb, the action of it expanding draws air into the tube — this is natural breathing. Notice how in this way breath is draw in, not forced in. This type of breathing also ensures that the full area of the lungs are involved in the process, allowing more oxygen and energy to have access to the bloodstream."[16]

The Secret of the Golden Flower states:

"One should not be able to hear with the ear the outgoing and the intaking of breath. What one hears is that it has no tone. As soon as it has tone, the breathing is rough and superficial, and does not penetrate into the open. The heart must be made quite light and insignificant. The more it is released, the less it becomes; the less it is, the quieter. All at once it becomes so quiet that it stops. Then the true breathing is manifested and the form of the heart comes to consciousness. If the heart is light, the breathing is light for every movement of the heart affects breath-energy. If breathing is light, the heart is light, for every movement of breath-energy affects the heart. In order to steady the heart, one begins by taking care of the breath energy. The heart cannot be influenced directly. Therefore, the breath energy is used as a handle, and this is what is called maintenance of the concentrated breath-energy."[17]

Breathing is of vital importance; it is the first step in the quest for self-realization. A very important step, the key to new states of being. Begin the journey by exploring the relationship of breathing to heart rate and to centering. It leads to better health, reduced stress, and ultimately to ecstatic states and metaphysical exploration, should you choose to pursue them. But it starts with breathing. For a detailed description of proper breathing practice, visit the Visionary Being website. It's as simple as breathing in and breathing out. What's

---

16 Breath Of Life: Calm Power Through Natural Breathing ~Joshua Williams
17 *The Secret of the Golden Flower* – Routledge & Kegan
    Paul, Wilhelm Translation, 1931, p. 41.

more,[18] it's the doorway to the Backward-Flowing Method.

The Backward-Flowing Method

When you detect the sensation of movement in the lower belly as you breathe (after practicing GFM for 100 days), you are ready to initiate the backward-flowing method. What is it that moves? It is more a sensation than an action, more of an essence than a substance that moves in the lower belly, a sensation that may be perceived as breath energy, and essence akin to psychic fuel. Whatever its energetic composition, it also has the properties of movement and direction. You may perceive it as a sensation or an essence, something you can feel, but not actually touch, hear, or see.

Whatever it's true nature, it's perceived differently by individual practitioners. That's the reason it's difficult to express with everyday language. I first perceived it as a current of air in the lower belly, but now I'm convinced, after many years of reflection and years of listening to various accounts, that it's an etherized or distilled form of sexual energy. Where does this energy come from? Is it breath? Is it energy? Is it breath energy? It's the result of Diaphragmatic Deep Breathing (DDB), the catalyst for the sublimation process — an indication that you are starting to harness your energies instead of wasting them.

DDB is the key to stabilizing the heart rate, but the key to causing the energy to flow upward to the brain is the backward-flowing method. It, too, works like pump priming. Reversing the direction of the breath energy begins the process of drawing distilled seminal fluid up the spinal column.

I like to call it breath energy or psychic fuel because it's the result that correct breathing practices have on the body's energy apparatus; correct breathing starts the sublimation process, in other words, a distillation process. Sexual fluids — semen or cervical fluids

---

18 Visionary Being - https://visionarybeing.wordpress.com/2009/12/15/
    breath-of-life-calm-power-through-natural-breathing/

— plus lymphatic secretions are transformed, or distilled, into pure Pranic energy by diaphragmatic breathing practices. This movement in the lower belly is a sensation you have probably never felt before. You will either feel it or you won't. If you don't, I encourage you to continue practicing until you feel the breath energy circulating. If you do feel it, read on. I will explain how the backward-flowing method works. The purpose of the backward-flowing method is to divert this breath energy (the distilled seminal fluid or, in the case of a woman, the distilled cervical fluid) to the brain. If you thought it had any other purpose, you were mistaken. It is the driving force of evolution — the Secret of Life, plain and simple.

The question most people ask after, "What is the backward-flowing method?" is, "How does it work?" The backward-flowing method is a process with a beginning, a middle, and an end. And like any process, it has to proceed step-by-step in proper order, like a scientific experiment. The first step is to reverse the breath. Reversing the breath triggers step two: drawing the distilled seminal fluid up the correct channel in the spine. It ensures that the process will unfold correctly, without harming or frightening the practitioner.

Some respondents ask me what's so special about restorative Golden Flower Meditation. They say any number of serious meditation methods include some sort of sublimation process. And they're right, some do. The difference is that the backward-flowing method works by drawing the distilled seminal fluid (breath-energy) up the spinal column, not by thinking or visualizing it. What do I mean by drawing? I've been asked that question many times. This is a very subtle technique whose implementation begins only at the moment when a practitioner perceives that this breath-energy has the property of direction. This occurs in the lower belly.

Although the backward-flowing method is the key to making it all work, it's a big step to consider, because there's no turning back. Using Golden Flower Kundalini Meditation to activate the Life Force is a restorative process — physically, mentally, spiritually—for me and for the ancients who studied and practiced this method in the past, as well as for modern practitioners. Yet, it is a life-changing step. It will affect your being from body to mind, from eating habits to sexual nature. The Pranic energy (distilled seminal fluid) will be diverted to the brain and used to create a new being with a rejuvenated body and an aptitude for greater metaphysical exploration and understanding. Once the process is underway — the distilled seminal fluid is diverted to the brain — sexual activity and intercourse, even for procreation purposes, have a debilitating effect, at least in the immediate aftermath following awakening. The brain needs a constant supply of Pranic energy, so you must conserve it.

Receiving signals from the body and the ability to interpret them is crucial to your success. Movement and direction is a perfect example of this type of signal. If you practice regularly, master diaphragmatic deep breathing, learn to slow down your breath until you can't hear it, you will be able to control your metabolic responses — heart rate, etc. Your being will reach a state of total stillness during meditation, a state of permanent attentiveness, a state of inner visualization, the point where breath takes over being. You will be able to observe sensations inside your body. These phenomena are real occurrences. In *The Future of the Body*, Michael Murphy points to them as examples of the metanormalities of everyday life.

When you become aware of this activity — that the breath energy in your belly has the properties of movement and direction — it will put you on notice that the time has come to decide whether you want to continue. Should you decide to go forward, all you have to do is command this Pranic energy to change directions. It will obey. It will appear to you that you have changed the direction of the flow of air in your breathing. Instead of moving down the back and up the front, you will command it to move down the front and up the back — the backward-flowing method!

How does "commanding the breath to change direction" work? Recently, a young woman started a dialogue about it over the

Internet. She came up with the phrase "directed intention." It's a phrase I think works well to describe the process.

Many people have asked me when they can expect this sensation/activity to occur. Many ask why it hasn't already happened for them. They even say they think it might be happening, but they aren't sure that they are able to recognize it. They ask me to help them.

I tell people that it usually happens about 100 days into the meditation practice, but before it happens, they must master each step, each technique in turn. In other words, there are a certain number of dependencies. How can an individual expect to be able to detect the property of direction in the flow of air in the lower belly if they haven't regulated their breath, slowing it down to the point of absolute stillness? If you do not hear your breath, you become that much more able to "feel" it, to become one with it. Once you become one with it, you can direct it.

But you must master deep breathing completely to the point where inhalation and exhalation become totally still. How long will it take to master deep breathing to the point where you observe the aforementioned "property of movement"? Whether it takes 100 days or 365 days, if you want to succeed, you'll have to continue until you can breathe without hearing your breath. Silent on inhalation, silent on exhalation.

As for me telling you if the activity has begun or telling you when it might begin, I can't do that. It's up to you to learn to communicate with your body. What I can say is that if you progress through the breathing exercises and learn to listen to your breathing cycle, you will eventually detect the property of movement, as if the air in your belly is moving. In fact, you will become aware of the slightest occurrences within your body.

Why is drawing the distilled seminal fluid (sexual energy) up the spinal column superior to thinking or visualizing or forcing it up the spinal column? Those methods can cause the distilled seminal fluid to go up the wrong channel, a condition that may induce severe pain or discomfort. In Kundalini: The Evolutionary Energy in Man, Gopi Krishna explores this issue in depth.

The backward-flowing method doesn't let this happen. Why? Because, once again, it's like pump priming. Changing the direction of the breath energy kicks off the sublimation process, opening the reservoir of seminal fluid and sending its distilled essence up the proper channel. It's a seamless, imperceptible process — the breath slowly drawing the seminal fluid out of its reservoir, distilling it, and sending it up the spinal column.

The whole process is a series of dependencies. Step one "allows" the next step to proceed without adversely affecting the process or the results, which are 1) Kundalini activation, and 2) Life Force energy arousal. However, one cannot reverse the breath energy without first detecting the property of movement in the flow of air in the lower belly (another dependency).

Heredity, Environment, and Karma

Here's a little theoretical background on where, when, and why kundalini visits some, but not other individuals.

We know about the influence of heredity and environment on the ontological[19] and psychological evolution of groups. To some degree, we can even predict the development of individuals.

For instance, the current US population is 325,000,000 (three hundred and twenty five million). A recent Surgeon General's report states that one in seven (1/7 | 14%) are, or will become, addicted. That would amount to 45M persons becoming addicted. The USA Today summary of the report states, "genetics accounts for about half of a person's likelihood of becoming addicted." Could this curiously worded sentence mean that the other half of the 45M will become addicted due to environmental factors? If this is true, it tells

19   Ontology: a branch of metaphysics concerned with the nature
      and relations of being. A particular theory about the nature
      of being or the kinds of things that have existence.

us that addiction is half heredity and half environmental so that:
- A person might become addicted because he or she was exposed to prescription drugs for medical reasons and, after treatment ended, is psychologically and metabolically unable to return to his or her former prescription-less life style, or,
- A person might have sampled the wares in a friend's medicine cabinet and become immediately dependent because his or her DNA receptors, inherited from a parent, had flipped a switch in the brain.

So where does Karma fit in? Setting aside the issue that Karma is not something that science acknowledges as real — not that science accepts the Christian notion of God either — it is part of the present topic.

What is Karma? This Internet definition states (in Hinduism and Buddhism): "the sum of a person's actions in this and previous states of existence, viewed as deciding their fate in future existences."

A definition, which, in our example, might impact an individual's chances of becoming addicted, or, in a more spiritual context, might influence an individual's chances of successfully arousing kundalini.

In a recent Symposium, we discussed the attributes that facilitate kundalini awakenings, one of which was the notion of the Field, or a kind of Quantum event that "bounces" the affected person out of his normal vibrational alignment into an alternate, random, alignment of matter and consciousness that ultimately produces a kundalini awakening.

The thesis of my presentation was that matter (sexual energy) and consciousness, in their own right, are not enough to guarantee a kundalini awakening; these elements must be accompanied by a Quantum event. This would explain why certain persons are unable to arouse kundalini no matter how hard they try. It would also explain why kundalini visits certain persons without their ever wishing for it.

It might also explain why some people resist addiction in spite of harboring the characteristics of the 17%. There is a random, aleatory aspect to the energy continuum that influences karmic certainties — reasons why some individuals escape poverty and others escape addiction when all environmental and heredity markers point to their becoming dependent.

Can we then overthrow the effects of heredity and environment in order to create an entirely independent new Being? Kundalini provides a biological basis — a jumping off point for karmic realignment.

Is Kundalini Safe?

Two questions were recently posed by a very astute student. Here they are with my replies:

There doesn't seem to be a root cause behind these 'improper activations.' Is kundalini safe? Is there an optimal method that assures safe landings? How do I know it will work for me?

Presuming it is safe, will it affect normal family life? Is there an optimal age at which to begin practicing?

Answer 1: You answered your own question, at least partially, when you stated: "... there doesn't seem to be a root cause behind these 'improper activations.'"

This is accurate. There are many forms of activations (triggers) and outcomes (effects). When Gopi Krishna and I spoke about my practice of Golden Flower Meditation method, he kept coming back to the Backward-Flowing Method (BFM), a technique based on sexual sublimation. He was aware of it, realized it might be the key to safe awakenings. How so?

All kundalini episodes are the result of some sort of sexual sublimation. It's how the sublimation process takes place that's crucial. The BFM assures the energy is drawn up the correct channel. How does it assure both the conversion of sexual energy into an elixir the brain can tolerate and the proper channeling of the elixir? The following is copied from the Golden Flower Meditation method:

"Some respondents ask me what's so special about Golden Flower Meditation. They say any number of serious meditation methods include some sort of sublimation process. And they're right; some do. The difference is that the backward-flowing method works by drawing the distilled seminal fluid (breath-energy) up the spinal column, not by thinking or visualizing it. What do I mean by drawing? I've been asked that question many times. This is a very subtle technique whose implementation begins only at the moment when a practitioner perceives that this distilled breath energy has the property of direction. This occurs in the lower belly.

"Why is drawing the distilled seminal fluid (sexual energy) up the spinal column superior to thinking or visualizing, or forcing it up the spinal column? Those methods can cause the distilled seminal fluid to go up the wrong channel, a condition that may induce severe pain or cause other problems. In Kundalini: The Evolutionary Energy in Man, Gopi Krishna explores this issue in depth."[20]

I followed this method in *The Secret of the Golden Flower* (SGF), updated it for modern practitioners in *Deciphering the Golden Flower One Secret at a Time*. I know it works. So did Gopi Krishna, so did the ancient adepts who contributed to the SGF.

How do I know it works for others? Tom Kinney has already addressed this.[21] I'd like to add the following: CHECK YOUR SYMMETRY. Symmetry is the best indicator of future success. Gopi Krishna spoke to this:

"Can we deny the fact that whether fortuitous gift, divine grace, or the fruit of Karma, in every case there is a close link between the talent or beauty exhibited and the organic structure of the individual."

Any difficulties I experienced were not those of poor implementation of the techniques, they were due to my asymmetry, detailed in *Deciphering the Golden Flower One Secret at a Time* and since

20 The Golden Flower Meditation Method
    https://www.goldenflowermeditation.com/the_method/
21 How I got started with The Backward Flowing Method - http://www.
    kundaliniconsortium.org/2012/11/how-i-got-started-with-backward-flowing.html

corrected by kundalini.

Answer 2: Questions concerning Start or Don't Start or When should I start can only be answered by you.

Nevertheless, I offer the following: it's very important to consider what life would be like should you awaken kundalini. Gopi Krishna told me sex would be amazing once the settling in process was complete. Was he correct? Depends on the individual. Kundalini inventories the body after activation and determines if there neural adjustments to be made and blockages to be cleared. Depending on the individual, this process takes the time it takes. Don't take kundalini for granted; there are challenges you must consider.

One thing is certain: Your life will change! Will you be able to manage the changes?

I would add "children" into the mix. Think carefully. I've had children, so have others. Just remember kundalini requires a large measure of your sexual energies. Is there enough to go around? Enough to spare? Living with kundalini is the least explored aspect of the whole experience; so many focus on the "transformational" aspects, believing once it happens, their work is over and kundalini will manage the rest.

The Proper Study of Kundalini is Kundalini

Why are so many books on kundalini in the West written by people who have never had a kundalini experience? In the East, it's the practitioners that students seek out, the ones with experience. Not those who sit in libraries, copying information from other sources, lord knows, how many times removed from an actual kundalini experience. And not just any kundalini experience — a permanently active one.

I've shared venues with other speakers lecturing on kundalini some of whom, it turned out, never had a kundalini experience. Strikes me as somewhat inadequate, but indicative of the outsized value we in the West place on second hand research, degrees, and diplomas. Now to get a degree, you have to get a good SAT score; you have to score well. And to score well, you have to understand the game, know what's expected of you. Do you have to think or act creatively? No. All you have to do meet expectations. In fact, the people that score well by meeting expectations carry this trait over into their careers. They know how to meet expectations, to score well. It's the quintessential definition of a YES man. That's what the SAT mentality creates. Individuals who are prepared to please.

What do Orson Welles, William Blake, Stanley Kubrick, Michael Faraday, Woody Allen, Jacob Boëme, George Bernard Shaw, Socrates, and Ben Franklin have in common? All of them are autodidacts. Self taught by doing, by on the job training.

Would you take flying lessons from someone who's never flown? Then you'd be dealing with opinion and not fact. And that's just what you get from a book that's been written by someone who's never had a kundalini experience: Opinions about how it might work as opposed to facts about how it does work.

I'm not against reading. I read a lot. Less that I used to, especially since I have so much kundalini material to work with. Reading and research are fine up to a point. Sri Ramakrishna said, "Do you know my attitude? Books, scriptures, and things like that only point out the way to reach God. After finding the way, what more need is there of books and scriptures? Then comes the time for action."

So why do so many people spend so much time searching for spiritual meaning when scientists tell them that, aside from anecdotal accounts, there is scant evidence that metaphysics are real? Probably for the same sense-of-urgency reasons that drive so many physical scientists to experiment on themselves, using their bodies as laboratories. Here is a sampling of three cases from Wikipedia:

"One evening in June 1984 Dr. Barry Marshall walked into the hospital lab, opened a test tube and added several eyedroppers of a light gray liquid to a glass beaker filled with broth. With a quick toss of the head, he swallowed the foul tasting concoction. Within 72 hours, he was doubled over in pain with a roaring case of clinical gastritis, a precursor to ulcers. Severe vomiting and stomach pain kept him awake for nights. He shuddered to think of what it was like for patients who had such symptoms on and off for years. But by the time he started the antibiotic/bismuth treatment, his system had managed to eradicate the germ."

"JBS Haldane, a notable British biologist, is yet another example of a scientist who conducted experiments upon himself. Haldane was a keen experimenter, and was more than willing to expose himself to danger in order to obtain the desired data. One such experiment involving elevated levels of oxygen saturation triggered a fit which resulted in him suffering crushed vertebrae. In his decompression chamber experiments, Haldane and his volunteers suffered perforated eardrums, but, as Haldane stated in What is Life, 'The drum generally heals up; and if a hole remains in it, although one is somewhat deaf, one can blow tobacco smoke out of the ear in question, which is a social accomplishment.'"

"Roger Altounyan developed the use of sodium cromoglycate as a remedy for asthma, based on khella, a traditional Middle Eastern remedy, with experiments on himself."

How do these relate to kundalini and consciousness? These researchers realized that the only way to test their discoveries was from the inside out, in contrast to the scientific method that prescribes experiments based on observation (the outside-in approach). If the remedy worked on them, they thought, it must work on others. And because they faced steadfast opposition from scientists taking the outside-in approach, this proved to be the only way of moving their work forward. They recognized the moment and they acted!

Yes, using the body as a laboratory is lonely, dangerous work. You have to learn to rely on your intuition and summon up abilities you never knew you had. Outside acceptance and validation are rare. What's more, even if you do reach your goal, don't expect a Nobel Prize.

It takes a big person to acknowledge their opposition was

ill founded: "Even Walter Peterson [Chief of Gastroenterology at the Veterans Affairs Medical Center in Dallas], long a skeptic of Marshall's theories, has come around. He says now, 'We scientists should have looked beyond Barry's [Dr. Barry Marshall] evangelical patina and not dismissed him out of hand.' Agrees Vanderbilt's Blaser, 'Science needs solid research, but it also needs someone with great vision. Barry had vision.'"

In any case, the inside-out approach, the one material scientists call anecdotal accounts, is valid. If it doesn't fit the strict requirements of the scientific method, it's not because a given metaphysical experience never happened, it's because we don't have the proper tools for measuring metaphysical phenomena at this point. We will... someday. It's too bad there isn't an open dialogue, because scientists and meta-physicists should be working together not only on the true nature of consciousness, but on methods of exploring it.

Just because someone tells you metaphysical experience is not valid doesn't mean it isn't — that your experience didn't really happen, that it's all in your mind. They said that to Dr. Barry Marshall, to Dr. Paul Erlich, to Dr. John Lilly, too. But they moved ever forward, in spite of the opposition: "When Barry Marshall finally presented his and Warren's findings before an international conference of microbiologists in Brussels in September 1983, he was greeted with some skepticism. Unschooled at such presentations and filled with boyish eagerness, he refused to respond to questions in the measured, cautious manner of most researchers. Asked whether he though the bacteria were responsible for some ulcer disease, Marshall replied, "No, I think they're responsible for all ulcer disease."

"Such blanket statements, backed only by small studies and anecdotal case histories alarmed many researchers. Microbiologist Martin Blaser, an infectious disease expert from Vanderbilt University who attended the conference, said, 'At that time, I thought the guy was a madman.'"

What makes scientists so skeptical? For one, it's their training, and that's a good thing. But when it comes to new horizons, such as metaphysics, they seem as closed-mined as the 15th century knuck-leheads who persecuted Leonardo da Vinci. Material scientists tend to lump accounts of metaphysical experience, including such widely occurring phenomenon as Near Death Experience (NDE), in with religion, forgetting, it seems, that kundalini and near death experiences occur across cultures, geography, and language to people of all religions, including those who profess no religion at all. Saying kundalini isn't biology, it's religion is the same sort of short-sight-ed comment directed at Dr. Barry Marshall when they told him bacteria didn't cause ulcers; stress and worry did...until he proved the conventional wisdom wrong, that is.

I'd love to tell you there's a quick fix, that raising kundalini is easy to do and easy to live with. From reading the letters people write to me, I know it isn't. It wasn't for me and it hasn't been for them. Activating kundalini takes time. Is it wrong to experiment? Not at all. The world today is a laboratory of experimentation. Millions of people, young and old, are working to achieve self-knowledge and higher consciousness. Some flounder; some go straight to their goal. All I can add is: Keep on trying. Take action. Try all and everything. But be prepared to discard whatever it is that doesn't ring true. Don't be a YES man in exploring consciousness. But don't be afraid it won't work either. Kundalini is coded into your biosystem. All you have to do is find the switch that triggers it. I used meditation, a seemingly benign pastime that ended up triggering biomechanisms (the sexual sublimation process) in my body that transformed my biological structure, my anatomy, and eventually my consciousness.

How do you recognize when the right system or technique comes along? You have to keep testing, listening to your body. The body knows (it's a biology laboratory), and if you're practicing — whatever that practice may be — your body will send you signals to interpret. It won't steer you wrong. It's akin to auto-diagnosis.

Practice makes things happen. If nothing happens, try

something else. Prefer primary sources to secondary. Talk to those who have already succeeded in a given practice, but do so with skepticism. Talk, read, think, travel, and remain skeptical. YOU are the proper study of YOU! All else is opinion and rationalization, not much good to you when the time does come. And it WILL!

Sexuality And Kundalini

In Gopi Krishna's book, *The Biological Basis of Religion and Genius*, what do you think the word biological refers to? No tongue twister, trick question here: the answer clearly is SEX, or the repurposing of sexual energy for evolutionary advancement within the space of a single lifetime.

> "It is sufficient to mention here that during the whole course of this (kundalini) transformation, in addition to the blood and other fuels present in the body, every particle of powerful reproductive fluid in the system is sucked up through the spinal canal to irrigate and feed the various nerve junctions and the brain. This entirely biological operation is carried out in such an unmistakable way that even a novice in physiology cannot fail to notice it. The semen in men is now produced in such abundance that a tiny stream rises day and night through the spine into the cranium to provide the richest and the purest food for the now heavily overworked brain cells. In women, the sexual energy and secretions involved in erotics are used as the fuel. This is a perfect example of the forethought and ingenuity of nature to keep the body equipped with all the necessities to make the completion of the evolutionary process, normally needing eons to accomplish, possible in the short span of one life."

~ *The Biological Basis of Religion and Genius* – Gopi Krishna

Everyday, this information is becoming both accessible and understood by more and more people, whether it's through exposure to books like *Deciphering the Golden Flower One Secret at a Time* or *Kundalini: The Evolutionary Energy in Man* or just by talking or exchanging information on web forums. People are beginning to understand this information and act on it. Sublimation, as a process for using sexual energy to awaken kundalini, is ubiquitously at your disposal. There are almost as many techniques as practitioners.

But sublimation is accompanied by a trade-off. According to Bonnie Greenwell:

> "During this time which is so intense, there will be moments when the sexual drive just disappears because all the energy — physiological, psychological, emotional — goes in a different direction. It's really important for a person not to take on a rigid belief system, but to listen to what their body needs right now. And if it wants, needs to be celibate, doesn't feel driven at all towards sexual experience, then honor that for the period of time if it feels that way."[22]

There are times when you can't share the sexual energy; kundalini needs it all to accomplish its evolutionary mandate. Ejaculating (the outward flow of sexual energy) during intercourse instead of sublimating it (the inward and upward flow of sexual energy to the brain) is deleterious and harmful not only to the kundalini process but to the body itself.

If some fail to arouse kundalini, it's probably due to the issue of adapting a particular technique to a particular individual. Or perhaps it's Karmic — the individual isn't ready. One lifetime too few perhaps. Or a technique that might work is out of reach, unknown to the initiate.

I get questions pertaining to sexual pathology — involuntary ejaculation, hormonal irregularities, inability to consummate, low semen count, erectile dysfunction — questions from readers considering kundalini as a possible means for overcoming their condition. Every type of sexual idiosyncrasy.

Yes, what about gays? Are they somatically or metabolically unable to activate kundalini? With so little discussion on this issue, it's important to reread Gopi Krishna's passage above. Nowhere does he say that certain groups or individuals are excluded from accomplishing this process. In fact, this process isn't about sexual energy

22 The Triggers in Kundalini Awakenings – YouTube

flowing out; it's about conserving sexual energy, about holding it in, redirecting it. And that's a big challenge right there because it supposes that interested parties — especially males — are going to refrain from ejaculation because it interferes with the activation process. It's a big hurdle. Many are infatuated with kundalini, but don't want to abstain from sex.

It's understandable that individuals who consider themselves "sexually irregular," either over- or under-sexed, or otherwise impaired, should regard kundalini as a possible solution. And while no group or person is excluded, some persons may need clinical treatment for the irregularities they cite.

However, when I'm asked if kundalini is a cure for such and such irregularity, there's little I can say. Fact is, I don't know. If I were to guess, I would say it behooves the individual to investigate his/her condition first. Think about treatment. See a pathologist. Consider the fact that some awakenings turn out badly. After all, if kundalini is only being considered as a remedy for some condition, it might indicate that the person is not truly purposed for the challenges ahead, not suited to the regimen kundalini imposes. You have to consider all sides of the issue. *The Backward-Flowing Method: The Secret of Life and Death* explores the challenges of living with Kundalini American-Style.

Take It Easy, You'll Get There – With Or Without Kundalini

You're worried that other people are making more progress on the spiritual pathway. You'd give anything for a quick fix to enlightenment. There's certainly no lack of tempting Shangri-La proffers: strip-mall yoga studios, checkout line spiritual magazines, water-cooler mindfulness discussions. The familiar optimism while you're at your umpteenth seven-day, total transformation retreat. And then, the return to the fray followed by a letdown.

Alas, there is no mythical Himalayan utopia, no happy land, isolated from the outside world. Only the drip, drip, drip of everyday life. Fox News, MS-NBC, news and fake news, saber-rattling, money-making, penny-pinching, love-starved, thrill-a-minute reality TV.

Rule One: Don't make your spiritual quest a competition.

You know you're different. You feel different. You are different. You're ready to make the effort, to answer the call: meditation, kundalini, mindfulness, yoga — some catalyst that will take you to the "there" — beyond duality.

Relax...you will get there: self-actualization, salvation, self-realization, enlightenment. You name it; they're one and the same — no matter the bells and whistles associated with the various competing spiritual trends. All roads lead to the same destination. Not in this lifetime, perhaps, but eventually.

If they're not for you, don't undertake pretzel-bending yogic contortions, declarations of faith, or kundalini devotions. You don't have to spend years of your life meditating like Gopi Krishna and myself.

Rule Two: Don't force it.

Why? Because the more strenuous the practice, the more likely you'll get caught up in something you never bargained for. It's not a race; it's not competitive. There are no medals for spiritual excellence. Not everyone is suited for exertion, be it cognitive, physical, emotional, or spiritual.

So what makes me say you'll get there anyway? Evolution, that's what! Ever thought about it? About the one-celled life forms we evolved from? About how long it took us to evolve from that lowly avatar to where we are today? That's right; we think we're the greatest. We hold dominion over all, don't we? Look around: things don't appear so secure, not as secure as we might desire or imagine. Maybe we haven't finished evolving. Maybe there's a lot of ground to cover.

Of course, you can try to jumpstart the process. yoga, Tai Chi, kundalini yoga, crystals, Scientology, mindfulness, witchcraft.

Does the process you're currently involved with work? Has it made a real difference in your life? Are you following through with it? Did you get all whooped up, just to watch it peter out? Practice relentlessly only to get no results?

I don't mean to be cynical about spiritual purpose. I know a lot of people are succeeding, just as others are not. But what are the increasing numbers of seekers really looking for? When you boil all the white noise down to first principles, they're looking to dissolve duality and merge with the Energy Continuum. In other words, Oneness — No matter the path, purpose, or practice.

Nevertheless, many sincere seekers fall by the wayside, which leads to disenchantment, disaffection, and discouragement. No need to berate yourself. Live an honest life, follow the Golden Rule and evolution will do the rest:

> "If it's a set of moral standards for daily life, what more do you need than the Golden Rule? 'Treat others as you would like to be treated' or its Judaic counterpart, 'What is hateful to you, do not do to your neighbor.' Most religions share this ethic of reciprocity. If the world's population observed it, it's hard to imagine crime or war existing. But that's another issue.
>
> "If the goal of religion is enlightenment or salvation, above and beyond a moral code for leading a good life, then the various religions have done a poor job. Wars, pogroms, crusades, jihads, persecutions, sexual molestations, inquisitions, witch-hunts are only some of their failings."[23]

Rule Three: "What is hateful to you, do not do to your fellow."

Sound familiar? It should. It's the Talmudic variation of The Golden Rule. Al the morality you need for life on Earth.

As for evolution doing the rest, all our best characteristics are slowly improved on and carried over to future generations in DNA. It's what Gopi Krishna called The Evolutionary Impulse. He knew

---

23 ~ "Finding God - Within Or Without" - JJ Semple - www. kundaliniconsortium.org/2017/04/finding-god-within-or-without.html

that kundalini energy, even in its mistakenly labeled "dormant" state, is still active. It must be, otherwise we would never have evolved at all.

Let's hope that the wonders wrought by our evolution get to play themselves out over the coming millenniums, that evolution does not become devolution, which, when we evaluate current events, is anything but a given. There's a lot to be vigilant about and it begins with the ability of the self to make good life, as well as, lifestyle decisions.

Develop your mind, body, and spirit to the best of your ability and you will get there. I promise.

It takes a lot of work, which sometimes means less effort and more letting go.

Rule Four: Forget doctrinal purity!

Imagine you're in heaven or a Tibetan Buddhist bardo state after death — a bodiless being. There's nothing to adhere to: no belief system, nothing to waste your time on, trying to convert or convince another Being.

In life, someone is always waving the rulebook at you. As a bodiless being — in heaven or in a bardo — there are no rules. Don't let anyone force their beliefs on you, and don't force your beliefs on anyone else. That goes for methods, techniques, systems, religions, politics, etc. Think for yourself!

Rule Five: Let go!

Kundalini Effects

"First I am a Zorba, and then I am a Buddha. And remember, if I have to choose between the two, I will choose Zorba, not Buddha... because the Zorba can always become the Buddha, but the Buddha becomes confined to his own holiness. He cannot go to the disco and become the Zorba. And to me, freedom is the highest value; there is nothing greater, more precious, than freedom."[24]

~ Osho

The Blueprint of your Physical Body

"We are all perfect at that split-second moment before conception. Of course, like a building before the foundation is laid, at that moment our beings are only blueprints. These blueprints — the numinous plans laid out for our incarnation — are perfect. At the moment of conception — the moment the egg is fertilized by the sperm — the body begins to take shape. It's the moment when, were we able to stand over our perfect blueprints, we might wonder if they can be executed as designed. From the moment we're born, any one of thousands of stimuli — within or out of our control — can alter our growth, assuring degrees of deviation from the blueprint for our unique bodily incarnation.

"After activating the Kundalini-Life Force, I was able to see the blueprint of my perfect body and compare it to my altered state. Amazingly, the Life Force recognized my deformity and immediately began to correct it. I witnessed it slowly reshape my anatomy to the exact proportions in the blueprint. So — and this requires a leap of logic — if I could see the original design for my body and it was perfect in every way, there must be some sentient agency that created this design. And even though my growth took a detour on account of my deformity, the blueprint continued to

---

24 cf. "Rajneesh aimed to create a "new man" combining the spirituality of Gautama Buddha with the zest for life embodied by Nikos Kazantzakis' *Zorba the Greek*: "He should be as accurate and objective as a scientist ... as sensitive, as full of heart, as a poet ... [and as] rooted deep down in his being as the mystic."[171] [195] His term the "new man" applied to men and women equally, whose roles he saw as complementary; indeed, most of his movement's leadership positions were held by women.[196] This new man, "Zorba the Buddha", should reject neither science nor spirituality but embrace both." https://en.wikipedia.org/wiki/Rajneesh#Renunciation_and_the_.22new_man.22

exist in some ethereal computer-memory-like storage, waiting for the day that I might learn of its existence and find a way back to it.

"Happily, GFM, the method of meditation I practiced, restored my deformed body to its original state, and, in so doing, proved both the existence of the blueprint and the restorative power of the Kundalini-Life Force. This sounds an awful lot like Intelligent Design, doesn't it? A permanent blueprint of our beings and a mechanism within the body capable of restoring it to its intended state."

~ Deciphering the Golden Flower One Secret at a Time - JJ Semple

I suppose some readers pass over the above without a second thought. One reader, however, challenged me to explain these words when he posted this inquiry, "Dear JJ: How does a person access their blueprint? It's not clear from your book."

I got to thinking, and I had to agree: It isn't entirely clear, but not because my description is poor — it's the best I can do — but because you can't see the mountaintop until you're on top of the mountain.

So what's the real issue? For one, the only way to describe a phenomenon like this is by liberal use of imagery: "perfect body," "template shroud," "sentient agency," "causal body overlay," "incarnated energy," "controlling field," "permanent numinous plans?" Two, we have to determine what this blueprint is before we can talk of accessing it.

I don't know any way of doing this without using more imagery. No words suffice or exist for those who have never experienced the energy continuum. But I won't compound the difficulty by adding more imagery.

When my kundalini awakened, I was able to see two separate bodies, one, my actual physical form; the other, my intended form that lay over my physical body like a template shroud. I knew it was there; I knew it was perfect. I knew the physical body could be "stretched" to fit this causal body, using it as a blueprint to restore my physical body to its intended form. So how did I know it?

I wasn't able to get to the state that allowed me to perceive the blueprint/aura until I had successfully mastered all steps of the method. Once I saw the blueprint, I realized it had always existed. It was responsible for my earthly incarnation. How so?

When someone says kundalini is "dormant" until activated in later life, it implies that if it is sleeping, it must have been there all along. An entity can't sleep unless it already exists. And that's the case with kundalini. In fact, it's as much a part of you as your flesh and bones. It created them; that's what the life force does.

> "After the process of creation of the body is complete, *Kundalini Shakti* is said to go into a dormant state. But it can become active again later in life as the spiritual process known as a Kundalini awakening. But rather than creating a new life form from a fertilized ovum, it now undertakes a process of renovation of the existing human body, particularly the brain and nervous system, so that a more advanced faculty of mind — cosmic consciousness or enlightenment — can be manifested."[25]

As previously stated, it's responsible for the blueprint of your being, responsible for the formation of your embryo, for your fetus, for your physical body up to the moment of birth, at which time it hibernates. Up to the moment of your birth, it stays one step ahead of your actual embodiment, carefully matching your anatomy to the three-dimensional form as prescribed in your blueprint.

> "There can be no doubt that the DNA contains the master plan for how every type of cell in our body is maintained and replicated. Nor can there be any doubt that the constitution of our cells determines many aspects of how our body functions. But the building of a fetus in the womb is a process many orders of magnitude greater in complexity than building a protein or enzyme in a cell. If no physical mechanism can be found that can coordinate and control this process, then the only conclusion that can be reached is that it is being done by a creative intelligence

---

25 Bradford, Michael. *Consciousness: The New Paradigm* (p. 83). Institute for Consciousness Research. Kindle Edition. https://amzn.to/2rDyI75

that is totally unknown to science at present."[26]

Nevertheless, throughout your life, *Kundalini Shakti* waits to be summoned from slumber and use its super-conscious intelligence to guide your now capital 'B' Being to a more enlightened state. If remedial metabolic, somatic, or anatomical work needs to take place, the awakened kundalini is able to call forth and access your original blueprint and use it as a pattern to restore your body to its intended physiological state, according to the blueprint.

Once my kundalini re-awakened, my nervous system found another level of activity, as if it had morphed from a chugging Model-T Ford to the Warp Drive propulsion of a Star Trek spacecraft. My mind's eye perceived my aura shimmering around my body.

See my aura? I had never been able to beforehand. Whole lifetimes without seeing one's aura is par for the course in most cases. It could have easily been mine. Yet when it happened, it was a feeling greater than enchantment; it signaled a complete breakdown of the duality paradigm. I realized I was a part of a greater whole, that I extended beyond the limits of my physical body into an infinite horizon. There are many other types of awakening experiences, many induced by other sorts of stimuli or triggers, but I only know mine.

I can tell you about it, I do in my books, but you shouldn't rely on me. In fact, the more you rely on me or anyone else, the less likely you are to actually experience any of this as anything but an intellectual exercise. A big part of the method — of any method — is the necessity of validating everything you see, hear, and feel, whether you hear it from me or whether you perceive it yourself. An even bigger part is practicing the method until you become a trained observer of the inner landscape. Complete the method — all parts, all steps — as per the instructions. When you do, you won't ask questions, you will have answered them the only way possible:

---

26 Bradford, Michael. *Consciousness: The New Paradigm* (pp. 81-82). Institute for Consciousness Research. Kindle Edition. https://amzn.to/2rDyI75

by hard work and practice. Only then can you expect to reach states attainable by completing the work.

What's more, there are no guarantees in this work; you shouldn't expect any. Success (whatever that is)[27] depends on your Karma, your efforts, your conditioning, and the method you use. Is GFM the only method that induces permanent kundalini? No, there are other methods and I encourage everyone to explore them. I can vouch for GFM; I can't vouch for any other method.

Sensing the blueprint and seeing the inner workings of my being only occurred after I was deeply into the process, i.e. months and months of working at it. It's not a question of fairness, that it worked for me, but not for you. It's a question of practice and training. Kundalini is not the private domain of certain adepts; anyone can achieve higher states of consciousness.

If you play around with a lot of methods, you may have some kundalini experiences, even a kundalini awakening. The question is: will it be complete enough for you to witness the inner workings of your being?

Is Kundalini Intelligent?

How Intelligent is kundalini? It's smarter than I am. I used to think I was the smart one. That's because I didn't understand the concept of the Primal Spirit as a component part of human ontology, even after reading *The Secret of the Golden Flower* (SGF) — the book that makes the distinction between it (the Primal Spirit) and its polar opposite (the Conscious Spirit). According to the SGF, the Primal Spirit is the formative energy responsible for our incarnation. When the Conscious Spirit activates at birth, it starts recording and processing the endless flow of information taken in by the senses.

---

27   You should have a goal and a roadmap. Many individuals don't; they
     dabble and flail about, then wonder why they're not successful. Success
     is dependent on many factors. If there was a magic Kundalini elixir, that
     would be great, but as of now, there isn't. Nevertheless, a good way to find
     out about the design for your Being is to practice Kundalini meditation.

And from this information it constructs your ego.

Bombarding the Senses - Wrap around conditioning

As a baby you perceive the world around you and begin to formulate judgments and hypotheses about what you see, hear, smell, taste, and feel. This entity offering me her breast is warm and smells good and the milk it provides tastes good. Later on as you refine your ability to process information, you learn to abstract events and situations: this entity (which I now identify as my mother) loves me, or, heaven forbid, if the experience is unpleasant, if your mother doesn't provide the comfort and protection you need, you attach negative labels: *my mother doesn't love me, my mother hates me.* And the beat goes on, until you are fully conditioned by the world around you, and you've forgotten the energy that created you — the Primal Spirit. The ego wants it that way, wants you to suppress this knowledge, all part of a defense mechanism for survival in the "so-called" real world.

At the age of thirty-five, I raised kundalini. Energy I didn't know existed started flowing through a neural subsystem in my body. I could feel and observe it. Almost immediately, I realized a change had occurred: *Kundalini Shakti* had replaced *Prana Shakti*. This hibernating subsystem had reasserted its dominance over my being. Not only would it heal my physical body and realign my metabolic and somatic systems, it would teach me how to manage my emotions, how to overcome ego conditioning, and how to make better life decisions.

I'd come across these terms many times during my yearlong study of the SGF, never really understanding what they meant. To me they were devoid of any substantive meaning. But when kundalini booted up inside me, not only did the energy of the Primal Spirit invigorate my body, it healed and restored it. I put two plus two together to make four, then five, then six, then infinity. Yes, the Primal Spirit deals in oneness and infinity.

Not only did this energy subsystem heal me, it did so intelligently. Which made me realize it had access to DNA and other evolutionary information about my being.

Of course, the ego doesn't like this. And given my exposure to years and years of conditioning, I was habituated to believing that "smart" started and ended with the Ego I'd created — that distortion of who It believed I was. No other entity — no part of me — was as smart as It was.

After a few months of living with kundalini, I realized the Primal Spirit knew more about my actual Being than my ego (the Conscious Spirit) ever would. Ignoring my conditioning, it went about its business with the same determination it used to create my body — fixing its broken parts, reengineering its subsystems. After all the Primal Spirit (*Kundalini Shakti*) built my body. It is the master contractor, all other systems are subservient. Now, recalled to command after a thirty-five-year period of hibernation, it picked up where it left off at birth. Back then, the ego didn't exist. And now that it did, it was incapable of admitting that it is a product of acculturation, conditioning, approval, and longing. The ego is a master of denial.

How do I know any of this to be true? Think back to that primordial time in the womb. What is the brain doing during gestation? Is the left brain functioning? Is the right brain intelligent? Does the word intelligence have any meaning during the time in the womb? I surmise that the situation is pretty much like Jill Bolte Taylor's account of left-right brain interactivity during her stroke:

"On the morning of the stroke, I woke up to a pounding pain behind my left eye. And it was the kind of pain, caustic pain, that you get when you bite into ice cream. And it just gripped me and then it released me. Then it just gripped me and then released me. And it was very unusual for me to experience any kind of pain, so I thought OK, I'll just start my normal routine. So I got up and I jumped onto my cardio glider, which is a full-body exercise machine. And I'm jamming away on this thing, and I'm realizing that my hands looked like primitive claws grasping onto the bar. I thought "that's very peculiar" and I looked down at my body and I thought, "Whoa, I'm a weird-looking thing." And it was as though my consciousness had shifted away from my normal perception of reality, where I'm the person on the machine having the experience, to some esoteric space where I'm witnessing myself having this experience.

"And it was all every peculiar and my headache was just getting worse, so I get off the machine, and I'm walking across my living room floor, and I realize that everything inside of my body has slowed way down. And every step is very rigid and very deliberate. There's no fluidity to my pace, and there's this constriction in my area of perceptions so I'm just focused on internal systems. And I'm standing in my bathroom getting ready to step into the shower and I could actually hear the dialog inside of my body. I heard a little voice saying, "OK, you muscles, you gotta contract, you muscles you relax."

"And I lost my balance and I'm propped up against the wall. And I look down at my arm and I realize that I can no longer define the boundaries of my body. I can't define where I begin and where I end. Because the atoms and the molecules of my arm blended with the atoms and molecules of the wall. And all I could detect was this energy. Energy. And I'm asking myself, "What is wrong with me, what is going on?" And in that moment, my brain chatter, my left hemisphere brain chatter went totally silent. Just like someone took a remote control and pushed the mute button and — total silence.

"And at first I was shocked to find myself inside of a silent mind. But then I was immediately captivated by the magnificence of energy around me. And because I could no longer identify the boundaries of my body, I felt enormous and expansive. I felt at one with all the energy that was, and it was beautiful there."

The above extract, previously cited in Margaret Dempsey's "The Master and his Emissary"[28] post, highlights the operational differences between right and left brain functioning, reveals what happens when the left brain (the Conscious Spirit) shuts down and the right brain (the Primal Spirit) is left alone to cope. Trouble is with the left brain shutting down, there's not much the being can do except to let spirit merge with the infinite. In the womb, it's different; the left brain is barely operative while the right brain uses evolutionary energy to create and embody a new being.

So how does kundalini manifest intelligence? It doesn't know addition; it doesn't memorize phone numbers, balance your checkbook, solve quadratic equations, or do crossword puzzles. It does, however, know the human body. It does know evolutionary energy. It does know DNA, which it "invented" without having to read a textbook. In fact, text books are only now scratching the surface of what the Primal Spirit "knows."

In my case, it sent out feelers to inventory my body; it received the results, analyzed and interpreted them, then sent back the requisite healing energy to repair the disorder. In my book, that's intelligence.

---

28 "The Master and his Emissary" - http://www.kundaliniconsortium. org/2013/03/the-master-and-his-emissary-divided.html

Does Kundalini Make You A Happier Person

Recently someone sent me an inquiry, "I've read your kundalini books and I'm beginning a meditation practice. But the question that keeps popping up in my head is: Does activating kundalini make you a happier person?"

Overlooking for a moment the semantics behind the expression "happier person," I responded with a resounding YES, in the sense that kundalini makes you a different person. What you want to make of this different person, how you want to mold him/her still depends on your basic character. What kundalini confers on you is the opportunity to meet, perhaps for the first time, the elusive, real YOU.

By stripping away denial and evasion tactics, an active kundalini allowed me to focus on the weaker aspects of my character. What I decided to do with this opportunity was up to me. But at least I now had focus. The stage was set for work.

This work can be extremely constructive, especially as concerns addictive or self-destructive behavior.

It's so easy to be cynical about change, self-discovery, and spiritual transformation; even Oprah Winfrey faces ridicule from the conventional press when she talks about her personal journey: "Ms. Winfrey shared no secrets, but she did repeat some of her most familiar, if impenetrable, platitudes, including "my personal journey is to fulfill the highest expression of myself here as a human being.'" Lack of understanding is rife. This language says more about the NY Times writer than it does about Oprah's sincere expression of self-discovery. So be ready for doubt, ridicule, and misunderstanding.

The advantage kundalini gives you is that the body becomes an ally. You are functioning at a higher vibrational frequency — at frequencies where drugs and alcohol no longer hold any appeal. The body begins to resist harmful substances. This is a place to start — at the bottom (the Physiological Needs level), an enormous advantage when you realize the hardest thing in life is taking the first step, especially when it means starting at the bottom.

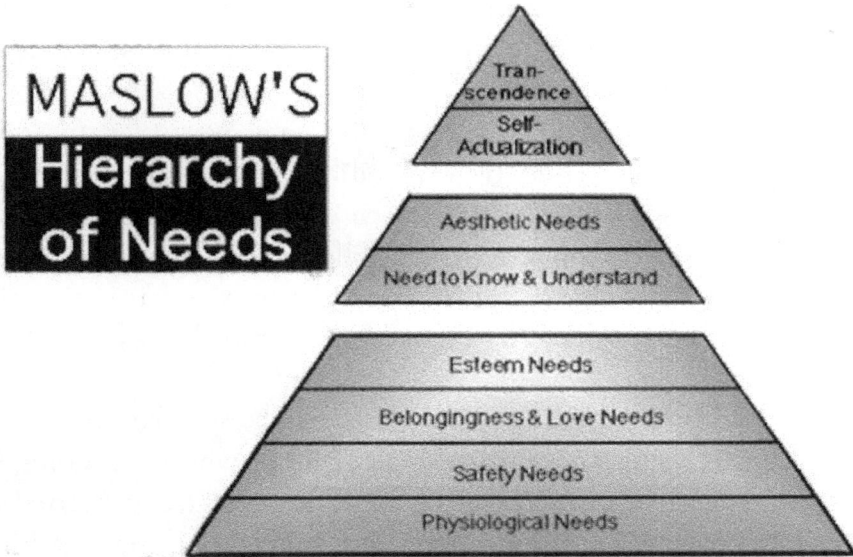

The Maslow Pyramid

Each stage in the pyramid is attuned to a different frequency. Yet, only by starting at the bottom can you can build a solid foundation — one stage at a time.

"Self-realization begins at birth; it is the journey as much as it is the destination." Eventually you realize there is no separation between the journey and the destination. Kundalini gives you a known place to start. It wipes the slate clean in that you are now functioning at a higher vibrational frequency, affording you an opportunity to insure that the journey is upward, providing you with a vantage point for putting things in perspective as you move along from country back road to the "spiritual" superhighway.

What does "starting at the bottom" really mean? How did it work in my case? When I wrote about starting at the bottom, the tried-and-true Maslow diagram popped into my head as a ready example of start and finish points. I began to think about the diagram I created in *The Backward-Flowing Method: The Secret of Life and Death*, a diagram that explained my journey, that it didn't just happen in a vacuum, that there was a karmic dimension to it — a vibrational dimension.

As you can see, this diagram's first stage *Search for the Secret Teachings* is characterized by exploration. In my case, it meant discovering and taking up yoga, which was not as readily available in the 1960s as it is today. My path followed the Maslow diagram to the extent that GFM provided me with a way of harnessing the power of the body — a feeling that I had to stop abusing it and get it working for me.

When I first started out, I had not the slightest iota of self-awareness. I didn't really know what I was doing or why I was doing it. I just practiced the poses. Little by little, however, things started to percolate upward. During my practice I noticed that my breathing exercises produced rumblings in energy centers throughout my body — sensations I had never before felt, which, as I continued to practice, became palpable and real. I had awakened a sleeping subsystem. I realized that breathing — an autonomic process I had always taken for granted — was the key to the changes taking place in my body.

Breathing became the center of my practice. Not only during my practice, but in every other activity: walking, driving, lying in bed. Little did I realize: more is less. Breathing is more powerful than strenuous physical exercise.

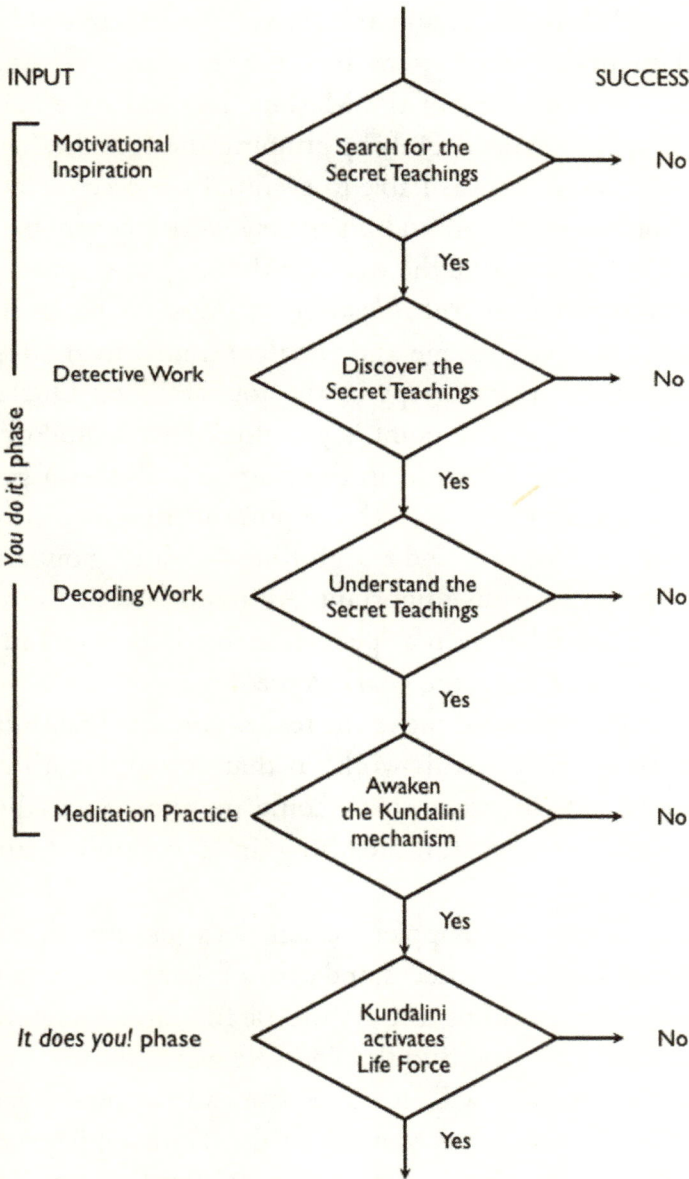

Where my path diverged from the Maslow diagram: I jumped over the *Belongingness & Love Needs* and the *Esteem Needs* stages. Had I been obliged to master these steps before attempting the final stages in Blocks Two and One of the Maslow, I would have been condemned to perpetual failure. Only by jumping ahead to the *Need to Know & Understand* stage was I able to eventually succeed (reach the top of the Maslow pyramid) and ultimately work my way back down to Block One to complete the work on the stages I skipped.

My route jumped from the *Physiological Needs* stage to the *Need to Know & Understand* stage and then continued to the top. It completely ignored the two steps at the top of Block One of Maslow. So what, you say? The point is you don't have to follow a specific order. It's not set in stone as in the diagram. Whatever gets you vibrating at a higher frequency! The important thing is getting there, and that entails a journey and a beginning — starting out and finishing. The sequence isn't as important. All roads lead to Rome. The differences are those between a "people-oriented" person and a "goal-oriented" person. I am more goal oriented.

So I chose yoga, which led me to the realization that breathing was the key to progressing in this work, in that correct breathing induced sensations and vibrations that I could monitor. Kundalini meditation became a means for breathing in a controlled and regulated manner.

As for the notion of a happier person, let's just say that if we concern ourselves with strict standards of happiness, we're a long way from understanding the nature of life, and therefore, probably on another path. The Buddha said Life was suffering, and he prescribed a path to deal with it. Does it mean happiness gets lost in the shuffle? Or that when you get to the Transcendence or the It Does You! stage, you have somehow, mysteriously reconciled Transcendence and Happiness? It means that as long as we inhabit bodies, we will suffer if we base our expectations on materialism as the key to happiness, a process a Buddhist might say, is an illusion.

So, is Oprah Winfrey's statement of devotion and service ("fulfill the highest expression of myself here as a human being") an illusion? Would being more aware, making better decisions, treating others as you would be treated make you happier? Would you even think about it in those terms? I didn't. Kundalini provided me with a known starting place, and many opportunities, one of which from whence, if I was not bound by expectation and desire, I could find happiness in very mundane undertakings.

Kundalini And Out Of Body Experience

My first Out Of Body Experience (OBE) occurred when I was twenty-one. Lying in a George Washington University hospital bed after an appendicitis operation, I was given a morphine injection. I wrote about it in my book, *Deciphering the Golden Flower One Secret at a Time*, from which, the following excerpt — a visit to the hospital by my girlfriend at the time, Madeline — is taken:

> JJ: "I was in this half-state between sleep and waking. A great glowing light filled the room. Suddenly, I was floating upward. When I reached the ceiling, I realized I could steer myself. I'm having trouble though. I command myself to roll over and I'm looking down at my physical body, asleep in the bed, and I realize that I'm in an altogether different body."
>
> Madeline: "So?"
>
> JJ: "So I stayed up there watching my body asleep in the bed. I knew I could leave the room, but I didn't know if I'd be able to get back. I knew I'd see amazing things, but I figured I had to return to my body, that I wasn't ready to take off and leave it."
>
> Madeline: "Hummph."
>
> JJ: "Well, it opened my mind... Perhaps, I shouldn't say 'mind' because the mind may not be part of it."

Until my kundalini awakening fourteen years later, I had no further OBEs. Since activating kundalini, I've had numerous Astral Body experiences and am now able to put myself into the state at will. How is that possible? OBE can be learned. Yes, you can train yourself to leave your body at will. In my OBEs, I have experienced many of the abilities to:

- Fly like a bird and even visit outer space,
- Walk through solid objects like walls, ceilings etc,
- Meet loved ones who have passed on,
- Grow spiritually and gain awareness of your true Self,
- Visit the Akashic Records and see the past and the probable future,
- Increase your psychic abilities,
- No longer fear death,
- Become a better problem-solver,
- Become a better person in all areas of your life,
- Engage with the pet (especially your cat) in an OBE,
- Heal yourself physically and mentally.
- Astral sex

Is an active kundalini necessary for OBE? It certainly doesn't hurt. Many kundalini adepts have shared most of, if not all of, these effects. But is it absolutely necessary? Aren't the effects of an OBE a subset of kundalini effects? Given the large number of OBE accounts over the centuries, I think they are. People have been experiencing OBEs without ever knowing about, or even having heard, the term Kundalini. In its own right, kundalini is perhaps more difficult to activate, especially on a permanent basis.

Again, I experienced the Out-of-Body state spontaneously — no deliberation involved, — and also as a deliberate result of kundalini. Perhaps, my first experience acted as a "warm-up" — a signal that this faculty would retire to the background until my meta-body was sufficiently reprogrammed, in my case, by kundalini, a condition that would eventually enable me to summon my Astral Body at will.

Recently with the explosion of self-realization studies and energy cultivation techniques, a critical mass of interest in Astral Projection and kundalini has appeared, which has led to Astral travel self-learning materials, available on the Internet.

I meet and talk with many people about meditation, NDE,

OBE, mindfulness, enlightenment, and kundalini. It's easy to distinguish a genuine seeker from a boastful pretender. Detached, yet present, emotionally composed, the seeker acts as a receiver and transmitter of metaphysical actuality, proving their capabilities over many years.

Should you become interested and wish to explore Astral Projection, one critical point to remember is: you must retain conscious control over all your impulses. Like my experience in the George Washington Hospital when I decided to pull back, you can exert the same kind of control. In other words, you can move forward incrementally, only undertaking astral travel as you are able to master your emotions, fears, and anxieties, etc.

Since awakening my kundalini forty years ago, I have applied the techniques of Astral Projection and consider them an effect of self-realization, the ability to recognize the subtle bodies that surround me and realize that they serve as a preview to the various states in the soul's never-ending journey.

Once you master it, there's no limit to the insights into the cycle of life and death that Astral Travel bestows on you, the traveler.

Kundalini and Occult Powers

I am often asked about kundalini and occult powers. It's an issue that fits well with Western conditioning — the idea that there must be some reward at the end of the rainbow, the notion that one who has fought the good fight deserves an exceptional reward. *Post proelium praemium.*[29]

Because it stimulates intensive neuroplastic activity, kundalini changes your being either permanently or temporarily, depending on the type of awakening. It may awaken certain talents or stimulate creativity. In fact, it usually does. It may also bestow certain powers, such as clairvoyance or metanormal cognition. However, to go into it thinking in terms of occult powers, hoping for some reward is

---

29 Lat. After the battle, the reward.

self-deception. It's not just counter-productive in a religious sense, it's psychological and social self-deception, too. Don't let *Bruce Almighty* fantasies distract you.

You don' need no stinkin' occult powers. What comes to you comes out of the being you already are. You can't make yourself more than you are; all you can do is refine what you already are. And that, in and of itself, is a lot. So just because you have a big ego, don't count on kundalini to improve your standing or your self-image. In fact, it will probably put your whole being in perspective for you — perhaps for the very first time.

If you've been thinking in these terms, consider the following: "Radha had attained *mahabhava*. There was no desire behind the ecstatic love of the gopis. A true lover does not seek anything from God. He prays only for pure love. He doesn't want any powers or miracles.

"It is very troublesome to possess occult powers. Nangta taught me this by a story. A man who had acquired occult powers was sitting on the seashore when a storm arose. It caused him great discomfort; so he said, 'Let the storm stop.' His words could not remain unfulfilled. At that moment a ship was going full sail before the wind. When the storm ceased abruptly the ship capsized and sank. The passengers perished and the sin of causing their death fell to the man. And because of that sin he lost his occult powers and went to hell.

"Once upon a time a sadhu acquired great occult powers. He was vain about them. But he was a good man and had some austerities to his credit. One day the Lord, disguised as a holy man, came to him and said, 'Revered sir, I have heard that you have great occult powers.' The sadhu received the Lord cordially and offered him a seat. Just then an elephant passed by. The Lord, in the disguise of the holy man, said to the sadhu, 'Revered sir, can you kill this elephant if you like?'

The sadhu said, 'Yes, it is possible.' So saying, he took a pinch of dust, muttered some mantras over it, and threw it at the elephant. The beast struggled awhile in pain and then dropped dead. The

Lord said: 'What power you have! You have killed the elephant!' The sadhu laughed. Again the Lord spoke: 'Now can you revive the elephant?' 'That too is possible', replied the sadhu. He threw another pinch of charmed dust at the beast. The elephant writhed about a little and came back to life.

Then the Lord said: 'Wonderful is your power. But may I ask you one thing? You have killed the elephant and you have revived it. But what has that done for you? Do you feel uplifted by it? Has it enabled you to realize God?' Saying this the Lord vanished. "Subtle are the ways of dharma. One cannot realize God if one has even the least trace of desire. A thread cannot pass through the eye of a needle if it has the smallest fiber sticking out.

"Krishna said to Arjuna, 'Friend, if you want to realize Me, you will not succeed if you have even one of the eight occult powers.' This is the truth. Occult power is sure to beget pride, and pride makes one forget God. An egotistic person cannot realize God. Do you know what egotism is like? It is like a high mound, where rainwater cannot collect: the water runs off. Water collects in low land. There seeds sprout and grow into trees. Then the trees bear fruit. "Therefore I say, 'Never think that you alone have true understanding and that others are fools.' One must love all. No one is a stranger. It is Hari alone who dwells in all beings. Nothing exists without Him.'"[30]

I'm not saying that kundalini could never bestow amazing metanormal powers on an individual. After a massive neuroplastic reengineering of the brain, anything is possible. All I ask those who ask me about occult powers is this: "Suppose you acquire such powers, how do you visualize your life with such powers? How do they change the way you live, the way you treat others, and the way you think about yourself?"

---

30 "Sri Ramakrishna on Occult Powers" (Sunday, September 21, 1884)

Living With Kundalini

"Those who are able to see beyond the shadows and lies of their culture will never be understood, let alone believed, by the masses."

~ Plato

Kundalini – Then and Now

Forty years ago, when I activated kundalini, I was a blank slate in more ways than one.

For one, I was a lost soul, immature and self-destructive. Two, I had never heard the term kundalini. To give you an idea of just how surprised I was to watch this seemingly alien energy take over my being, the book with which I practiced kundalini meditation, *The Secret of the Golden Flower*, does not even mention the term kundalini once, even though it's an ancient method for awakening it. Not one mention. Nada.

Instead, it uses the term "Primal Spirit" to denote *Kundalini Shakti*, the creative, intelligent life force energy — in opposition to "Conscious Spirit," which is a stand-in for the ego. The book outlines a meditation method — which I dutifully practiced for over a year. At the same time, it presents some venerable insights into ontology, specifically insights on the battle between the Primal Spirit and Conscious Spirit and how, if you follow the method correctly, you will awaken the Primal Spirit (*Kundalini Shakti*) and it will dislodge the Conscious Spirit (the ego) and take its place as the ruler (the guiding intelligent consciousness) of your being.

Basically, it states that under the thrall of the Conscious Spirit, you have been going about life all wrong. This is an idea common to many spiritual methods, i.e., Ouspensky's *Fourth Way*.

Activating the Primal Spirit fixes this. Little did I know that these words would be prophetic, that over time, *Kundalini Shakti* (Primal Spirit) would do exactly that — completely overhaul my being.

Of course, it's not very meaningful until you're actually living it.

Not that, once awakened, kundalini takes care of every aspect of your life. No, it's a gradual process. I had to first surrender to it, before it changed me somatically, metabolically, anatomically, hormonally so that, as a result, I watched these organic changes affect my emotional states, my cognitive capacities, and my spiritual nature, allowing me to see and perceive metaphysical activity and experience a conscious, energetic shift in being. It was as if I'd been functioning at one-eighth of my potential and kundalini had opened a host of growth opportunities. The awakening experience resembles a nuclear reaction as matter, in the form of sexual energy, collides with consciousness in a kind of quantum event. I could not sit back; I had to work at each phase of my life and being, but I finally had the tools as well as the gift of understanding.

Back then, forty years ago, in the early 1970s, there were no kundalini support systems, no formulas for activating this energy, not that awakening kundalini or the Primal Spirit was my actual goal. For most of my practice, I considered the discussion about the Primal and Conscious Spirits to be so much allegorical babble. It was only when I started feeling sensations inside my body — the awakening of certain energy centers — that I began to take what I had been reading seriously. The allegorical, mystical contents began to make empirical sense.

When I started the practice, I was living in Paris. As the sensations I felt began to affect my body, my brain, and my sexual nature, I realized I would have to change my environment — which to me, meant either going to an ashram or, like my role model, Milarepa, find a place to work alone. Realizing that finding someone who understood my situation was problematic, I chose the latter course, becoming a solitary seeker/practitioner.

I found an old house in the south of France that I rented for about forty dollars a month and with my meager possessions — a few records and books — I moved into a house in Languedoc, about ten miles from Lodève, where I stayed for over a year until kundalini finally awakened. The details of this experience are set down in my book, *Deciphering the Golden Flower One Secret at a Time*.

Today, the solitary retreat is out of fashion. And yet, there's a lot to recommend it. It was the norm for thousands of years. Buddha, Jesus Christ, Lao Tse, Milarepa, St. John of the Cross, Meister Eckhart — all traveled the solitary path. All experienced the exhilaration, as well as the pain, doubt, loneliness, and despair that accompanies the mystical experience.

In the solitary context, you learn to figure things out — without Twitter, Facebook, Google Hangouts, blogs, Meetups, chat rooms, or digital bulletin boards. And without disparaging any of these, I do believe the time-tested solitary path works well because it turns you into a spiritual detective, makes you self-reliant.

But, today, given the interconnected, interdependent paradigm we live in, it's hardly practical. Today, my $40 a month fortress would cost a thousand dollars a month.

Nevertheless, since those bygone days of 40 years ago, not only have the number of individual kundalini accounts increased exponentially, they have done so regardless of geography, culture, language, political or religious affiliation. What's more, these accounts share many of the same effects. People state that they experience the same effects or results over and over, time after time. Kundalini affects them in the same ways. What does this mean?

It means that kundalini is no longer dependent on any of the institutional orthodoxies of our day. Anyone can raise it. You don't have to be trained in science, education, religion, business, politics, or even meditation. You don't have to be a cult follower. As a matter of fact, it's probably better if you aren't under the influence of any orthodoxy — religious or otherwise. Why? Because you can do it on your own.

Kundalini is a branch of biological science in search of validation and it should be approached as such.

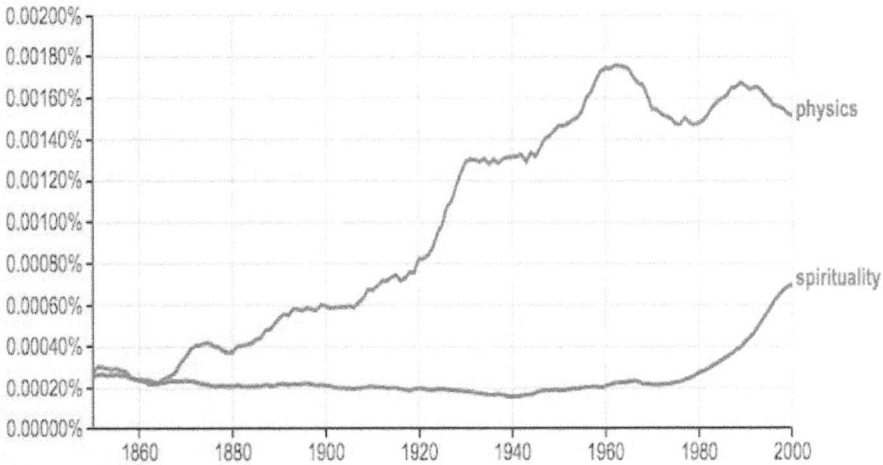

Science and Religion Cross Paths

Somewhere around 1930, there occurred a major cultural and social milestone: science passed religion as a field of interest. As you can see from the above Google NGram, which tracks mentions of words and terms in books and other publications, the two lines of interest crossed in 1931: there started to be more talk about science and less about religion. A major tectonic shift.

A second shift, a big surge of interest in spirituality occurred in the 1970s. As you can see in this second NGram, the gap between physics and spirituality narrowed.

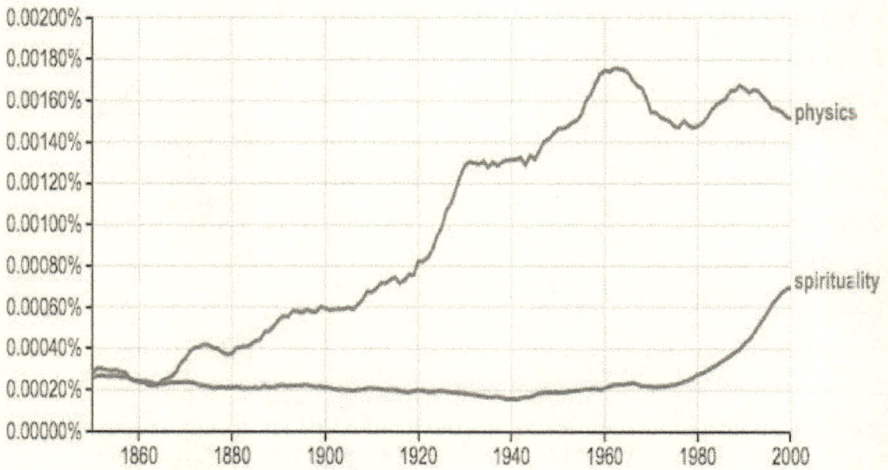

Spirituality Catches Up to the Physical Sciences

As interest in spirituality increases, interest in religion decreases, and although the following chart shows us that the one is not going to overtake the other any time soon, it does show a narrowing and a clear picture of a movement or an impulse on the rise.

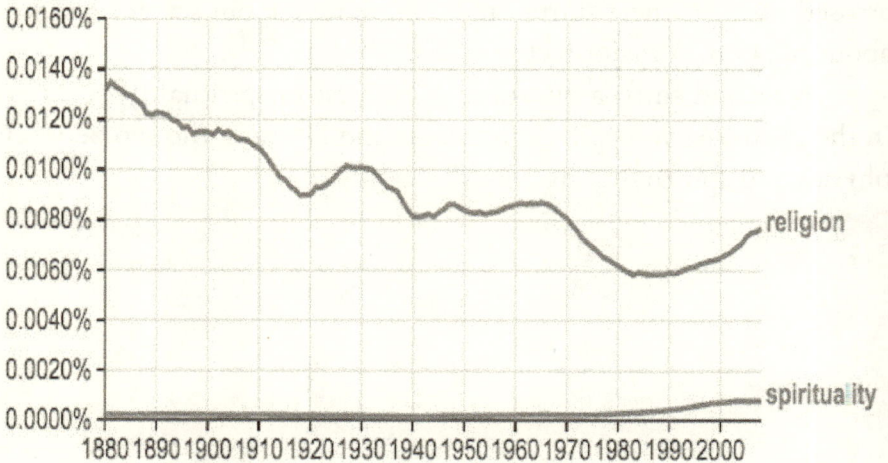

1970 - What Happened to Religion

Gopi Krishna recognized this shift. It was reflected in his writings on sexual sublimation and the biological nature of kundalini, that kundalini is:

- A biological phenomenon with metaphysical overtones, but without a causal connection to any religion,
- One of the predominant drivers behind this shift.

And there are two possible hypotheses for the increased interest in kundalini:

1) The notion that an energy continuum some call consciousness is causing greater numbers of Quantum events that consist of the release of distilled sexual energy into the brain in more and more people which awakens kundalini with greater frequency. Kundalini is now being passed on and activated through genetic improvements at a greater rate, and, as such, we no longer have to strive to awaken it because nature is doing the job for us. In effect, we're being pollinated by an evolutionary impulse. Or,

2) Quite simply more people are practicing the mindful arts and meditation methods that lead to kundalini activation.

Examples of the first hypothesis are found in the rise in spontaneous kundalini events, caused, it seems, by any number of triggers — from drugs to sexual encounters, from doing nothing at all to eye-gazing, and many more. At present, we don't know a lot about the reason for these events, but we are beginning to study them.

A case study that illustrates the second hypothesis is the work of Dr. Herbert Benson, the creator of the Relaxation Response, a movement that divorced meditation from religious influences.

If you think about it, the popularity of pastimes like meditation has motivated the disassociation of religion and spirituality. As more people began to meditate to relieve stress, EKG and other stress-related tests showed us there was a science behind meditation; it effects could be measured.

And that's why more and more people meditate. Because it's become a secular pastime, which has removed the barrier for many individuals put off by having to adhere to some religion in order to participate. Meditation became an acceptable self-improvement activity, like aerobics.

Doctor Benson imported his method from the East, making sure it remained agnostic. Agnostic and relatively safe. By this, I'm referring to the fact that he only imported the first two steps of the venerable Eastern method — diaphragmatic deep breathing and control of heart rate. I wondered why he had left out the final step — the backward-flowing method, the step I discovered in *The Secret of the Golden Flower* and was finally able to master.

I figured he had left it out for one of two reasons: either he didn't understand it, or he was afraid its implementation would be problematic for the average Westerner.

My analysis is echoed in *Halfway Up the Mountain: The Error of Premature Claims to Enlightenment*, a book by Mariana Caplan.

> "Unfortunately, but inevitably, in the mass importation of Eastern spiritual traditions onto Western soil what has been imported are the visible, tangible practices."

In other words, formulas, but not the cultural matrix from which they arise. So while stress-relief meditation, or meditation-lite, has continued to make headway, most kundalini meditation methods have no real substantive connection with the Eastern traditions from which they sprang. In the West, kundalini activation methods are fragmented and frequently at odds with one another.

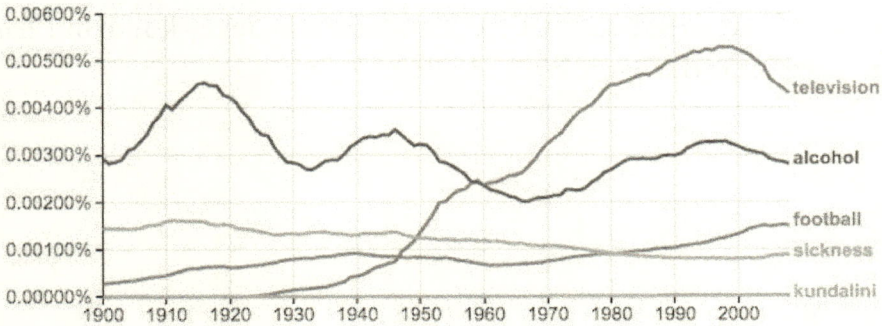

The Sudden Interest in Kundalini

The will is there, and so are the signs of progress — as evidenced by the growth in all types of kundalini awakenings. Kundalini has influenced the Global Shift of Consciousness.

However, as you can see by the following chart, when kundalini is matched up against some of the major social preoccupations of our era, there is very little name recognition, much less understanding of its properties:

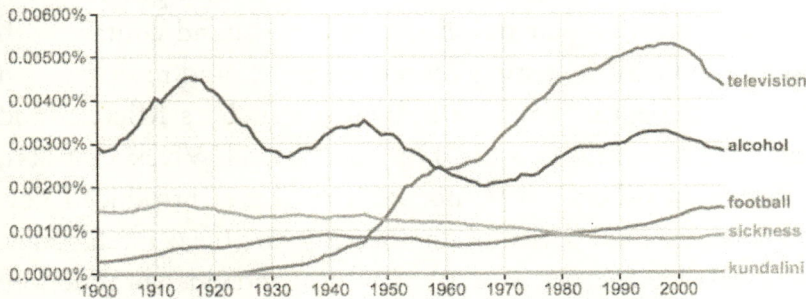

Comparing Kundalini Against Major Social Preoccupations

Moreover, when you mention kundalini in the same breath as many of the sacred cows of the spiritual movement, kundalini has nowhere near the name recognition:

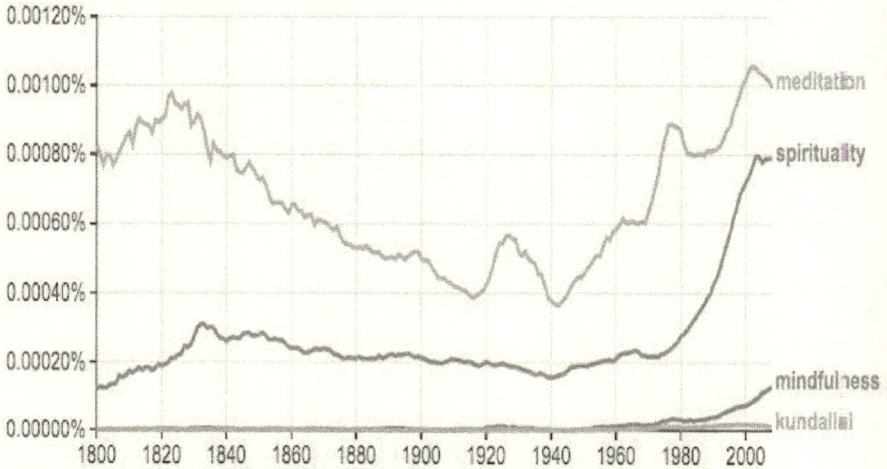

Comparing Kundalini Against Recognized Spiritual Trends

If it is to be positioned as a subject that scientists are eager to explore, it needs to achieve critical mass.

We cannot stand idly by; we must perfect safe and repeatable methods for awakening kundalini and we must document the various triggers and effects of the kundalini experience.

Fortunately, a passing of the baton from an older generation of explorers like myself, a generation that had first-hand contact with Gopi Krishna, the 20th century's foremost writer and researcher on the subject, has begun. Younger individuals such as Michael and Linda Molina, Corinne Lebrun, Duncan Carroll, Vivek Govekar, Neven Paar, and others I have not yet met, have introduced new skill sets into the mix: software engineering, artificial intelligence, innovative website creation, documentary film and video production, scientific analysis, collection, collation and compiling of kundalini experiences.

We look to these young persons to spearhead the repositioning of kundalini as a subject that achieves the critical mass necessary to eliciting scientific interest and peer review.

Kundalini - The Ultimate Teacher

Either it never crossed your mind or you never thought about kundalini as a powerful teaching instrument. Nevertheless, it is... What does it teach you? Well, it's not like going to class and being pumped full of information; there's no curriculum, prerequisites, exams, or schedules.

Learning From Kundalini

A lesson is being taught all the time — either right before your eyes perhaps or at a deeper subconscious level. It's up to you to tune in. Kundalini provides you with the opportunities; you have only to "enroll." Right now, there's a lesson going on in the background. If you're oblivious to it at the moment, as you integrate kundalini, your being will tune in subliminally.

Let's start with the basics and how kundalini teaches you on the visceral level, about your body, how to treat it, nourish it, fortify it. How does this work? I learned about eating correctly in several different ways.

First, I noticed I was attracted to certain foods and certain types of markets. Foods I'd never before eaten. Walking through the market, inspirations of food combinations popped into my head. I'd buy instinctively without forethought, and when I got home, discover that the foods went together.

Second, kundalini gave me instant feedback about foods I'd been eating since childhood, foods that weren't good for me. One example was cheese. I started to sweat at night. By the process of elimination I learned that cheese was the culprit, so I eliminated cheese. Same with other foods. Now I'm able to avoid the foods that aren't good for me, at the same time select those that are and combine them as they were meant to be combined.

Sleep, exercise, and supplements are also some of the basic

lessons I've learned. Kundalini teaches you about your limits. The Golden Mean. Never to overeat this or overdo that. Sex, too, falls into the basics category. Kundalini needs sexual energy to continue its work. Ignore this and you'll find out — as Gopi Krishna and I did — that wasting sexual energy through ejaculation has debilitating effects.

Kundalini Bestows Creative Gifts

Another aspect of your being that kundalini stimulates is creativity. This, because it immediately starts sending therapeutic, curative, evolutionary energy via the nervous system throughout the body and brain. Painting, composing, singing, and writing capabilities are acquired without effort or study. I'm not saying that a person with a tin ear is suddenly composing operas, but relative to the before, the after is auspicious.

Imagine a wholly creative race of beings. No war, negative emotion, racism, phobias, or bullying. Yes, there's a long way to go, but channeling fear, doubt, and shame into creative activities helps change your low-esteem, lower-case "b" being into a capital "B" Being.

Kundalini And Addiction

Believe it or not, kundalini educates you on addiction, too. It's not that you somehow start listening to the little voice in the back of the head and give up your addiction voluntarily; kundalini rewires the nervous system, short circuiting the dopamine response that governs all addictions.

The Ontology Of Kundalini

Ultimately, kundalini instills a greater cosmic consciousness. With this consciousness comes the realization that death — like life — is only another state of existence...your Being in an alternate manifestation, one that vibrates at a different frequency. How do you know this? You know because kundalini meditation has escorted you through a variety of vibrational states during your practice and you have resonated with them. You know there is a limitless universe, an energy continuum vibrating just beyond the human eye's ability to perceive it. Not readily visible, but real all the same.

My Daily Workout

Everyone does some form of exercise; even advanced couch potato-ism, or the utter lack of exercise, is a statement on exercising. Okay, maybe it's only to take a stand against it. Maybe it's laziness. Whatever. It is what it is. All I can do is present my meager workout and the reasons behind each component.

By most workout standards, mine isn't very impressive.

I'm not out to set records or build washboard abs; I'm merely seeking to create a rounded approach to preserving my body. After all, most of my exercise is accomplished during meditation: action through non-action — when the kundalini is at its most invigorating. Seizing control of my being, taking inventory, sending healing energy throughout my Being.

I don't do each and every routine each and every day; the ones I choose are a function of how I feel. Kundalini guides me. I listen.

I've been doing the same yoga routine for many years now; it's the centerpiece of my workout. As for walking, I'm blessed to have a choice of terrains, from fog-bound redwood forests to moody seascapes to sparkling bird sanctuaries in the low country marshlands.

I spread it out over the day, in no particular order, but usually start with the Nauli after I get up, adding various pieces during the day:

The Nauli

I've been doing the Nauli for over 60 years and I credit it with gastrointestinal health. The gut is your most sensitive body part; care and exercise are critical in avoiding obesity and degenerative disease.

"Nauli is one of the Kriyas or Shatkarma (cleaning exercises) from yoga. The exercise is claimed to serve the cleaning of the abdominal region - digestive organs, small intestine and is based on a massage of the internal belly organs by a circular movement of the abdominal muscles."[31]

The Nitric Oxide Dump

The Nitric Oxide Dump takes only five minutes and can be done throughout the day, especially if you're tied to a computer and sitting most of the time. Get up, push your chair back, and proceed with the four simple exercises. Space each series at least two hours apart.

"The Nitric Oxide Dump is one of the most recommended workouts that can aid with improving overall health. It allows your body to increase nitric oxide (NO) production, since your levels of it decrease with age. High-intensity interval training (HIIT) exercises like the Nitric Oxide Dump may seem intense, especially for those who are elderly, but most people can actually perform these exercises at any age and still reap major benefits. Before trying the Nitric Oxide Dump, however, talk to your doctor first to check if your body is ready to handle such high-intensity exercises."[32]

Nordic Track

Somewhere along the way, I come back to the present and spend 5-10 minutes on the Nordic Track. Not one of the new fancy ones, the classic wooden Cross Country Skier.

This device is the closet thing to real cross-country skiing. Yes, it seemed expensive at the time ($400), but I've had it for 25 years, long enough to amortize the cost. No, it's probably not in vogue. So what? It serves. And once you start gliding, close your eyes and you're in the Jura Mountains.

Mini trampoline

The mini trampoline is not violent exercise, but it helps

---

31 https://en.wikipedia.org/wiki/Nauli
32 Copied and cited directly from: https://www.mercola.com/calendar/2018/fitness.htm.

balance, breathing, and agility. I've been known to do the Nitric Oxide Dump while bouncing.

Earthing or Grounding

Recently, I've added Earthing, which, from the way it works, would seem to be completely passive. Yet it's quite active in that it's constantly infusing my body with the Earth's energy.

According to Earthing literature:

"Earthing is a fast-growing movement based upon the major discovery that connecting to the Earth's natural energy is foundational for vibrant health."

In keeping with my sensitivity to all energy sources, both positive and negative, I feel a definite tingling sensation as the Earth's energy flows into my body. Earthing products bring the healthy equivalent of walking barefoot indoors to your high rise condo or your second floor bedroom. Check out the science behind it.

Throughout history humans walked barefoot and slept on the ground. But modern lifestyle, including the widespread use of isolative rubber- or plastic-soled shoes, has disconnected us from the Earth's energy and, of course, we no longer sleep on the ground. Fascinating new research has raised the possibility that this disconnect may actually contribute to chronic pain, fatigue, and poor sleep that plague so many people.

The remedy for "the disconnect" is simple. All you need to do is walk barefoot outdoors whenever possible and sleep, work, or relax indoors in contact with conductive sheets or mats that transfer grounded energy to your body. People who do this on a regular basis say they sleep better, feel better, and have more energy during the day. This simple practice is called Earthing, also known as grounding, and it is both a technology and a movement that is transforming lives across the planet.[33]

The main thing is: you must remain health-consciously vigilant. Take charge of your health care. Manage it yourself, to the best of your ability. Here's a good reason why Number One (YOU)

---

33 What Is Earthing? https://www.earthing.com/what-is-earthing/

needs to look after your own body and your health.

> "British pension providers are asking insurers to identify people likely to die young in a bid to reduce the amount of retirement income they have to pay out. Pension trustees ask people to provide private medical information. The data is then given to an insurer which may take on the brunt of the liabilities of the pension scheme if it believes members will die shortly after retirement."[34]

Slant Board

I finish the day on my slant board. It's been around for a while, but active, it isn't. And although it is passive, I can feel a lot going on inside me as I lie head below my feet. That's due to the resetting effects of gravity, pulling organs back in their proper positions as I lie with my feet above my head.

Ten to fifteen minutes and all my organs are back in their correct places. Blood is circulating in new, refreshing ways, and for a moment gravity has been held in check. Mine is made out of foam, and, it seems, is now no longer available.

My Take

We need the will, both individual and collective, for better health. A desire that influences, and ultimately diminishes, the surge in preexisting conditions. After all, what are preexisting conditions but exposure to the various adverse, degenerative conditions of modern life?

Surely they are not the byproduct of a cosmic numbers game, where an individual's health conditions are handed out before birth, the universe determining who gets the short end of the stick. I would like to believe that free will plays a predominant role in human health. Individual and collective will power can shape our health — get us to the point where fewer people have these conditions. Is it easy? I don't know. But it is possible.

That's my workout: desultory, almost without purpose.

---

34 Insurers seek to cash in on unhealthy lifestyles

Stimulate The Phagocytes

Vivek Govekar explored the cosmological role of vibration, when he affirmed the following, "What is the nature of reality? Albert Einstein, that wise sage, once remarked, 'Nothing happens until something moves.'[35] This is quite literally true. Nothingness is the pure potentiality, the unborn absolute in its un-manifest form. When vibration happens, the nothingness gives birth to all that is."

This reality is the basis for all physical science, philosophical, and metaphysical exploration, ancient and contemporary. It covers nature, ontology, our bodies — all of existence, the energy continuum.

Let's take a look at some recent man-made discoveries in neuro-energetic stimulation including, vibrational stimulation devices, muscle activation and training techniques, Rife devices, neuromuscular alignment, oxygen intake enhancement, Earthing, and supplements have on the body and Being.

Since I activated kundalini, I have been able to feel the effects of supplements and neuro-energetic devices. The ones that are authentic immediately shift my kundalini motor into high gear, allowing me to distinguish between an adverse reaction and a positive one.

For instance, the Scalar Wave Laser, a device a friend loaned me, instantly stimulated my kundalini. Same goes for Earthing equipment, the difference being that, according to the designers, the Scalar Wave Laser focuses energy to match the vibrational frequency of a designated body organ while Earthing simply grounds the body to Earth's electro-magnetic field, allowing the forces of nature to tune the body. In both cases, the body's vibrational output is "tuned" by the equipment — vibration picking up on the frequency of other vibrations.

Earthing is perhaps more interesting. Why? Because a Scalar Wave Laser costs upward of $2000, requires batteries, charging, and

---

35 https://www.youtube.com/
    watch?v=leIqnnfTV3k&list=UUwfWXsz7Ox8RIVi01g9gtMA

maintenance while Earthing equipment is passive and, depending on the equipment you select, costs a mere $100-200. Yet, its effect on my body when I am grounded (using a piece of their grounding equipment) is almost as powerful as the Scalar Wave Laser.

I cite these as examples of the cause and effect relationship these devices have with the human body, at the same time as a warning against quackery, still as prevalent today as it was in early days of the 20th Century, as satirized by George Bernard Shaw's great play/movie: *The Doctor's Dilemma*.

> "As a relatively recent and cogent example within the age of science, in George Bernard Shaw's (typically) lengthy 1911 Preface to his 1906 play *The Doctor's Dilemma*, and the play itself, reflected the similar situation at that time. The essay and play are delightful, and if you have time or interest you'll enjoy reading it (or viewing the great 1958 movie with Leslie Caron, Dirk Bogarde — and the inimitable Robert Morely).
>
> "Here's Shaw's take on the state of medicine and medical science at the turn of the 20th century. We think you can translate it into 21st century equivalents. In those days the causes were bacteria (the 'genomics' of the age), and the magical approach was to *stimulate the phagocytes* which would enable the body to cure everything. In their desperation most people, 'to save themselves from unbearable mistrust and misery…fall back on the old rule that if you cannot have what you believe in you must believe in what you have…what you want is comfort, reassurance, something to clutch at, were it but a straw. This the doctor brings you. You have a wildly urgent feeling that something must be done; and the doctor does something.'"[36]

Scalar Wave Laser

I attended a training session with the inventor of the Scalar Wave Laser, whose workings basically boil down to setting the device to a particular vibrational frequency — one to which a specific organ is attuned — in order to benignly stimulate and/or positively affect said organ.

36 http://ecodevoevo.blogspot.ca/2015/03/stimulate-phagocytes-distant-mirror.html

That is the premise. During the session, all of the attendees were given a laser device to experiment with. The devices have very sophisticated program settings, allowing the user to "tune" areas and/or organs. I felt the effects immediately and then during the following week, as I experimented further, I continued to feel it working. The question is: working on what? Since I was not sick, I can't say that it cured or maintained any particular part of me.

During the breaks in the training session, I asked the participants if they could feel the actual energy. No one was able to say he/she "felt" anything, but many said the device relieved a given symptom. I wanted to find out whether they could detect the energy as I could, and although my survey was not scientific, I concluded that while the device may have stimulated energy in others as it did in me, they were unable to feel it. For them, it worked, but only behind the scenes, in the background, like some illicit computer program that transfers fractions of cents in thousands of customer accounts to an offshore account. If you're the beneficiary, you wake up one morning and you're rich!

I was especially impressed one evening during my reclining meditation. This is the moment the kundalini revs up, sending enormous amounts of sublimated energy up the spine to my brain, which in turn starts all manner of neuromuscular activity throughout my body. "What the heck..." I decided, "I've used my body as a laboratory for the last forty years. Why not test the laser device by placing it on the lower belly?" The staging area for my nightly energy build up!"

I set it to its most general selection and immediately felt a quantifiable intensification of kundalini energy coursing through me, which increased neuromuscular activity by a factor of three. This continued during the twenty-five minutes I remained in a deep Theta state.

All of which goes to show that these devices, at least the ones I mention here, do work. I first noticed the effects of outside-in, as opposed to inside-out energy sources, that affected my body after taking a Ginseng supplement back in the early nineties. Why shouldn't the awakened kundalini respond to other energy sources? Food, of course, stimulates kundalini. I've discussed the subject many times in my books; so has Gopi Krishna. But this was something different. I felt like a human energy detection machine. Get near to or ingest an energy substance and I could quantify its power and assign a value. Why not? That's what kundalini is all about — refining internal energy sources and discriminating among external sources. Vibration picking up on the frequency of other vibrations.

I've never been inside a nuclear facility, but I have been in a large automotive plant. Upon entering the plant, I started to feel like Superman when he's exposed to kryptonite, as if that factory's electro-magnetic field was draining the energy out of my body. I had to get out.

It's empirically clear to me that some substances/energies are toxic and some are benign. Would that each one of us could detect these properties! We might have an altogether different appreciation of environmental issues if we could feel toxicity in our bones. Imagine how we might be moved to recalibrate our thinking on wildlife were we able to feel the effects of encroaching development on the remaining pockets of wilderness. Imagine being able to feel the negative effects of junk food at time of ingestion, instead of waiting for diabetes to set in. It's a matter of sensitivity. Kundalini has made me into a test device; I like it that way.

Muscle Activation Techniques (MAT)

I have talked with MAT trainers and watched them work on my son for various basketball injuries. Jason, one of the trainers I talked with, tells me it's difficult to explain. The trick, he says, is in the doing. You won't understand the effects through any cognitive process. Only after treatment do you get feedback from the body. Exactly how my forty years of kundalini has transpired — continually using the body as a testing ground. Not settling for intellectualization. David, another trainer, says it's all 1s and 0s, as in computer programming. Touch a certain muscle in a certain way and it responds. I won't go into the details; these links contain overkill information. Nevertheless, I understood immediately that they don't treat symptoms, they treat causes, something that Western medicine has severely neglected, especially when you consider these recent findings on surgical intervention:

> Joint pain, Function not Always Better after Surgery (Reuters Health) - "Only about half of people who have a knee or hip replaced see meaningful improvements in pain and disability in the months after surgery, a new study from Canada suggests.
>
> Researchers found people who had worse knee or hip pain to begin with, fewer general health problems and no arthritis outside of the replaced joint were more likely to report benefits.
>
> "'I think this study really represents the general picture that often people do not have arthritis in just one joint,' said Elena Losina, an orthopedic surgery and arthritis researcher from Brigham and Women's Hospital in Boston."

PPM Mouthguard Theory

The first PPM device[37] I encountered cost $700; they had to be specially fitted by a dentist. That was two years ago. Since then they've come up with a do-it-yourself model that costs only $30. I bought one and tried it. I wanted to see if my ability as an energy detector also covers this sort of device. I want to see if it affects my kundalini and if it improves Strength, Balance, Explosive Speed, Agility, Endurance, and Recovery, as touted on their website. Like Earthing, the science behind this device also has its roots in anthropology in that it harks back to the time before eating utensils were developed:

Archaeological evidence suggests that most human beings had

---

37   The entire 2010 Super Bowl winning New Orleans Saints football team was outfitted with a PPM device.

an edge-to-edge bite, similar to apes. In other words, our teeth were aligned liked a guillotine, with the top layer clashing against the bottom layer. Then, quite suddenly, this alignment of the jaw changed: We developed an overbite, which is still normal today. The top layer of teeth fits over the bottom layer like a lid on a box.

This change is far too recent for any evolutionary explanation. Rather, it seems to be a question of usage. An American anthropologist, C. Loring Brace, put forward the thesis that the overbite results from the way we use cutlery, from childhood onwards.

What changed was the adoption of the knife and fork, which meant that we were cutting chewy food into small morsels before eating it. Previously, when eating something chewy such as meat, crusty bread or hard cheese, it would have been clamped between the jaws, then sliced with a knife or ripped with a hand -- a style of eating Professor Brace has called "stuff-and-cut."[38]

The model I have is for on-contact sports, such as golf, tennis, yoga, track and field, skating running, etc. It works by realigning the jaw to permit a greater flow of air.

In addition to the above factors the manufacturers say they have tested, I would like to see them do some accuracy testing, as in golf drives, archery, basketball free throws, etc. If my hunch is correct, by optimizing neuromuscular alignment both MAT and the PPM device should improve bodily symmetry, which in turn, should affect accuracy. So much of this emerging science has not been developed in the lab, but through intuitive hunches during years of on-the-job experience — individuals working empirically with 1s and 0s in the laboratories of their own bodies.

Material science is falling behind. Kundalini, Scalar Lasers, Earthing, MAT, PPM are in the vanguard of utilizing vibrational energy and neuro-energetic stimulation in order to improve health and human potential and offer alternatives to medical procedures that often bring no respite. In the future, it seems certain that medical treatment will include some sort of vibrational therapy, syn-

38 Teeth like a guillotine: How the fork created the overbite - http://www. dentistryiq.com/articles/2013/03/teeth-like-a-guillotine.html

chronizing of vibrations to re-calibrate faulty organs.

Raw Foods and Kundalini

The Kundalini/Raw Foods connection is based on Prana, the natural Life Force substance we need to perfect our beings during our life on Earth. To live, we extract Prana from our environment. The Chinese word for Prana is Chi; the closest English equivalent for this substance is Life Force Energy. If we don't get enough Prana, our bodies begin to degenerate prematurely. Very simply, to reach our potential, our bodies need to ingest only the purest elements — pure food, pure water, pure air. "Diet, not pills, may still be the best bet for brain power."

Prana exists in all living elements. Due to social conditioning, however, most people know very little about Prana, Chi, or Life Force Energy, and still less about how to extract it from the environment. Does Prana really exist, you may wonder? Perhaps you aren't aware that people who were weighed just before dying actually lose about six ounces when weighed again moments after death. What accounts for this weight loss? Researchers believe it reflects the loss of our vital Life Force Energy, leaving the body at the instant of death.

And, as Einstein proved, Energy, whether it's derived from a light socket or a nuclear reactor, is Matter, and matter is measurable. Our "vibrational essence," our Prana is measurable. In effect, human beings are energy intensive mechanisms — and after a kundalini awakening, a veritable Prana factory; we extract it, we store it, and we use it up. The object is not to squander it uselessly. So how do we extract Prana from our surroundings in its purest form?

Raw Foods contain Prana. So eating Raw Foods is a great way to obtain substantial quantities of it. Why Raw Foods? Raw Foods contain living enzymes and are highly alkaline in content and nature. If, like many in modern life, you can't be 100% raw, you can still consume a mostly alkaline diet. Why doctors don't test for pH levels at the same time the nurse takes your temperature and blood pressure is beyond me? It's the easiest way of determining chemical imbalance, and maintaining overall health. Acid foods lead to a stressful lifestyle; alkaline foods are full of Pranic energy that fights stress.

Even more Prana exists in pure air. The problem is we lack the correct breathing techniques for extracting it. Diaphragmatic Deep Breathing (DDB) — and its key technique, the backward-flowing method — is an acknowledged alchemical process for distilling Prana from the air we breathe. Unfortunately, information about the backward-flowing method is harder to get than information about Raw Foods. Not only has there been an information blackout, the whole idea of meditation is counter-intuitive. "Sit quietly in a room, contemplating my navel? Fat chance! Especially when all my buddies are at the gym building up their abs. I don't care how much it costs; I need to get into the gym!" Sorry, that's not the way health, or longevity, works.

The Backward-Flowing Method and Raw Foods

Kundalini Meditation (GFM) is the most powerful exercise on the planet and the backward-flowing method is its most powerful technique. The goal of the backward-flowing method is the permanent activation of the *Kundalini Shakti* Life Force. The basis of GFM is the backward-flowing method. Taoists refer to this process as The Microcosmic Orbit. The guiding intention of these techniques is action through non-action, or less is more. This is also counterintuitive, that an action based on stillness and deep breathing could actually be more powerful than the strenuous efforts undertaken in the noisy, energy-depleting atmosphere of your local gym.

But even the most powerful mechanisms are vulnerable from within. Yes, you can be well on your way to activating kundalini, and yet, for lack of proper diet, fall short. Why? Quite simply, you may be slowly poisoning yourself with the wrong foods. It happened to me. Even after I'd activated my kundalini, I began to have trouble with digestion as I grew older. I wondered why? Why was I constipated? Why did I need supplements and colonics? One day I heard about Raw Foods and instinctively knew it was the answer. Even when I can't eat 100% raw, I'm always alkaline-conscious, making sure I keep a high alkaline pH. When I started eating Raw Foods, it kicked my kundalini into high gear. I felt light on my feet once again. Raw Foods and Kundalini — perfect partners for distilling Prana!

If you do nothing else, keep tabs on how you use your energy. As *The Secret of the Golden Flower* reminds us:

"An ancient adept said: 'Formerly, every school knew this jewel, only fools did not know it wholly.' If we reflect on this, we see that the ancients attained long life by the help of the seed energy present in their own bodies, and did not lengthen their years by swallowing this or that type of elixir. But the worldly people lost the roots and clung to the treetops."

Evolution, Symmetry, and Sexual Selection

Wikipedia defines evolutionary psychology as attempting "to explain psychological traits — such as memory, perception, or language — as adaptations, that is, as the functional products of natural selection or sexual selection. Adaptationist thinking about physiological mechanisms, such as the heart, lungs, and immune system, is common in evolutionary biology. Evolutionary psychology applies the same thinking to psychology."

In *Deciphering the Golden Flower One Secret at a Time*, I wrote about physical symmetry not only as an indicator of sexual selection, but also as a prerequisite to activating permanent kundalini:

"The goal of GFM (kundalini meditation) is to standardize the outcome of the Kundalini-Life Force activation process. In other words, to make one kundalini experience indistinguishable from another. And although this may not be 100% possible at the moment, I believe that GFM comes close to meeting this objective. Why? Because it's based on the backward-flowing method, a technique perfected by the ancients over a long period of time, several centuries, in fact. Validation is simply a function of more individuals practicing GFM in the future.

"GFM demands commitment, self-discipline and concentration of the kind you'd expect from a doctorate level program. How do you know if you're ready? That's the tricky part. Your state of readiness is not something I, or any other person, can determine. Only your body can tell you. And it will, if you know how to listen to it. To a degree, symmetry is the predictor.

"Symmetry means being the same, or evenly balanced, on each side of the body. Over the last few years, biologists and evolutionary psychologists have looked at the animal kingdom, and they've made a few discoveries about symmetry, and how it relates to beauty and fitness."

"First, the more symmetrical an animal, the more likely he is to attract a mate. One scientist found that he could turn attractive male swallows into unattractive male swallows (and also ruin their chances of a good sex life) by clipping their tail feathers with scissors.

"Secondly, symmetry influences fitness. Horses that are more symmetrical run faster than horses that are less symmetrical. In one study, biologists measured some ten features on 73 thoroughbreds — features such as the thickness of the knee, or the width of the nostrils. The differences they could measure were quite small, and probably had nothing directly to do with how fast the horse could run. In fact, symmetry is probably a good indicator of general health and strength. Our imperfect world is full of nasty chemicals and germs. Only those individuals that are lucky enough to inherit a sturdy genetic makeup, and are also lucky enough to get good nutrition while they're growing, will end up being more symmetrical."

A now-defunct website entitled, "Mathematical Proof On Why Trying To Attract Women Fails" sought to prove that it's not worth perfecting a line and/or a persona to attract female sexual partners.

The best approach is to let nature take its course, in other words, rely on your natural symmetry that allows you to apply the mathematical concepts of symmetry to the faces of various movie stars.

For evolutionary psychologists this is serious business; for young men on the prowl, it's another kind of serious. What happens if your features don't conform to the strict mathematical requirements of physical symmetry as conveyed in this research?

"Developmental instability (DI) refers to an organism's ability to develop the appropriate species-specific phenotype despite genetic and environmental perturbations that tend to disrupt development, such as mutations, interbreeding, toxins, parasites, injuries, and DI is often operationalized as fluctuating asymmetry (FA), a composite measure of an individual's deviations from symmetry in traits that are symmetrical at the population level, without regard to side. Interest in DI stems in part from the wide range of studies demonstrating that humans with greater FA may show reduced fecundity, health, social dominance, and mating success. However, there is substantial variability in the strengths of associations across studies, and reasons for inconsistencies are poorly understood.

"To date, greater FA has been reported in a variety of neurodevelopmental disorders and has also been linked in humans with traits such as intelligence, jealousy, and physical violence. More specifically, individuals with greater FA have been reported to show relatively lower general intellectual functioning and to express more jealousy in mating situations. Furthermore, greater FA predicts fewer self-reported lifetime sexual partners and fewer episodes of physical violence.

"Given these behavioral correlates, one would expect FA to vary systematically with aspects of brain anatomy and/or physiology. Identifying specific neural correlates of FA would facilitate our understanding of the mechanisms linking the genetic and environmental determinants of FA with individual differences in behavior. To date, studies linking neural variation with FA in humans are sparse. In general, FA appears to be associated with

atypical functional lateralization of the human brain."[39]
So what if you suffer from Fluctuating Asymmetry? Are you
SOL? Well, if you read my kundalini memoir, you know I lost my
symmetry as the result of a childhood accident. I guess that's why
I was never able to walk into a room and make heads turn, male
or female. And yet, contrary to the findings of evolutionary psychologists, I experienced reasonable success with women. Did I feel
insecure around beautiful women? Who doesn't? But I never felt the
necessity to develop a line. I was as successful with women, average
to beautiful, as they were with me. What accounts for this?

Certain men and women don't require the absoluteness of
perfect symmetry in order to connect; they are able to go beyond
what Chris Anderson describes in the following passages:

"I'm sure you've asked a female friend before what she looks
for in a man and I'm also sure you were a bit puzzled by her answer."

"I just want a guy who's real."

"All I want is a guy who treats me decent."

"All I care about is that he doesn't cheat on me."

"Her response doesn't make much sense on the surface because
pretty much you and all the people you know pass these
seemingly low-bar requirements. She might as well have been
saying it's so hard to find a guy who has 2 hands and 2 feet. We
immediately dismiss what she said as crazy talk."

Or, as George Roundy explains to Lester Karpf in *Shampoo*
(1975), "I'm a gonna tell you about what they got against you.
Christ, they're women, aren't they? You ever listen to women talk,
man? Do you? 'Cause I do, till it's running outta my ears! I mean
I'm on my feet all day long listening to women talk and they only
talk about one thing: how some guy fucked 'em over, that's all
that's on their minds, that's all I ever hear about! Don't you know
that?"[40]

Clearly, we've evolved quite a bit since this film was released.

39 Evolutionary Psychology – ISSN 1474-7049 – Volume 6(4). 2008. -614
40 *Shampoo* (1975) Hal Ashby, director; Julie Christie, Warren Beatty

Statements like the above would be shouted down today. Nevertheless, it's been my experience that some beings — men and women
— are able to connect on a higher plane, right here on earth, as
a result of higher consciousness or elevated spirituality. How often
do these connections occur? Not very often. But when one does
occur, it's immediate and evident. It's beyond physical symmetry;
it's a kind of Karmic symmetry that enables two people to connect
in spite of the laws of physical attraction, which, according to evolutionary psychologists, are the ultimate determinants of selection
and therefore should be immutable *Gattaca* (1997)-type, DNA deal
breakers.

> Remember:
> "The greatest book in the world, the Mahabharata, tells us we all
> have to live and die by our karmic cycle. Thus works the perfect
> reward-and-punishment, cause-and-effect, code of the universe.
> We live out in our present life what we wrote out in our last. But
> the great moral thriller also orders us to rage against karma and
> its despotic dictates. It teaches us to subvert it. To change it. It
> tells us we also write out our next lives as we live out our present."
> ~ *The Alchemy of Desire* - Tarun J. Tejpal

What to Do While "It Does You!"

There seems to be a polemic building around the notion that
"spiritual" work (meditation, energy cultivation, mindfulness,
prayer, attending workshops, seminars, and retreats) takes care of
underlying emotional and psychological issues, so you don't need to
undertake any type of behavioral work to complete the self-realization process:

> "... the vast majority of us who are engaging in spiritual practice
> are making a similar mistake. We tend to put far too much
> emphasis on the need to "work out" our personal psychological
> issues as part of our spiritual path.
> "The way this plays out practically is as follows: let's say that
> you take up a spiritual practice in earnest, and you notice in the

course of that practice that you're deeply defended against life and intimacy. You won't let other people see you. You always wear a social mask which hides a deep-rooted insecurity.

"The trouble is that although this "archaeological dig" into the depths of your psyche might lead to greater self-understanding, it won't necessarily make it any easier for you to be vulnerable, authentic and present. Indeed, it might even take you further away from authentic intimacy with life by making you more self-preoccupied than before.

"It's important to recognize that this tendency toward self-preoccupation isn't our fault. This habit grew out of our over-psychologized culture which basically told us that we were all damaged by our childhood and that we have "inner wounds" that need to be healed in order to become happy and fulfilled as adults."

~ *The Mistake Most of us Make on the Spiritual Path* – Craig Hamilton

This appears to run counter to Margaret Dempsey's hypothesis that some psychic work may be needed, not so much to overhaul the psyche, but to help the individual recognize the ego indoctrination process:

"So before any spiritual work is attempted, I strongly recommend individuals, especially those who have been on a spiritual path for many years, do a transformative, self-development program. In my case it was the Forum from Landmark Education, but there are others. It's not important which one is done. What is critical is doing something to deal with the sloppy thinking in which one presumes that simply by meditating or doing yoga one is going to transform the ego that stands in the way of awakening.

"Trying to transform the ego on one's own is like a thief turning detective to catch the one who is the thief; it can't be done and leads to frustration and disillusionment."

~ The First Stage of Spiritual Awakening: Know Yourself – Margaret Dempsey

To answer the question "What to Do While 'It Does You!'" I created a diagram of the process that attempts to illustrate what happens when you reach the It Does You! stage. In short, it really does DO you! I'll not serve it up again for reconsideration.

That is to say the Kundalini-Life Force energy starts re-engineering your being (body, soul, mind, ego, all) and you can sit back and let it work its evolutionary magic, or as Craig Hamilton says, "... feel instantly connected to the heart of Life and energized by the impulse of evolution itself."

The challenge is, at least for me, that I have been living with this energy for over 40 years, exploring, as time went by, many facets of my being, and I don't believe that delving into the various aspects of my being has been counter to the It-Does-You! work that kundalini carries out on a daily basis. In fact, doing this work has helped change my Being. No longer was I simply a body and a mind, but rather a Being with a capital "B," connected to an energy continuum, like the scent of a pine forest is connected to living trees.

That said, I can see how too much self-exploration — a trend offshoot of the Freudian gotta-go-through-Analysis lobby so prevalent in American society during the 50s and 60s — might short-circuit an individual in the You-do-it! phase, leaving him/her prey to what Hamilton terms "inner wounds." Nevertheless, once you reach the It does You! phase, there's no harm in pursuing insights into how the mind and the ego work, especially as pertains to the finer aspects of social interaction. In my case, I never felt the need for psychoanalysis; I got the point of it after reading Eric Berne's *Games People Play*.

The work I've done on myself since kundalini took over has been pretty much confined to self-remembering,[41] which is geared toward self-control, the key to success in the material world, and I'm not using the preceding term in a materialistic sense. I mean it in the sense of learning to respond instead of to react.

Other than that, any polemic brewing over the question of

41   Recently reinvented as, mindfulness

what to do while pursuing self-realization is a non-starter. I think all three of us (Hamilton, Dempsey, Semple) are basically saying the same thing. It depends on where you are in the journey:

- If you're in the You-do-it! stage, beware of distractions that blur your sense of purpose.
- If you're in the It-Does-You! stage, you should have developed the perspective and the awareness to manage the important aspects of your life.

Seminal Retention And Kundalini

One way of telling if kundalini is genuine is by how it affects you after ejaculating.

For many men, an after-sex timeout to revitalize the body is commonplace, normal, and natural. For kundalini adepts, however, ejaculation has a difference-of-kind effect, usually characterized by a complete somatic depletion — a de-energizing that grips the whole body and demands more than just a little respite. It is this condition that both Gopi Krishna and I wrote about: he in *Kundalini: The Evolutionary Energy in Man*; I in *Deciphering the Golden Flower One Secret at a Time*. Both of us experienced this effect and both of us noted the immediate need for nourishment as a means of replenishing the pranic life force.

In the aftermath of my first post-kundalini sex, I felt as if I was imploding, as if the constant, daily rebuilding work kundalini was performing on me had been so adversely affected by ejaculation that I needed an immediate influx of pranic energy to reverse the threat to my metabolism. I felt like someone had pulled the plug and the contents of my braincase were trickling down the drain. It was a feeling akin to fear or surprise, the type of sensation that grips the whole body in an instant of shock. A panicky notion that I was dying. Food. I needed food. I went to the refrigerator and quickly gobbled four containers of yogurt, which started to repair the damage and eventually calmed me.

Why does sex affect kundalini adepts like that? Simple.

Kundalini doesn't like sharing the distilled sexual energy that it produces, i.e., the life force; it wants to send it all to the brain. Procreation is one thing; sexual sublimation is another. Ejaculation affects the newly anointed adept as it affected Gopi Krishna and me, and when it does, woe to he who ignores the signals.

Gopi Krishna explains

"As we have seen in our previous discussions, it is not easy to prescribe behavior and diet for the future evolution of the brain. Although I also spoke about sex before, I now would like to be a little more explicit. Inasmuch as all our modem theories about sex, including the ideas expressed by Freud, do not take evolution of the brain into account, we can therefore say that they are incomplete.

"The moment it is established that the brain is evolving biologically, it will then be seen that a part of the reproductive energy is consumed in this evolution. I have given the proof, genius and the illuminated mind. For the last three thousand years the Indian savants knew it, as did the Greeks and the Egyptians. They knew that genius and illumination come from transmuted sex energy.

"Freud puts it in a different way. He says it is libido and that all creative activity and mental disorders arise out of the libido. But he has not defined libido. For him, libido is psychic energy in its subtle form, in its psychic form.

"But it has a somatic aspect also, as Reich correctly put it. It is anchored in the body, his libido. He has clearly mentioned this. But since science has no awareness of a phenomenon that has been in evidence for the last thousands of years, that it is the transmutation of sexual energy that leads to creativity, then naturally all current theories about sex are incomplete.

"What is recommended by some psychologists or by some clinicians about unrestrained sex is therefore not only fallacious, but highly dangerous for the race.

"In the ages to come, people will determine what part of the energy goes to the brain and what part they can utilize for procreative or for pleasurable purposes. There is no doubt that there is nothing in the world so enchanting, so alluring, so inspiring as sexual love. It has inspired some of the greatest thinkers. It is the women whom they loved who inspired some of the greatest writers, thinkers, politicians, conquerors of the world. There is nothing comparable to love for the happiness, health and evolution of mankind.

"But it has not to be abused, because this energy is designed by nature both for evolution and procreation. And evolution must have its share. It would be saner to conserve the energy, even to be a celibate than it would be to overspend it. This is the reason why celibacy has been recommended in religions. Otherwise there is no reason. Why should religion in some way insist that you have to be celibate unless the energy is used in some way?

"But we need not go to that extreme. The rational, normal, and natural course is to adjust our life so that we allow that part which is meant for our evolution to be used for that purpose.

"There are some facts that show that nature is always giving us warnings. For instance many people, after the climax, after the expenditure of the energy, feel a sense of disgust or coldness, antipathy, or great tiredness. That is a warning from nature that they have overdone it. If, after the sexual climax, a man feels as energetic as before, it means he has not used or taken from the amount needed for evolution."[42]

Why is this important? Because many people don't realize that enlightenment or self-realization (that elusive state so many people are searching for) actually has somatic, anatomical, and metabolic components. They believe that enlightenment is attained through activities like meditation, prayer, mantras, faith, visitations and not through any contributions of a somatic or metabolic nature. But why wouldn't an individual's body be involved in all aspects of the evolutionary process?

People who say they believe that kundalini exists, but that it has no place in ascending to higher spiritual states don't realize that

---

42 "Gopi Krishna Talks About Sex and Love" - http://www.koausa.org/Kundalini/sex.html

kundalini is not something you believe in. It's a physical actuality, like a heart attack or an orgasm — a biological process whose effects vary.

People may also believe in holdover medieval myths that the body must be scourged in order to attain spiritual grace. Not so, if anything the body must participate in the process through yoga, meditation, and other energy cultivation techniques. Isn't it ironic that reaching the sublime requires a contribution from our sexual apparatus? The sacred is nourished by the profane.

Now, I'm not saying that everyone should be trying to activate kundalini — given the many unexpected effects that most people aren't prepared for, most people shouldn't — only that kundalini has played, and will continue to play, a crucial role in human evolution...and therefore more study must be directed towards its true workings.

So can the two purposes — evolution and procreation/pleasure — coexist? Can the trial and error quest for self-realization coexist with what Gopi Krishna called "unrestrained sex?"

The answer is yes. And that's where seminal retention techniques come in. Seminal retention allows you to conserve the seed during intercourse. Why would you want to do this? For all the reasons stated above, plus the fact that times have changed. The quest for self-realization does not need to conflict with the sybaritic tendencies and self-indulgent practices associated with sex in contemporary living. Harmonizing the two — self-realization and unrestrained sex — requires learning and practicing seminal retention techniques, which by the way, actually add to the pleasurable aspects of intercourse. Nevertheless, it's not an easy course to follow. Concessions by both partners are required. Sexual habits are difficult to change and harder to break. However, having experienced the debilitating effects of ejaculation, it's not something you allow to get out of control.

Transphysiological Energy Activation

Back in June 2011, I wrote an essay on labeling spiritual constructs and how labels restrict meaning, making cooperation among individuals exploring similar methods and techniques more difficult than it need be because they feel beholden to the subtext of meaning of the particular path they've been indoctrinated into.

Take kundalini, for instance. Even though it's a biological process, it's approached and understood in many other unrelated ways — as a religious offshoot, as a myth, as an emerging science, as a ritual. It's a term whose connotations control the way it's perceived. For example, I've met persons who are unable to discuss kundalini because the term somehow suggests a cult and a host of negative connotations. Their minds are prisoners of false associations. If I say kundalini, their minds register cult. They are closed to kundalini as a biological process.

Even if people aren't turned off by a given term in its raw state, they still tend to infer meaning from their own immediate experience. Until, of course, the process is described in scientific language, which is itself an arduous task. Survey the various authorities on kundalini and you realize each one has its own special perception of the phenomenon behind the term, which, of course, leads to the inability of the various authorities to cooperate.

There are obvious reasons for this: the term Kundalini has a spiritual derivation. The process has been documented by most of the world's religious and mystic traditions. Each one has its own terminology and practices, which they defend against all other usages and observances. A veritable Babel!

Yes, the term Kundalini is the reigning champ, but its connotations, as noted above, overwhelm the appeal to attract serious scientific investigation. Why should we consider science over religion? Kundalini is a biological process, first uncovered by early religious seekers, who, because of the startling effects it induced, attributed its consciousness-enhancing effects to spiritual causes. At the time, the scientific method had yet to be discovered. Biology was unknown, for the most part. The only rational explanation was an irrational one: that the Gods must be responsible, that the Gods had conferred special powers on certain individuals.

We owe those early explorers a lot: Milarepa, Lao Tse, Jesus, Siddhārtha Gautama - the Buddha. Props also to modern investigators, Osho and Gopi Krishna, the 20th Century's most prolific writer and researcher on kundalini.

The term Kundalini has served us well. Until now...

Now we need to focus our research and practice on the biological aspects of the process. To this end, Cristian Muresanu has put forward a new lexicon of terminology to do exactly that. Will it take hold? I don't know, but I applaud the effort he's put into it. *Transphysiological Energy Activation*[43] is the term he proposes. He's already published a first post on the subject, one that deals with the medical condition he faced and how his infirmity led him to the Transphysiological Energy Activation process. Check out his back-story.

Love's a Skill

I've often wondered about Love, what it actually is. It seems so intertwined, so many of life facets operating on so many planes. How to define it? Especially when it's bandied about so freely. Witness talk show hosts and guests in familiar mutual self-promotion mode: *I love this guy*-type statements. *Love you, man.*

The pull of youth to couple with another human being — to feel and be felt, to smell and be smelt, to kiss and be kissed. How those passions progress over thirty or forty years of marriage. How the young look at their parents and can't wait to move on with their own lives. How their parents see themselves in their children. How the two find it impossible to communicate their feelings.

---

43 http://www.kundaliniconsortium.org/2014/03/reversing-incurable-chronic.html

How frequently Love is used as a Twitter hashtag — how it peaks and dips at certain times in the 24-hour cycle.

Definition of #love

May refer to romance, relationships, familial love and any person, thing, situation or event that makes you feel all giddy inside.
[More...]

#love 24-Hour Trend Graph

Upgrade Analytics

Estimated Tweets Per Hour (Based on 1% Sample)

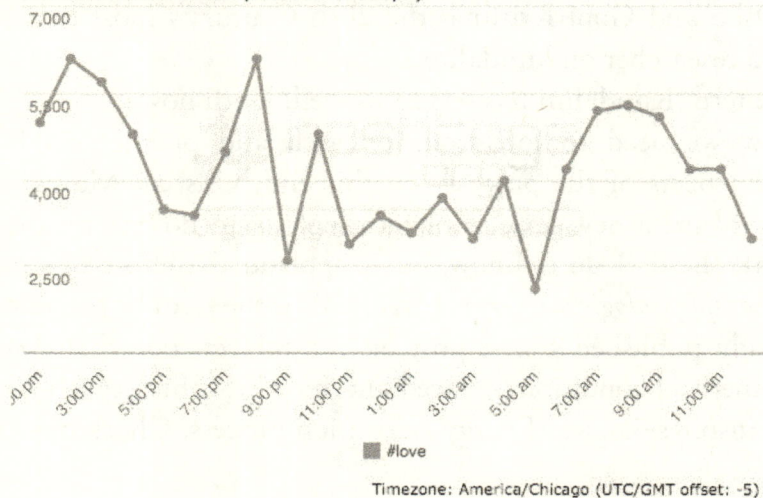

Timezone: America/Chicago (UTC/GMT offset: -5)

How the word #Love — even though it's sincerely meant by many a conveyor and felt by many a listener — somehow gets lost in the sentimentality that repetition engenders. In a popular song lyric, for instance:

What's it all about, Alfie, is it just for the moment we live?
What's it all about when you sort it out, Alfie?
Are we meant to take more than we give
Or are we meant to be kind?

And if only fools are kind, Alfie
Then I guess it is wise to be cruel
And if life belongs only to the strong Alfie

What will you lend on an old golden rule?

As sure as I believe there's a Heaven above, Alfie
I know there's something much more
Something even non-believers can believe in

I believe in #love, Alfie
Without true love we just exist, Alfie
Until you find the love you've missed
You're nothing, Alfie

When you walk let your heart lead the way
And you'll find love any day, Alfie, Alfie
© *Alfie* - Music & Words: Burt Bacharach, Hal David

And yet, when Dionne Warwick, Whitney Houston, or Barbara Streisand reaches the payoff line, 'I believe in love, Alfie,' it sends a chill down our backs and we forget about definitions and believe we really know what it means. Then, when the song is over, we ask ourselves, once again, What does it mean? Is it "I believe in (#hashtag) Love, (fill in your lover's name here) or is it remaining married for forty years and being able to live and laugh together?

And even though we understand in our minds that a big part of it is only a hashtag cliché, we know, there are occasions when it transcends banality. Nevertheless, until a few days ago, I didn't know what love was, and now I do: Love is a Skill.

A few days ago, in a meeting, a writers group was discussing the meaning of love, going through the usual changes, the sharps and the flats of our various triumphs and failures, until someone said they'd heard phrase, *Love is a Skill* and it resonated. And, it fell into place for me, because I looked back and realized how unskilled I'd been for most of my life. At that same instant, I reflected on how love, when treated like a skill, is closely tied to self-remembering.

It's the difference between Reacting and Responding, a shift from emotional to cognitive, or mnemonic. Reacting is immediate; Responding is the moment one uses to remember one's self before rejoining the fray. It is, in fact, stepping outside the fray, seeing the fray as an enactment with all the players, one's self included, strutting and fretting on a stage. A true out-of-body experience.

So if love is more than a hashtag, it must be different than Tin Pan Alley love, just as passion and lust are different than sitting around the kitchen table discussing the family finances, and coming out of the discussion without once raising one's voice.

There's a lot of talk about civility today, and rightly so: That instead of calling people names and thinking of them as #Assholes, we need to see people as unskilled or inexperienced in the various arts and sciences of love and/or the practices of civility.

Sex is one thing; Love is another. Not to say that sex has no place in Love; it does. But it's not the only thing. Yes, it's the thing we get lost in (like we get lost in a song), the thing that gives us immense pleasure (like a roller coaster or other sensation). But sensations are tied to thrill seeking; we tire of thrills as we tire of repetitive chores.

Love is the skill — the art and science — of not tiring, of dealing with other human beings, playing a hand of cards, shuffling them around expertly: the money card, the sex card, the prestige card, the power card, the race card, the health card, the pride card, etc. Some decks have more cards than others; some players have to play more cards than others at any one time. It's the hand you're dealt with and how you play it. What does this have to do with kundalini?

Progressively, kundalini gives us an ethereal, subtle body that allows us to detach ourselves in order to observe the daily enactments, instead of getting swept up in them. It helps us to understand the realities of the physical plane, instead of idealizing them. And that's why I don't believe there's such a thing as a #Soulmate because this notion, when built on sex alone, crumbles over time, as the body debilitates.

Could it exist? Yes, if, when the sex card no longer has value for one partner, the other is able to acquiesce: one partner plays a card, the other knows how and when to play the right card in return so as not to leave the other partner in the lurch. It requires empathy: a mutual stepping back to witness an enactment from outside the body — an ability kundalini readily confers upon those it favors.

Want another example? How about Rodgers and Hart's 1938 torch song in waltz time, featuring Hart's special brand of cynicism, *Falling In Love With Love*:

Falling in love with love is falling for make believe;
Falling in love with love is playing the fool;
Caring too much is such a juvenile fancy;
Learning to trust is just for children in school.

I fell in love with love one night when the moon was full;
I was unwise with eyes unable to see;
I fell in love with love, with love everlasting;
But love fell out with me.

Kundalini In Society

"Speak it into existence. Keep talking about it until it happens."
~ LaVar Ball"

How Kundalini is Perceived

If you're out there, dealing with kundalini, how do you explain it to others, to yourself? Do you even try?

Recently, I had the opportunity to test this. I wasn't giving a talk or a presentation on kundalini; I had been invited to join a community discussion group with five or six other men and I was attending my fifth or sixth session. Discussion usually skirted around cultural and any number of other progressive topics, but it never touched spiritual matters. And I never brought one up.

One day, however, one of the participants — I later discovered he was battling cancer — brought up the afterlife question in a way that flowed seamlessly into the existing context. I can't remember word for word what followed, but I did seize the opening to comment on my research into human energy potential and energy cultivation techniques, as well as my findings on evolution.

Someone asked me if I could prove it. I cited NDE and kundalini as examples of consciousness existing outside mind and body. I underlined that my hypothesis was the result of research done in the laboratory of my own body, and it was supported by many similar accounts from all over the globe. Some members continued the discussion; the man who'd started it wanted to hear more. But several others began shouting that kundalini had no scientific value; it was only a cult.

A cult, a religion, a philosophy, a practice, and an exercise regimen. It's been called all of the above, as well as many less flattering names. One man kept shouting, "It's a cult, it's a cult!" I spent two minutes trying to explain that kundalini was a biological process, that I had no religious affiliations, and that kundalini, despite the unfortunate connotations attached to its name, was the driving force behind evolution. I mentioned that my kundalini experience had begun with breathing exercises, and then morphed into profound consciousness experiences I have documented in several books.

I stated that my experience was not the result of any religious practice or a belief system. In fact, I told them I practiced no religion nor did I hold any position on God.

I explained that kundalini triggered many physical, metabolic, somatic, cognitive, psychological, and other effects in my being, right down to the cellular level, on which I could elaborate if the group was interested. I told them these effects had nothing to do with religion. They were the by-products of the biological energy kundalini produces and they resulted in my becoming immersed in an Energy Continuum, not unlike the Unified Field physicists speak of. My experience inspired me to learn more about higher consciousness, energy cultivation, and the role of kundalini in evolution. I added that the effects were largely unexpected and showed me that keeping an open mind was paramount if we are interested in the forces behind evolution.

"Cult, cult!" he shouted.

"It's not a religion or a cult," I said. "You can't be 'converted' to kundalini any more than you can be converted to a heart attack or an orgasm; they just happen. Some kundalini arousals are triggered by deliberate practices, like meditation; others are autonomic or spontaneous."

Needless to say, the discussion ended there and that was the last meeting I attended. What's the point? If a person is so closed-minded he confuses biology with religion, there's little room for dialog.

Nevertheless, of the two most excitable critics, I learned that one was a virulent atheist who could not conceive of any middle ground between belief and non-belief in God or in the actuality of metaphysical phenomena and the other had been raised in fundamentalist surroundings and had it up to his chin hairs with religion.

Both were college professors.

"In the same way that science has been unable to anticipate discoveries that radically changed our understanding of how reality works, it has also been blind to the possibility that another faculty of mind beyond the intellect has been evolving in us. This blindness is mostly due to the fact that it is extremely difficult for the intellect to conceptualize any faculty of mind more advanced than itself.

"The same must surely have been the case when the intellect began to evolve. The early proto-humans that preceded Homo Sapiens doubtless had no concept of the intellect about to evolve in them. But this lack of awareness could have had no bearing whatsoever on the process of that evolution. Similarly, just because we have little or no idea what faculties of mind may evolve in us in the future does not change the possibility that such faculties will eventually come into our possession.

"If we consider the intellect as being the most recent evolutionary development in our mental capabilities, then what shape would a new faculty of mind, that transcends it, likely take? The intellect uses logic, reason, and inference to process information about the external world gained through sensory input. Consciousness, according to Quantum Theory, has the ability to force subatomic particles to take physical form. This would suggest that it is more primary than matter, and must therefore have an independent existence of its own." [44]

So how do you explain kundalini? How do others react to your explanation? What have you learned from people whose minds are closed to any investigation of the hypothesis that biology is an expression of consciousness or that extrasensory perception exists? Do you insist there's an energetic component distilled from sexual secretions in every human, which, if properly directed to the brain, is capable of awakening powerful extrasensory capabilities and higher consciousness? How do listeners react when you explain that trans-forming an embryo into a fetus and thus into a fully-grown person is

44 Bradford, Michael. *Consciousness: The New Paradigm* (p. 51-52). Institute for Consciousness Research. Kindle Edition.

not some sort of mechanistic process, but is actually executed from a blueprint of your being that existed before your conception? What happens when you cite examples of "consciousness as an aspect of Creation independent of matter?"[45]

Kundalini and Pop Culture

Yoda, The Matrix, Spiderman, and Batman. Why has our popular culture become so permeated with tales of super heroes? Do our subconscious imaginations know something our conscious minds don't? The Dark Side and the Light. Can pop culture predict the future? Does the truth about the future of humanity lie hidden in the epic struggles of comic book heroes or in blockbuster super hero movies? Is there a secret to life?

I ask because a pop essence has infused our culture, producing a yearning for something more powerful, more liberating. Since the 1940s, Hollywood has featured movies in which people:

Come back from the dead to instruct the living (*Ghost, Heaven Can Wait, Topper*);

Have guardian angels (*It's A Wonderful Life, Here Comes Mr. Jordan, The Bishop's Wife*);

Acquire super magical powers (*Star Wars, Superman, The Matrix, X-Men*).

If they do it in the movies, and it's seeped into our consciousness to such an extent, there must be something to it. Doesn't fiction foretell reality? Is not actuality rooted in dreams? If there's nothing to it, then why has so much time and money been spent stimulating our imagination? Why do we spend so much time on stories and fables about the acquisition of extraordinary faculties? Quite simply, because not only is there increased interest in the evolution of mankind, there's also an outsized fascination with the acquisition of superhuman abilities.

We shouldn't be indignant with Hollywood. The purveyors

---

45 Ibid, p. 52).

of dreams — pop culture trendsetters and advertising wags, writers and storytellers — are merely channeling the phenomenon of unconscious or collective yearning. What is unconscious yearning? It's a symptom of the evolutionary impulse that Gopi Krisana celebrated in his books.

Unconsciously, we have always yearned for higher states. Our popular culture has given us Avatars to aspire to: Batman, Superman, The Hulk, Wonder Woman, Captain Marvel, Daredevil, Spiderman. Heck, Robert Louis Stevenson's best-selling work, *Strange Case of Dr. Jekyll and Mr. Hyde* (1886), was little more than a veiled kundalini awakening gone awry.

Eventually, we will morph into more spirit-based beings. What will this entail? Well, in the first place let's look at where we've come from. Only in this way can we understand where we're going. We evolved from one-celled animals, tiny invisible creatures. Look at where we are now. What a progression of form and capability. Yes, it took millions of years, but the progression has been amazing. Who says we won't continue to evolve — take on new forms, add more advanced capabilities.

Evolution has allowed us to dominate our planet. To do this, we needed raw aggressive powers, a type of behavioral nature that could not be deterred by any threat to our survival. Immediate survival was the role of the reptilian brain psychologists and anthropologists often talk about. Once on the road to dominance, a mammalian brain was added. This evolutionary adjustment added an emotional component — a capability that allowed our species to develop a strong sense of identity based on simple emotions such as, surprise, fear, anger, sadness, joy and more developed emotions like remorse, awe, pride, optimism, shame, guilt, love.

Now, to evolve to the next stage of being do we need such powerful emotions? Can we survive in world with less need for aggression and less space per individual, possessing, as part of our beings, emotional states that frequently lead to trouble: wars, family breakdown, addiction, crime, greed, hate crimes? Emotions that many times — more often than not — lead us in the wrong direction.

Perhaps pop culture, as it relates to the eventual metamorphosis of our species, can shed some light on the subject. I say eventual because it's not for today. But, if and when it comes, what form will it take?

To illustrate the form this new human being might take, I'll break down a pop culture icon and show how, beneath its many layers of metaphor it contains hidden patterns of unconscious yearning. This icon is none other than Don Siegel's 1956 masterpiece, *Invasion of the Body Snatchers*, starring Kevin McCarthy and Dana Wynter.

Pods Being Delivered

This review from the Internet Movie Database (IMDb) by Brandt Sponseller sums up several of the film's allegorical levels.

> "Much has been said about the parallels between Invasion of the Body Snatchers and the 'communist paranoia' in the United States in the late 1940s and early 1950s, especially as it was

directed against Hollywood by the House Un-American Activities Committee. However, there is another very interesting subtext present that isn't often mentioned. The film can also be looked at as a philosophical exploration of personal identity. Just what does it take for people to be themselves? Is it how they look, act, the things they say? Is it not the case that people are constantly transformed into something they weren't just hours ago, or even moments ago? Among the many ways that these kinds of ideas are worked into the script is that sleep is a metaphor for unconscious physical change over time. It would be easy to analyze each scene in the film in this manner, going into detail about the various implications each plot development has on the matter of personal identity."

Reading this review, I couldn't help thinking about the common phrase: "He wasn't himself." A phrase often applied to persons who lose emotional control due to personal tragedy or disaster. I don't know if that's the direction the author of this review was going in, but control of emotion is really the underlying theme of this movie. Except for human emotion, the original being and its Pod counterpart are alike in every way. Unbeknownst to the screenwriters, who may have thought they were making a statement about Communist witch-hunts, the real and hidden theme of the film is a change in being based on mass kundalini awakening. The next great leap forward in human evolution.

I know this goes against everything you've ever heard of or thought about this film. It goes against our revulsion and fear of the Pod People, and our inherent tendency to side with the good guys, who in this case, are us, even though there are no superficial differences between the characters in their Original or Pod avatars. To us, our emotions, our ability to feel love especially, is the single attribute that sets us apart from them, that makes us "right" and them "wrong". At least, that's what the authors would have the characters believe, and through them, us. In one scene, a doctor, played by Larry Gates, explains this to Miles and Becky, who are so terrified at the thought of being stripped of their humanity, they can't even listen. They don't know kundalini from nothing. That's because the authors didn't either. But unconsciously they took us far beyond Communist conspiracy and McCarthyism. They didn't know it but they were describing the next stage of human evolution, one where humans, if we are to survive, will no longer need to express emotion in the wanton, destructive ways we do.

Let's step back for a moment and reflect on the psychology of the screenwriter's creative process. Since the inspiration comes from the author's subconscious, it's reasonable to believe that he had no conscious awareness of the deeper layers of meaning. In the case of *Invasion of the Body Snatchers*, it's probable that the author wasn't knowingly aware of the symbolism of a kundalini awakening, especially if he was preoccupied with the subtextual theme of McCarthyism. Yet, the story has all the earmarks of this experience, at least in allegorical terms. People who fall asleep, only to awaken as new beings that are superior to the old. New beings that threaten the old order because of their superiority. Their superior emotional control, capacity to cooperate, to communicate, to get along, resistance to illness, longevity. The Pod represents the awakening process, the slow formation of the more perfect being, and the results are clearly superior physical beings.

Resistance, however, is hysterical, even illogical. The author is saying that in spite of the fact that the transformation process is painless and produces a superior being, we should be afraid of it. Why? Because our emotions make us "human." No mention is made of the destructive power of our emotions. In spite of the fact that today our emotions get in the way of just about everything we need to accomplish.

So, am I saying that we will not succeed as a species unless we can learn to govern our emotions? Up to the industrial revolution we needed powerful emotions to extend our "perceived" dominance over nature. Now we are moving in another direction. In the film, one of the characters talks about emotion as one of the elements that makes us human, that without it, we would not be human. Who knows what it is to be human? We don't even know where we became human. That we came from the mud, evolved from lower forms is certain, but when did we become human and who's to say that the human being of today shall not evolve into further avatars with even greater powers of awareness? Is our evolution finished? Is our brain incapable of adding entirely new nodes — as it did long ago when it added the neocortex?

> "Evolutionary developments generally start with a few individuals of a species, scattered in time and location. Over long periods of time these developments eventually become a widespread, then permanent feature of that species as a whole. We would therefore expect that this new evolutionary faculty might already have shown itself infrequently in some individuals of the human race.
>
> "The three primary characteristics of this new faculty would therefore be: 1) a direct perception of consciousness as an aspect of Creation independent of matter, 2) an ability to acquire knowledge from that consciousness without the use of the intellect, and 3) an extremely infrequent distribution of individuals with this new faculty over a long period of time."[46]

These pop-culture avatars spring from the depths of our creative imagination, even to the point of laying out a blueprint, in storyboard form, for our transition to a new state of being. That people should interpret the blueprint as something to be feared is only normal. Evolution does not come easy. As Mikhail Turovsky said, "The first ape who became a man thus committed treason against his own kind."

In neuro-biological terms human potential is limitless and our subconscious mind knows it. Where does the subconscious mind get its information? From time to time, the kundalini nudges our subconscious. Some of these contents come to us in the form

---

46 Bradford, Michael. *Consciousness: The New Paradigm* (p. 52). Institute for Consciousness Research. Kindle Edition.

of dreams and inspirations of various sorts. In men of genius, it endows them with extraordinary creative powers. These contents are not mere figments, but the signs of a deeper reality, one constantly beckoning to us to push the boundaries of consciousness, what Gopi Krishna called the Evolutionary Impulse.

Is Compromise Possible? - A Kundalini Worldview

With tropes like, "This is the dirtiest campaign ever" being amplified to a fanatical degree by the Media and the Internet, it's possible to think it may be so, until you remember the pundits have been saying the same thing about the last 20 election cycles. So I think it's safe to predict that the next presidential campaign will sink to even lower depths, waste more time that could be used for getting things done, and throw away more money for the wrong reasons.

It's not so much about the beliefs and positions of the left or right as it is about the growing distance between the two camps that makes compromise close to impossible. What's wrong with that? What's wrong with opposing camps hurling invective and personal insults at each other?

You've heard the expression, "It's not personal, it's business." It's an expression that makes a lot of sense when applied to the nation's business, the business of running the country, which amounts to government doing the greatest good for the greatest number of people, even if that sometimes means doing nothing. Personal connotes doing something for your own immediate gain; government connotes a rationale that involves something larger than the individual.

Sitting around the table negotiating takes patience, civility, and a degree of mutual understanding — what George H. W. Bush called a kinder, gentler mindset — the capacity to put oneself in the other's position. So what's happened to cause our society to move from positions of relative cooperation to complete estrangement? Not that the political forces in this country haven't always opposed one another's policies. They have. But when things were on the line, they compromised.

Estrangement leads to perpetual gridlock, a condition that's expanded geometrically since the 1970s, whose stifling nature we've all but accepted as the new normal, except when using it as a talking point to blame the other side.

Can anything short of a Napoleon-like dictator get the nation focused on fixing the things that need fixing? That's what Donald Trump is telling us: that only a strong leader can put things right. But we know what happens when a country resorts to a so-called strong leader.

The people who wish for it soon realize they've got more than they bargained for. There's a memorable passage on this subject in Elia Kazan's *Viva Zapata!* (1952), a film that tackles ambition and abuse of power:

> Zapata (to his followers): "You always look for leaders, strong men without faults. There aren't any. There are only men like yourselves. They change. They desert. They die. There are no leaders but yourselves. A strong people is the only lasting strength."

"A strong people..." How did we lose our strength? I'm not talking about military hardware, world hegemony, or economic supremacy; I'm talking about integrity. And when you succumb to every temptation out there, you lose it. I've summarized this issue previously;[47] no need to repeat. Only to add to the above that we're not alone; the rest of the world is right up there with us, chasing the same illusions: money, power, wanton sex, domination, self-aggrandizement — all the elements Freud said destroys a man. And if they can destroy a man, they can destroy a nation, a world, a planet. Just look at the frequency and prevalence of incarceration, mass murder, addiction, war, new diseases, racial hatred, sex crimes, wanton violence.

I used to believe the rapid increase in spiritual investigation, as typified by the growing number of kundalini awakenings, would somehow put us on the right track. No more. Why? There doesn't seem to be enough time to slow down the headlong, worldwide rush to self-destruction.

Not by any of the accepted orthodoxies can we change course:
- *Religion can't do it*: There are more religious wars now than ever before, and on a grander, worldwide scale.
- *Education can't do it*: There are a lot of intelligent people, but the true test of intelligence is not IQ; it's what you use your intelligence for. The more people who graduate; the more they disagree; the more they indulge self-interest.
- *Politics can't do it*: Any institution beholden to money interests and driven by them is bound to fail.
- *Science can't do it*: It's one step forward and two steps back. For every Salk vaccine we get napalm and the atomic bomb...with runaway profit margins. A cure for every ill, never mind the side effects.

If these orthodoxies were capable of change, they would have already changed things — they've been at it long enough. My guess is, over time, our brains become hard-wired in one of two ever-more-bitter positions: Right becomes Alt-Right and Left becomes Alt-Left. Over generations this breeds a strident, militant, self-righteous inflexibility.

Kundalini can change this wiring, rewiring the brain to a

---

47 https://www.commonsensekundalini.com/science_
    spirituality/capitalism-kundalini.html

more flexible worldview, a more temperate, more tolerant human being, one whose consciousness extends beyond the puny, insubstantial ego. In order to do so, time is essential; it also running short.

Football, Concussions, and Kundalini

By all accounts, the incidence of concussion at all levels of the game of football is steadily rising and the leagues, from Pop Warner to the NFL, don't know what to do about it. On the one hand, they are looking for technical solutions, i.e., better helmet technology, better equipment, and medical innovation. On the other, stiffer penalties for hits inducing concussions, improved protocols for identifying and managing concussions and their effects.

However, from week to week, there seems to be about the same number of players disabled by concussions, usually by players who launch themselves through space at high speed to collide with their victims at angles that snap the neck and rattle the brains, at the same time. However, there doesn't seem to be one type of hit alone that causes a concussion. In some cases, concussions occur without a direct hit to the head: by a severe snap of the neck, for instance.

The fact that the helmets are constructed of nosecone, hard plastic means that the G-force of impact is compounded by the hardness of the helmet casing. The critical factors in inducing a concussion seem to be: the angle of the hit, the hardness of the helmet, and speed and G-force of the incoming player. The fact that the victim also wears a helmet in no way mitigates the impact or the damage to his neural network.

The brain's moving on impact is not the only factor involved. The whole spinal column, from coccyx to the cortex, is connected in one long neural network. I know because I was blindsided in high school football, lifted off my feet and deposited on my butt, which dropped from a height of four feet to the ground. Not only did I see a shower of stars, I felt a searing pain from the base of the spine all the way up to my brain. I was temporarily incapacitated — and no hit to the brain was involved. How much harder are the hits in the NFL than the hit I incurred that day? 40:1? 100:1? And we were wearing leather helmets, not the plastic warheads today's players wear. I didn't even feel the primary impact to my ribs; landing on my coccyx, a secondary effect, caused the neural disruption and total whiteout.

An array of leather helmets, the fashion in 1947 (JJ Semple: first row, 2nd from right)

What do football concussions have to do with kundalini? If it affects the brain, then it concerns kundalini, a phenomenon devoted to revitalizing brain cells, not destroying them. I have no evidence that kundalini could assuage the effects of concussion. As far as I know, no studies have been done. But I do wonder if it might not be effective. After all, that's its whole purpose: restore and reinvigorate the neural network. Here's a passage from *The Biology of Consciousness*, citing the case study of an athlete who activated kundalini. In this passage, he is talking with his yoga teacher:

"He asked me if I'd ever had a concussion while playing a sport. To my recollection, I never had, but there were times I felt groggy after a hard hit. He told me that the objective of certain yogic practices was to revitalize damaged brain cells, that the changes in metabolism produced during these exercises actually had neurological benefits.

"'Do you mean that certain forms of yoga could actually cure my depression and headaches?' I asked.

"'I am not a doctor or scientist, but I have witnessed the benefits of yoga in my own practice. The reason I studied yoga was because of the head wounds suffered in wartime. Fortunately, I was young enough when I began to practice for it to revitalize me.'"

I'm not saying kundalini could treat concussion effects, I don't know. Number one, I'd go back to using leather helmets. Two, I'd investigate kundalini meditation, which were it to be adopted, would probably solve the problem in that anyone raising kundalini would lose interest in football altogether and move onto other pursuits.

This Is SO Silly

As concerns kundalini, I'm a big fan of making a common front. Not that all parties have to agree on all things kundalini, it's just that when so many people are now experiencing something as life-changing as kundalini, you'd expect it to lead to a tremendous scientific breakthrough. And it probably will...someday.

In the meantime, it would be productive if the individuals involved in promoting and evangelizing, researching and teaching, writing and speaking about kundalini could find a way to collaborate, share, cooperate, and mutually support one another. After all:

"...it's all about transformation through activating human energy potentials and yet...and yet, proprietary instincts keep us apart. We share this one goal — transformation via the energy-cultivation properties of kundalini — and yet we don't trust each other. Our baser instincts separate us, classify us, make us suspicious of one another and protective of the meager territories we stake out for ourselves. It's like the 49ers of old, rushing into the gold fields to stake a claim, spending more time defending a claim than mining its precious treasure.

"There are many systems out there. It's hard to keep score in this new age of ours. The only thing that matters — it's not our instincts or our pride — are the systems that work and the systems that don't work."[48]

For example, in the past I've been asked to place links from our sites to other kundalini websites, which I'm more than willing to do, but when I ask for a link to one of our sites in return, I'm met with a vacuous refusal — a response that completely floors me.

Think about it, soliciting a favor and then refusing to reciprocate is saying, *My content is somehow more worthy than yours; I have the right to judge you, but you don't have the right to judge me.* What is the source of this thinking? It certainly isn't kundalini. Kundalini has broadened my horizons, not diminished them. Most of the kundalini people I know say the same thing: Kundalini lightens as well as enlightens, as in lightening the Being, making it more rarefied and the mind more flexible.

You may disagree with me and my research on kundalini, and that's fine; I probably disagree with some of the ideas you propose, but I'm more than willing to exchange links between our respective sites. If your site meets the basic standards of quality, we'll link to it.

Moreover, I'm open to discussion and finding common ground. After all, when a phenomenon meets as much outside resistance as kundalini does, forming a common front makes a lot of sense. Intolerance is not only silly, it's suicidal. A common front makes people stand up and take notice, which leads to peer review and serious scientific study.

Just about everyone I know has a different take on kundalini. The Trigger and Effects they experienced were also different. But

---

48 Sacred Cow Terminology Obscures Real Meaning, JJ Semple - The Kundalini Consortium, Wednesday, March 20, 2013 - http://www. kundaliniconsortium.org/2013/03/sacred-cow-terminology-obscures-real.htm

those differences don't mean we can't listen to or support each other, especially since, where kundalini is today has more to do with science — it's biology, in case you didn't know it — than with religious doctrines or belief systems.

Recently, we included a post by Cristian Muresanu, which provoked so much outrage that it was deleted from certain FB pages after I posted it there as an alternate approach to kundalini. When queried, the administrator told me, "I know all I need to know about kundalini."

That's a real scientific approach. A manifestation of clear thinking and open-mindedness.

When first approached by Cristian, I listened to him and tried to place his experience in context with what I know to be true i.e., my experience. What struck me was the similarity of many symptoms and his ability to identify inner sensations and movements, even though he used a completely different name for his experience. That's right, he doesn't inflexibly refer to his experience as kundalini; he uses the term Transphysical Energy Activation. And so what? It's not the term that's important, it's the experience.

As for the pictures of the spoons and the cellphone sticking to his head in his post, yes, you can become outraged, or you can take a scientific approach, asking Cristian to duplicate his experiment in front of witnesses, after first assuring all the elements are legit. And you can video it.

Anything but outrage! In fact, less outrage and less compartmentalization, and more tolerance, more acceptance. An energetic opening, a meditative lucidity, kind of like what Osho wrote:

"So be concerned with meditation and not with kundalini. And when you are aware, things will begin to happen in you. For the first time you will become aware of an inner world that is greater, vaster, more extensive than the universe; energies unknown, completely unknown, will begin to flow in you. Phenomena never heard of, never imagined or dreamed of, will begin to happen. But with each person they differ."

Overcoming Addiction

Have you ever watched *To Catch a Predator*, the Dateline-NBC show with Chris Hansen? The show that breaks for commercial with the guy lying face down on the ground and a large policeman's knee in his back.

These men, the ones busted on Dateline-NBC, don't seem able to control themselves. And that's the real story. After being on the air for months, with all the attendant publicity and buzz around the program, men still show up to meet the 13-year old girl. They are willing to risk everything. Like moths to a flame, they can't help themselves. They're addicted.

The first step in overcoming any type of addiction is admitting. Without admitting, the addict simply rationalizes his behavior or makes up lies. But with the police waiting outside with drawn guns and transcripts of the chat logs, there is little wriggle room.

Part of the admitting process is understanding the addiction. But rational people don't always act rationally. In fact, many addicts go back to the chat room as soon as they are released by the police.

Not every addict ends up in desperate straights. That's why it's so hard to admit to addiction. It's easy to fool yourself and others. But the curtain always comes crashing down — eventually.

The problem is we don't have a good grasp of what addiction really is. Is it a behavioral anomaly or a disease? Until now, we've tended to separate addictions into two categories, one behavioral, the other substance-based. But what if all addictions: those in the substance category that we deem diseases like cigarettes, alcohol, or drugs and those in the behavioral category that we label moral failures like gambling, overeating, shopping, or sex all stem from the same type of brain activity?

According to New Scientist writer Helen Phillips, "Several studies of the brain and behavior back the idea that there's very little difference between what goes on in the head of a gambling addict and that of a crack addict. Yet, there's a common perception that overindulgence in certain behaviors is all down to individual choice. If you are overeating, oversexed, gambling away your earnings or spending all you time Online, you are more likely to be considered morally abhorrent than the victim of a disease. Calling these problems 'addictions' has triggered debates about whether our society or our biology is to blame."

Substance addictions have attendant withdrawal consequences, from physical indicators like sweats, nausea, cramps to psychological problems like hallucinations, depression, and moodiness. Alcohol sufferers experience DTs; drug addicts can expect physical breakdown and "cold turkey" sessions; cigarette smokers are so hooked that not even a serious lung condition is reason enough to make them quit. According to researchers, behavioral addicts suffer the same symptoms.

Drug addicts have drug addiction treatment centers to seek help from, while those afflicted with various behavioral addictions also have addiction facilities that specialize in dealing with such issues.

Yet in many instances, the consequences of behavioral addictions are in some ways even harsher. For overeating there is rejection, radical surgery, diabetes, and social ostracism. For gambling there's prison, debt collection, financial ruin. For sex addicts, the ones who commit serious crimes, there is sterilization, castration or prison. Yes, in case you didn't know it, radical solutions like castration are widely discussed and promoted.

Because he hasn't been caught in some serious transgression, the addict keeps coming back for more, especially since, as cited by New Scientist writer, Helen Phillips, "both drugs of abuse and pleasurable behaviors trigger the release of the same chemicals (dopamine) and gene regulators in the brain."

So what do research, medicine, psychology, yes, and even law enforcement, offer sex addicts in the way of remedies? A variety of tools and treatments, from therapy to medication to sterilization to castration. Some of the therapies actually suggest that abstinence be part of the treatment. Abstinence?

Abstinence is the equivalent of relying on the little voice in the back of the head every time a person tells a lie, or every time an alcoholic ends up in the gutter, or every time a thief holds up a liquor store. Yes, the little voice is there all right, but the liar, the alcoholic, and the thief have long ago pushed the mute button. Their addiction has drowned out the voice in the back of the head.

Well, many of the men who appear on Dateline-NBC seem normal. Many are talented, creative, and gainfully employed: doctors, rabbis, teachers. The only thing holding them back from completely functional lives is their obsessions.

To break an addiction, we need a technique that doesn't rely on the voice in the back of the head — the conscience as some call it. But, you say, that's impossible because you just claimed the sexual addict is unable to obey any moral imperative. Is there a treatment the addict can self-administer? And, if so, why would he choose it?

The harder he works to satisfy the urges that rouse him, the longer he continues to evade admitting his problem, the less he'll be looking for treatment. But if he gets to the point of admitting and wants to take control of his own destiny, to avoid entering the system and its enforced treatment programs that include: therapy, medication, prison, sterilization, and castration, there is sublimation. A process whose side effects are wholly positive and whose cost in dollars is zero.

Does the sublimation process change the way a person fantasizes over his obsessions? No, it's not possible to take over someone's fantasies and redirect them. That was the theme of Stanley Kubrick's famous film, *Clockwork Orange* (1971), using drugs and punishment to reprogram an offender. It didn't work; reprogramming blows the mind. Rather than reprogramming the mind — a process that kills creativity — sublimation diverts a distilled form of sexual energy into the brain. Implemented successfully, it changes the arousal patterns the individual feels. How does sublimation work?

Instead of flooding the brain with dopamine — the addict's reward for pressing the "pleasure button" — the body's chemical substances are recombined and used for worthier purposes, such as self-healing, overcoming addiction, and expanding consciousness. All addicts — dopers, drinkers, smokers, overeaters, gamblers, shoppers, lechers — pursue their addiction to trigger the dopamine response. That's right, the reward takes place in the brain, not the penis, or the stomach, or any other part of the body. The craving that starts in the mind is the brain's pleading for dopamine.

Sublimation, too, affects brain chemistry, but in a different way. Proper sexual sublimation diverts distilled seminal fluid up the spinal column into the brain. The introduction of this new element into the brain changes the brain chemistry such that the organ itself is completely transformed. Once transformed, the addict's consciousness as well as his attitudes and worldview changes, too. He has a chance to start over. Rebirth. Rediscovery. Recovery. A new Being.

Think of it as an opportunity to grow, to become the REAL you. Read Gopi Krishna's *Kundalini: The Evolutionary Energy in Man* and other books about awakening experiences. Notice I use the work "awakening." That's because kundalini promotes a complete makeover, not just physical, but cognitive, psychological, emotional, spiritual. The "awakening" is just the beginning. There are years of learning and accepting, until he finally realizes the kundalini is intelligent; it has his best interests at heart.

If this addict — on the threshold of a kundalini awakening — could look back at himself as he is today from a time forty years in the future, he'd wonder who the person was that was so obsessed with sex and say to himself, "What a waste of good semen! All that porn, all that lust, all that wasted sexual energy! I could have been using it to build the REAL me."

But how does an addict, in the full denial of his addiction, find any information on self-realization, much less information on kundalini? It's the smallest needle (no pun intended) in the largest haystack. Add to this the addict's blindness to everything besides his addiction and the odds seem impossible. And yet, many addicts are spiritual people. They're just looking for salvation in the wrong places. If they could only get a glimpse of their alternate Self — a higher consciousness version of their being — after practicing energy cultivation techniques, they might work their way free of their affliction.

Sublimation utilizes no instruments, no surgical procedures, no medication. It requires no sworn oaths of chastity. For me, it was the result of Golden Flower Meditation. I used this method over forty years ago; it changed my entire being. The whole and complete method is discussed and elaborated on in my book, *Deciphering the Golden Flower One Secret at a Time*.

So, what does this method entail? Basically learning to breathe in a certain manner during meditation practice, a voluntary physical action which in turn produces a series of reactions that culminate in the activation of the kundalini mechanism. No more, no less. It's an entirely physical process.

And it doesn't end there. Kundalini doesn't just change your body; it changes your entire being. Living with kundalini makes your body sensitive to negative stimuli: alcohol, drugs, cigarettes, bad food. Any ingestible substance that might harm your body. One by one your addictions drop away. You'll know exactly which substances harm your body and you'll take steps to avoid them.

In addition, you'll begin to make better life decisions. The fact that you are no longer addicted clears the mind. Gradually, you become a better decision maker and problem solver. You are more able to live in the moment.

The sublimation process changed my being and personality. It produced a creative repurposing of brain chemistry. The very chemical process that once marked me for addiction was altered. Instead of dopamine — the brain chemical addicts crave — my brain was fed a new substance, an elixir distilled from seminal fluid. Sounds strange, perhaps, but if you long for a healthier life and greater overall creativity, you'll marvel at its restorative properties.

Kundalini and Literary Criticism

Some folks may think I'm stretching it a bit in relating kundalini to literary criticism. Please bear with me.

The following is a comment on a book review of Peggy Payne's kundalini novel, *Cobalt Blue*.

"Despite repeated searches, I've been unable to find recent fiction on the theme of kundalini – when I've looked for novels on 'spiritual awakening' they've seemed to be more general, and aimed at the spiritual seeker rather than the literary reader. Hats off to Peggy Payne for what appears to be a sexed-up, highly imaginative work of commercial fiction, [*Cobalt Blue*]. The only novel explicitly dealing with kundalini that I'd ever read, The Serpent Rising (1988) by Mary Garden — about a vulnerable young woman's hellish exploitation by an unscrupulous guru in '70s India — has since been republished (2003) as the harrowing autobiographical account that it is.

"For some reason, anything kundalini-related seems to get grouped with new-age/spiritual or, conversely, mental illness titles, which as far as I can see, renders the phenomenon more or less invisible in any mainstream literary context. I suppose this is also somewhat true of the theme of out-of-body and/or near-death experiences (outside of the fantasy or horror genres); though with regard to films, Clint Eastwood's excellent and perhaps covertly political Hereafter strikes me as an exception. One person indirectly involved in triggering my own journey of awakening, a teacher of yogic practices, used to read sci-fi & watch fantasy movies — to find, I assume, analogies for his own, atypical experience of reality. I wonder if you have any thoughts as to what might account for the seeming invisibility of kundalini-related fiction?"

My first reaction was to ask: why read fictional accounts of kundalini by persons who have never experienced it when there are so many excellent real life non-fiction accounts? But then I got to thinking about the nature of literature and literary criticism, and what it really consists of.

I projected myself back to high school and a term paper I wrote on Sinclair Lewis. My approach to this type of project left a lot to desire. If I read the book — many times I didn't — I then went through a haphazard process of trying to figure out what the theme was and to build a credible case around what I decided it was, flavoring the whole with plot summaries and a few timely quotes from the text. We weren't taught concepts like premise, character, and conflict. All we had was plot and theme. Not that our teachers weren't intelligent; they were. They just didn't know about those concepts, and either did I until I read Lajos Egri's book, *The Art of Dramatic Writing*, many years after graduating.

So how does kundalini enter into literary criticism, or the understanding of human nature? Let's take Sinclair Lewis' novel, *Dodsworth*. It's a story about a Midwestern couple, set in the late 1920s. Rather than write my own summary, here's Wikipedia's excellent excerpted version:

> "Samuel 'Sam' Dodsworth is an ambitious and innovative automobile designer, who builds his fortunes in Zenith, Winnemac. In addition to his success in the business world, he had also succeeded as a young man in winning the hand of Frances 'Fran' Voelker, a beautiful young socialite. While the book provides the courtship as a backstory, the real novel begins upon his retirement. At the age of fifty and facing retirement as a result of his selling of his successful automobile company (The Revelation Motor Company) to a far larger competitor, he sets out to do what he had always wanted to experience: a leisurely trip to Europe with his wife. His forty-one-year-old wife, however,

motivated by her own vanity and fear of lost youth, is dissatisfied with married life and small town Zenith, wants to live in Europe permanently as an expatriate, not just visit for a few months to allow Dodsworth to visit some manufacturing plants looking for his next challenge. Passing up advancement in his recently sold company, Dodsworth leaves for Europe with Fran but her motivations to get to Europe become quickly known.

"On their extensive travels across Europe they are soon caught up in vastly different lifestyles. Fran falls in with a crowd of frivolous socialites, while Sam plays more of an independent tourist. With his red Baedeker guide book in hand, he visits such well-known tourist attractions as Westminster Abbey, Notre Dame Cathedral, Sans Souci Palace, and the Piazza San Marco. But the historic sites that he sees prove to be far less significant than the American expatriates that he meets on his extensive journeys across Great Britain and continental Europe. He eventually meets Edith Cortright, an expatriate American widow in Venice, who is everything his wife is not: self-assured, self-confident, and able to take care of herself.

"As they follow their own pursuits, their marriage is strained to the breaking point. Both Sam and Fran are forced to choose between marriage and the new lifestyles they have pursued. Fran is clearly Lewis' target here while Sam ambles along as a stranger in a strange land until the epiphany of getting on with his life hits him in the last act. Sam Dodsworth is a rare Lewis character: a man of true conviction and purpose. Purpose and conviction can be relied on significantly as the book (and film) concludes with the two main characters going in quite different directions.

"Set from late 1925 to late 1927, the novel includes detailed descriptions of Sam and Fran's tours across Europe. In the beginning they leave their mid-Western hometown of Zenith, board a steam liner in New York and cross the Atlantic Ocean. Their first stop is England. They visit the sights in London and are invited by Major Clyde Lockert to join a weekend trip to the countryside. Later on, when Lockert has made an indecent proposal to Fran, they depart for Paris, where she soon engages in a busy social life and he takes up sightseeing. When Sam decides to go back to America for his college reunion in New Haven, Fran spends the summer months on the lakes near Montreux and Stresa, where she has a romance with Arnold Israel. Once Sam picks her up in Paris, they agree to continue their travels together, touring France, Italy, Spain, Austria, Hungary and Germany. Their marriage comes to an end, when she falls in love with Kurt von Obersdorf in Berlin. Whereas she stays on with her new love, he criss-crosses Europe in an attempt to cope with his new situation. When Sam happens to run into Edith in Venice, she persuades him to accompany her on a visit to a village in the vicinity of Naples. As Fran's fiancé calls · off the wedding, Sam joins his former wife on her voyage back to New York. Only three days later he is back on the next ship to meet Edith in Paris."

My high school paper on *Dodsworth* was very primitive. I don't recall much of it. I do recall reading it and other books and wondering where and how to begin my paper. Even with the books I liked, it was difficult. We were told not to simply recount the plot because the book itself contained the plot and it was no use in regurgitating it. So how was I supposed to analyze a book without summarizing plot points?

I didn't understand that stories — whether in book, film, or theater form — were studies in human nature and you could get from character to conflict to premise by examining each character's nature. And how each character's nature — his/her compulsions and desires — inevitably precipitated conflicts with other characters. And that the character's compulsions were emotions usually stirred by incoming chatter of the senses. Subliminally, perhaps I understood these dynamics, but I didn't have the fancy labels — conflict, character and premise — through which to examine them.

What are the character issues in *Dodsworth*? Who are Sam, Fran, Edith? If you look for the character's motives and desires, this leads you to the conflicts with others, within themselves, with external forces (the economy, the Gods, etc). Get the conflicts, and you come up with a premise: Vanity — especially in middle-aged individuals — leads to degradation.

No point in going through the conflicts and the cross purposes in this book. All books are pretty much the same: victims, persecutors, witnesses ever at each other, changing roles from time to time. No point in tallying the fatal character flaws that lead some to their ultimate destruction — because they're basically the same: *Macbeth, Othello, Raskolnikov, Sister Carrie, Anna Karenina*, all prisoners of their senses and their compulsions.

We may learn about human nature by reading, attending plays, and viewing films, but the foibles usually amount to the same kind of triangular relationships detailed in Eric Berne's *Games People Play*. In fact, you can use his model to break down most personal relationships, if that's what your goal is. The problem is: Human nature isn't much improved since the first novel was written, since Shakespeare's *King Lear*, since FW Murnau's 1927 silent film masterpiece, *Sunrise*.

The question is not: when will we see an improvement in human nature? We won't; not anytime soon. The question is: If we were to somehow cast out all our devils, remake ourselves in God's image, what would that do to the literature, film, and theater industries? Which brings us back to the kundalini novel, in which we are no longer trying to rectify human nature, but are attempting to enhance consciousness. Where is the conflict in spiritual novels? What might their premises be? Certainly not the same as the various games characters have played in novels, plays, and films up to now. The kundalini — or spiritual novel — would have to do away with the three-cornered persecutor, victim, witness paradigm that marks most fiction. Or would they? If these types of novels don't yet exist, how can we determine what they will or will not consist of?

Nevertheless, it seems to me that great novels have already incorporated spiritual elements to a certain degree. The Russians are best at this: *Crime and Punishment, Anna Karenina, The Brothers Karamazov*. And Shakespeare, of course.

Is there a spiritual component to *Dodsworth*, an element of enhanced consciousness that takes the characters beyond their shortcomings to some sort of transcendence? Each of the principles goes through changes. Fran regresses from accepting housewife to vain social-ingratiator, acquiring very little self-awareness along the way. Edith is self-assured to begin with and doesn't want anyone in her life who might introduce problems. Sam is creative, yet his creative abilities have been affected by his attachment to Fran. Once he ends that relationship, he is free to explore his creative ideas. Let's hope that Sam and Edith won't get on each other's nerves at some point in the future and repeat the previous scenario. As for improved consciousness, perhaps not, even though they may attain a high level of emotional stability.

Is there spiritual progress in *Cobalt Blue*? Although the main character is quite self-aware, the fact that the author misunderstands how kundalini functions ultimately dilutes any significant spiritual growth. Had she applied kundalini correctly, Andie Branson, the heroine might have been dealing with sexual sublimation rather than nymphomania. But that would have been a harder novel to write: sexed-up trumps doctrinaire adherence to fact every time. The theme? Writing about kundalini without experiencing it produces mixed results.

Writing is an intellectual process, and therefore, perhaps, less susceptible to ecstasy. At least compared to music, which is an immediate, more "soulful" means of expression. Whether it be John Coltrane, Gustav Mahler, Mozart, or Puccini, the transcendent themes of their music reverberate in your body; you feel them viscerally. The writing process makes it difficult to incorporate transcendental experience because it demands more intellectualizing — writing and rewriting. Is there a type of "soul" writing in our future? A style/process that communicates more directly, soul to soul, rather than filtering content through the mind?

JJ Semple Interviews Peggy Payne, author of Cobalt Blue

I read *Cobalt Blue* after author Peggy Payne and I reached out to each other in an attempt to define the similarities and differences between kundalini fiction and non-fiction. Today, non-fiction outweighs and outsells the fiction category, but that may change as more and more authors investigate kundalini, either by experiencing it or by reading about it.

Before Christmas, Peggy and I agreed that I would send her questions about how she was able to work the kundalini theme into Cobalt Blue. Here is the Q&A:

JJ: There's kundalini and kundalini. The strip mall kind and the Gopi Krishna kind. Are you're at all familiar with the differences? To what degree?

PP: I feel strongly about making no judgment on anyone's spiritual experience. Certainly I've read the literature: Gopi Krishna, Lee Sannella, Irina Tweedie, Stanislav and Christina Grof, Muktananda, your own work, JJ Semple, and many others. Also, early Christian mystics who described similar experiences.

As for "strip mall kundalini," I once attended a workshop where I was informed that we had all had our kundalini raised (I didn't believe that for a second.) So I know what you mean if you're talking about glib bandying of the term.

However, much more important to me than making any such distinction is to respect each person as the expert on his or her own experience.

JJ: In which category do you place Andie?

PP: Andie's experience rocks her to the bottom of her soul. At the time of her first experience, she has never heard the word kundalini. She doesn't know until near the end of the story what has happened to her. For most of the story, she is in the midst of an enormously disruptive ordeal that unmoors her from everything she thought she knew about herself. And to make things much worse, she is fighting it.

JJ: Unless I've misunderstood your background, it seems that you don't have direct experience with energy cultivation techniques like kundalini meditation. How did you become interested in kundalini as a subject for Cobalt Blue?

PP: I've studied reiki, done some kundalini yoga as well as other kinds in India and the U.S., attended various workshops on energy, and been a meditator for many years.

But when I finished my early drafts of Cobalt Blue, I, like Andie, didn't even know the word kundalini. I had overheard it used once at a party in a two-sentence exchange behind me. Noted it, but didn't know what it meant and didn't look it up.

Then years later, I thought I'd finished my novel and was sitting out on my porch by myself one night listening to the rain. A thought popped into my head: "It's kundalini." The next day I did a little research, and I found that this force fit the story that I'd already written, that it was roughly comparable to experience others have had. This gave me a new understanding of what this woman — and, vicariously, I — had been dealing with. (It was a ferocious hard novel for me to write.)

I don't claim anything as dramatic as a kundalini awakening for myself. Only twinges. I found this in a journal I kept years earlier in India doing research for my previous novel, Sister India:

"Throughout the morning I keep noticing a sensation I have felt here before, a small physical thrill that I cannot explain. It comes from simply looking around me. It's like an electric pulse, made of molten color, the brilliance of all the silk saris at once; and it pushes past my fatigue and travels along the wire that hooks together body and soul. Jet-lagged and short of sleep though I am, that jolt keeps pushing through. I welcome it. It's somehow part of what I've come here for."

JJ: I found Cobalt Blue an easy and fun read. You write very well. I especially liked the way you developed Andie's place in her artist community and her relations with others. Talk about your approach.

PP: Thanks, JJ. Her place in her artist community came naturally to me. I've been in the same weekly writers group for thirty-two years. And I share office space with a dear friend; other writers and artists also rent in the building from time to time. I'm part of a close-knit group of supportive fellow artists. It's a great thing. I'd hate to try to do this work without it.

JJ: Kundalini entails a repurposing of sexual energy by preventing it from flowing out through masturbation or intercourse, and instead, diverting it up the spine to the brain. If this is an accurate analysis of how sexual sublimation works — and documented experiences from ancient Indian and Chinese to modern practitioners say it is — what made you think that Andie might go on a sexual rampage when conservation of sexual energy is the only way to avoid debilitating effects associated with the loss of sexual energy (Prana)? Or, to put it another way: after awakening, heretofore unused functions in the brain become active and warn male and female kundalini adepts (by sending biological signals) about the harmful effects ejaculation has on the body. Do you think someone could go against the biological changes in brain function that kundalini induces and actually waste large quantities of Prana?

PP: Andie is no adept. Her awakening happens in jolts and ragged pieces at a time when she is depressed and her life is already in disarray. Its genesis is the meditative practice of painting, even doing work she considers routine. She thinks she's ill and her biological signals are utterly swamped by confusion, emotional uproar, and the powerful sexual sensations that so many people experience in kundalini awakening. But without a teacher or any kind of guidance or knowledge, she finds herself compulsively acting on the mad sexual impulses. That's very upsetting and frightening to her.

Yes, the sexual energy should be transmuted. But for a long time, Andie is in the throes of a "wrong rising" and an effort to suppress what is happening.

Finally, however, a valuable spiritual development comes about through sex as she begins to regain some control. It gives her a body-and-soul recognition of the passion to merge with others, to know herself as one with other people, to give up, if briefly, her separateness.

JJ: Nevertheless, even if my take on the triggers and effects of kundalini don't jibe with Andie's actions, I found your hypothesis very interesting to the degree that I cannot positively say that the effects she manifests (her sexual behavior) could never happen as a result of a kundalini awakening. Have you thought about that? About the subconscious urgings that caused you to take her in that direction?

PP: I didn't feel I had any more control of her than she did of herself. As so often happens with novels, the story and the character had their own life to live.

I do feel strongly that sex and spirituality are vitally intertwined. Sex and spirituality are central to my other novels as well and I write a blog on the subject.

And subconscious urgings? Well, having been a teenager in the years of the frustrating sexual Double Standard, I was perhaps due to erupt in some way. (I'm 65 now, BTW)

JJ: What's more, if a person did go on a sexual rampage like Andie's, she would probably act in much the same way. Who's to say?

PP: Exactly. I think our imaginations know things that our minds and bodies are still catching onto.

Kundalini and Poverty: Same People, Different Situations

It's often suggested to spiritual seekers that there's no way to care for the poor and reach for spiritual release at the same time. Individual souls are on an individual journey; each person must fend for his/her own soul, find his/her own path. That the outer trip is fraught with insurmountable snares and therefore one should concentrate only on the inner trip. The notion here is that evolution will take care of the less fortunate. A rising tide raises all boats, so to speak.

Back in the 1970s, Isaac Bentov developed this "rising boats" theme along similar lines as today's kundalini people, who say kundalini is accelerating evolution by writing changes in consciousness into DNA.

So where does that leave America's poor? Or the poor and disabled around the world, for that matter? Should the rest of us be trying to help?

In 2004, CNN ran a special on Poverty in America that focused mainly on women — how easy it is for them to become homeless and impoverished while working more than forty hours a week.

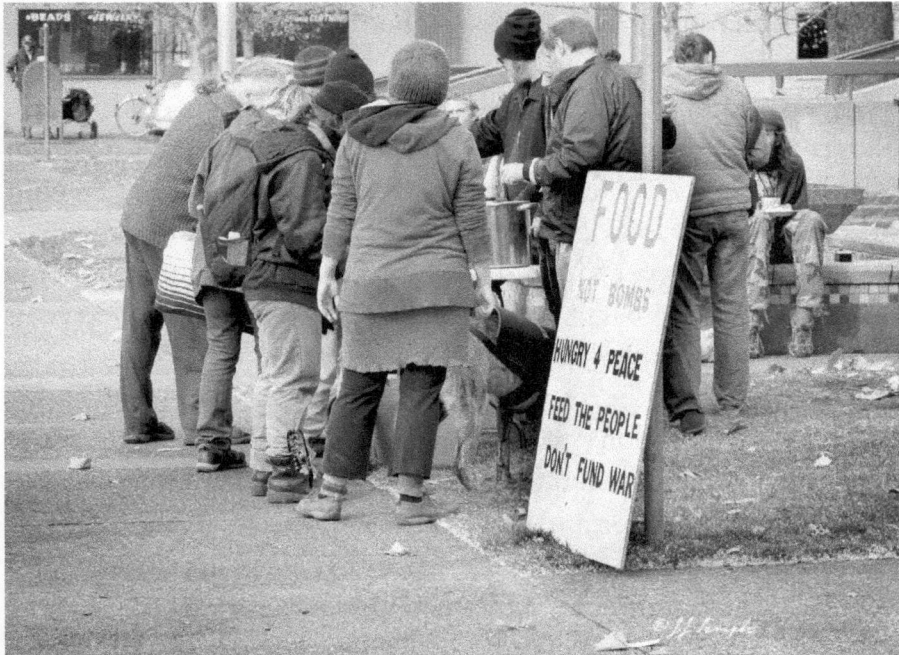

Rich Cities; Poor People

Yes, it's hard to believe that poverty has spread to the proportions it has. Life is precarious. We are all under constant threat of annihilation: war, terror, hunger, joblessness, poverty. The Bible warns us not to forget the unfortunate, but somehow we do. In fact, its parables illustrate the fragility of life, even at the highest levels.

Yet, our egos tell us we've come a long way. We're in the home stretch. There's nothing more to accomplish, nothing wrong with wealth. And, per se, there isn't. Just like intelligence, it's what you do with it that counts. Only by balancing the material with the spiritual can we achieve success. The rest is ego driven. Yes, ego was needed in primitive times. No longer at a primitive stage in evolution, we're still in survival mode, but the rules are changing. We no longer need more. In fact, less is now more! The ego will continue to serve a purpose, but it must be sublimated.

Bentov says we will all be enlightened — after a million more years of evolution. Probably exist in bodiless form. I think we will, if we are able to meet the challenges of survival.

If we didn't inhabit bodies, all our problems would vanish. Negative emotion, war, greed, violence, prejudice, fear would not exist. But we DO live in bodies that control our perceptions and our so-called needs. How do we manage persons whose abundances are boundless living next to persons who have nothing but a shopping cart full of plastic bags? What mechanism in the brain makes us believe we need more than our neighbor?

Bentov says the people in mental hospitals are the highly evolved. We just don't know how to communicate with them. And because they do not perceive the world on the same terms as "normal" people do or are unable to communicate in the language the material world, we institutionalize them. I don't know if he's joking, but every time I encounter a person with alcohol or drug addiction issues, I come away believing they are searching for redemption, that their issues are more spiritual than material. But they're stuck in an escape syndrome of drugs, alcohol, addiction, domestic violence. They are searching in all the wrong places and they can't find their way out.

When I ask a street person why he/she needs to "get high," they reply in much the same terms as a spiritual person explains why he meditates. It's not by accident that they use the term get high. Both seek release from material concerns.

Although I don't see meditation catching on in homeless shelters any time soon, I don't believe that conventional treatment methods are working either. Poverty has become an endemic issue; it's sapping our resources, bequeathing more of the same to more and more people, many of them yet unborn.

And now that countries and states are legalizing not only pot but also heroine and other drugs, more and more people are going to give up and drop out permanently. It's no longer a question of reform; we need a change of consciousness — a high built on true spiritual foundations. Without drugs or alcohol.

Bigger government isn't the answer. That hasn't worked in the past and it won't work in the future. The answer is people turning away from physical gratification, exploring the metaphysical potential within each of us.

Realistically, many eons of evolution are needed before the tide raises all boats. Of course, I'd prefer generations to eons. Let's surprise each other!

Types of Kundalini

Jesus said: "There are many standing at the door, but it is the solitary who will enter the bridal chamber."

~ Saying 75 from The Gospel of Thomas

What Type of Person Awakens Kundalini?

That is a question that cannot yet be answered scientifically. Anecdotally? Yes, perhaps. Generally, however, I don't see a lot of Type-A, mesomorphs involved in self-realization. Of course, I may be wrong; I can't see the total picture; nobody can. But if I'm not wrong, why might this be true, why are so many seekers ectomorphs?

First of all, you may not be familiar with the following terms pertaining to physical types: mesomorph, ectomorph, endomorph. I first ran across them in Robert De Ropp's 1968 book, *The Master Game: Pathways to Higher Consciousness Beyond the Drug Experience*, given to me by my father as I was about to kick off my European self-realization adventure. It was the first book I read that approached higher consciousness from the perspective of Western psychology and science as opposed to Eastern yogic influences, although the book does include its share of materials on Eastern traditions.

I haven't read the book in over forty years; I lost it along the way. Around 2001, I bought a copy, but never got around to rereading it. Nevertheless, certain ideas in the book have stayed with me.

JJ Semple (1964) – The Quintessential Ectomorph

In a section entitled Physical Type, De Ropp writes about the above body types and their related temperaments.

"Sheldon's (W.H. Sheldon) basic theory is that temperament is related to physique. This is intuitively understood by every experienced novelist and playwright. Shakespeare's three prototypes, Falstaff, Hotspur and Hamlet, correspond both physically and temperamentally to Sheldon's three physical morphs and three temperamental tonias. Falstaff is the extreme endomorph. He is shaped like a barrel, typically oval in outline. Hotspur, the fiery fighter, is the extreme mesomorph, muscular, broad-shouldered, narrow-hipped, triangular in outline. Hamlet, the irresolute thinker, is lean and angular, linear in outline, the typical ectomorph."

He goes on to describe the temperamental characteristics of each physical type and how the quest for self-realization fits with the ectomorph profile.

Endomorphs, De Ropp says, are labeled viscertonics (gut dominant) and characterized by: excessive food intake, excessive relaxation, excessive complacency, excessive amiability.

Surprisingly, De Ropp is harder on mesomorphs or somatotonics (muscle dominant) than on either of the other two types. "They delight in vigorous action, the overcoming of external obstacles. They have powers that less rugged individuals may envy, have a high capacity for physical endurance, a low sleep requirement; they are relatively insensitive to pain, noise, distraction, and the feelings of others." They are characterized by insensitivity and blind obedience. De Ropp quotes Sheldon, "Somatonic people tend to lack introspective insight. They tend to enter upon the most tragic of human quests, the quest for lost youth. One of the cardinal indicators of somatonia is a horror of growing old."

The ectomorph physique, on the other hand, is nervous system dominant. This cerebrotonic individual says Sheldon, "...finds both his delights and his defenses in the system and the detail of his own consciousness." People high in cerebrotonia are often "seekers."

I don't believe we can assign a given individual to any one category. We share traits across all of them. At the same time, there probably is predominance of one type in each of us. I know that I started life as a somatotonic (mesomorph), but, due to a childhood accident, I morphed into a cerebrotonic (ectomorph). And yet, I've retained many mesomorphic attributes in the body of an ectomorph. This enabled me to complete the kundalini awakening process successfully, which, back in 1971 when I went through it, was a solitary undertaking, best accomplished by a loner like me with the temperament of an ectomorph and the action-oriented drive of a mesomorph.

Body type and temperament are related to symmetry, which is related to successfully activating kundalini. Again, mine is only one experience; any type can awaken kundalini, but I've encountered more ectomorphs/cerebrotonics along the way than any other body or temperament type. That this type is governed by the nervous system is a dead giveaway because it's the nervous system that handles the anatomical, somatonic, and metabolic work of the kundalini awakening process.

Don't believe a person can morph from one body type to another? In *Deciphering the Golden Flower One Secret at a Time*, I document the process of changing body and temperament types.

The Master Game

A few days before writing this essay, I had a lengthy telephone conversation with Emerging Sciences Founder Michael Molina on the subject of where and how kundalini fits in with higher consciousness. Is it a cause? An effect? A prerequisite? An arbitrary happenstance?

Why are the triggers and effects so varied? Why are there so many ways of activating kundalini? And so many sundry ways it affects the individuals who ignite it through energy cultivation or those who are struck by it involuntarily?

Is it a kind of loose cannon in the forward surge of evolution? A willy-nilly, will-o-the-wisp facilitator of higher consciousness?

At one point in the conversation, while discussing energy-cultivation triggers, I suggested that there seemed to be physiological and temperamental components that influence the ways individuals approach the challenge of releasing it. I noted that once task-oriented persons like myself begin the search for self-realization, it becomes a quest that includes testing energy cultivation techniques (GFM in my case) until one or another method induces energy sensations inside the physical body. In my case, once I detected energy activity inside my body, I knew I had found a method worth pursuing. Where it might lead or any dangers it might present were unimportant; I knew I'd pursue it to the end — whatever that might be.

People-oriented individuals, on the other hand, readily participate in more inter-personal activities. They seek reassurance in groups and gurus whereas I steered clear of them, seeking to validate my findings much like the Buddha did, through a solitary meditation practice. This approach taught me that the journey is as important as the destination, and that the more I forged ahead alone in my unsupervised practice, the easier it was to face up to its unrelenting challenges.

While talking with Michael about the characteristics of task- versus people-oriented persons, I remembered *The Master Game,* by Robert S. De Ropp, a book that played an interesting role in my life.

In 1970, when I was leaving for Europe, endowed, at that time, with only a cursory interest in yoga, my girl and I stopped in Connecticut to say goodbye to my father, very surprised that, at the moment of my departure, he handed me a copy of De Ropp's book, subtitled, at that time, *Higher Consciousness Beyond The Drug Experience.* Now, in its latest release, it's been re-subtitled, *Pathways to Higher Consciousness.* Such was my father's concern (i.e. my use of drugs) that he felt the book might redirect my interests from the drug culture to something more spiritual, nudging me to aim a bit higher. That was 1970, a time when drugs had started flowing freely and parents were given to manage a whole new set of worries. In its most recent edition, the editors have posthumously shifted the book's focus to higher consciousness as it presents a wider field of interest than drugs alone, although De Ropp, much like myself, declares in earlier chapters that drugs can play a role in sensitizing the individual to more lofty explorations, and the games they represent. Nevertheless, he is not an apologist for psychedelics:

> "They [drugs] can never, no matter how often they are taken, enable the investigator to change his level of being. Their continued use represents a form of spiritual burglary which carries its own penalty, an irreparable depletion of the substances [kundalini, for example] needed for real inner work and a total loss of the individual's capacity to develop. Carefully controlled experiments with the drugs are justified if they lead the exper- imenter to the conclusion that the fourth and fifth states of consciousness are possible for man. This realization may serve to

awaken him to the existence of the Master Game, the only game in life that is truly worth playing."[49]

Little did I know that within two years I would not only stop using drugs and alcohol, I would awaken kundalini, something my father was never able to conceive of or process.

As it happened, however, my kundalini awakening might well have been kick-started by the book my father gave me, for I devoured it on the plane to Paris and it led to further study and practice.

During the conversation with Michael, I went to the book case for my copy of *The Master Game*, mentioning to him that I hadn't read the book in over forty years, but I seemed to remember De Ropp's writing about the factors that determine the likelihood of an individual's becoming a spiritual seeker and, if so, how the physiological and psychological factors discussed in his book manifest themselves.

It was the chapters on Games and Types that most interested me because they examined the issue of why some awaken, some do not, and some are not even interested:

TABLE I

Meta-games and Object Games

GAME	AIM
Master Game	awakening
Religion Game	salvation
Science Game	knowledge
Art Game	beauty
Householder Game	raise family
No Game	no aim
Hog in Trough	wealth
Cock on Dunghill	fame
Moloch Game	glory or victory

"Life games reflect life aims. And the games men choose to

49 The Master Game: Pathways to Higher Consciousness ~ de Ropp, Robert S., Gateways Books & Tapes. Kindle Edition, p. 48.

play indicate not only their type, but also their level of inner development. Following Thomas Szasz (more or less) we can divide life games into object games and meta-games. Object games can be thought of as games played for the attainment of material things, primarily money and the objects which money can buy. Meta-games are played for intangibles such as knowledge or the 'salvation of the soul.' In our culture, object games predominate. In earlier cultures, meta-games predominated."[50]

De Ropp's hierarchical table of games tells us that the highest is The Master Game, whose goal is Transcendence, Awakening, Enlightenment, self-realization or any of the various synonyms we apply to higher consciousness states.

He also tells us that the game we choose indicates our personality and physical type, from which we can deduce that, if we know our type, then, using the following chart, we can predict the game we are most likely to play. I won't go into the exact equivalences here; they're sprinkled liberally throughout his book. Suffice it to say: Know the game, deduce the type; know the type, infer the game. Very neat.

---

50 The Master Game: Pathways to Higher Consciousness - de Ropp, Robert S., Gateways Books & Tapes. Kindle Edition, p. 12.

TABLE IV
Components of Type

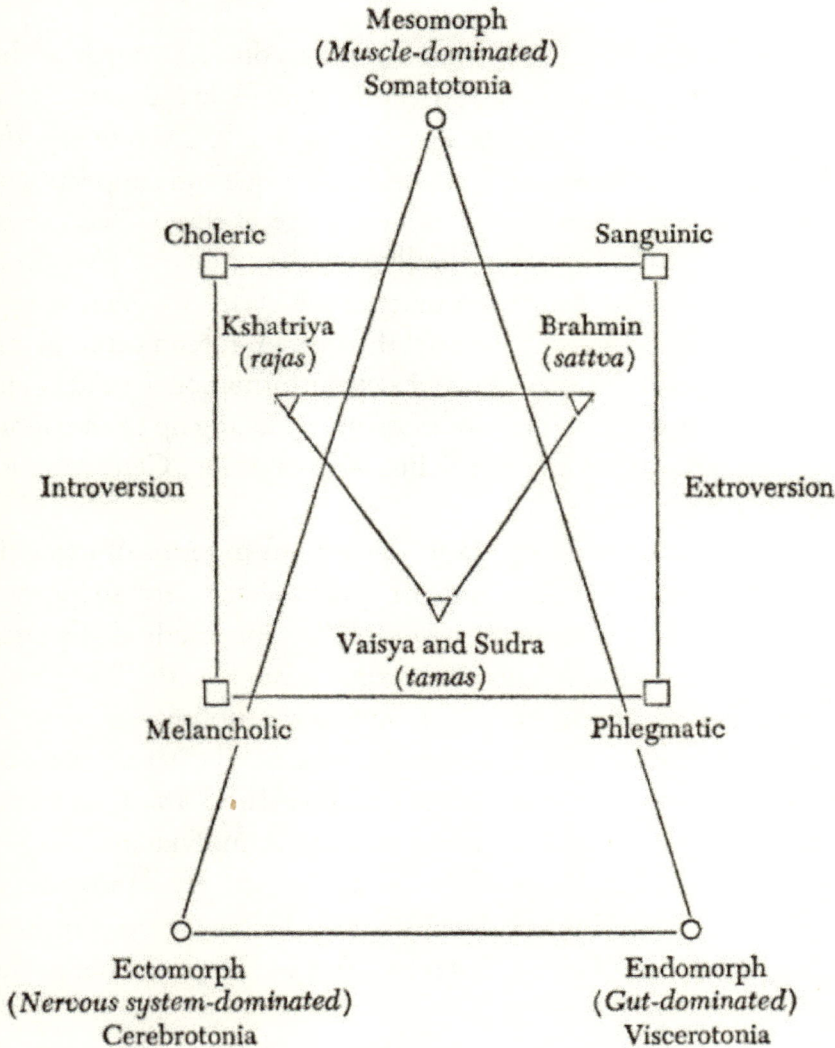

Mesomorph
(*Muscle-dominated*)
Somatotonia

Choleric   Sanguinic

Kshatriya   Brahmin
(*rajas*)   (*sattva*)

Introversion   Extroversion

Melancholic   Phlegmatic

Vaisya and Sudra
(*tamas*)

Ectomorph   Endomorph
(*Nervous system-dominated*)   (*Gut-dominated*)
Cerebrotonia   Viscerotonia

Where Ate You on The Chart?

He even overlays his physical types with the ancient Greek humors (Choleric, Sanguinic, Melancholic, and Phlegmatic), as well as the Hindu Gunas (Sattva, Rajas, and Tamas), warning us appropriately:

> "He who tries to play a game for which his type does not fit him violates his own essence with consequences that are often disastrous."[51]

Applying these notions to my own case, I consider myself to be a cross between mesomorph and ectomorph. Why? Because of a childhood accident — documented in my book, *Deciphering the Golden Flower One Secret at a Time* — my physique and temperament took a detour from meso- to ecto- at the age of seven. Because of that turn of events, I became ideally suited to pursue self-realization, so much so that I started a practice which led to a permanent kundalini awakening in my early thirties. A mesomorph in an ectomorph's body, the morphological transformation I underwent allowed me to retain the qualities most apt for facing up to the rigors and challenges of releasing kundalini — Sanguinic, Cerebrotonic, Introverted, Sattvatic.

The most profound kundalini activations in terms of meta-effects are deliberate, not accidental or spontaneous; permanent, not temporary — the result of a proven meditation method. Essence meets Matter in a kind of Quantum event. Sexual energy flows, or is drawn, up the spine to the brain as a result of the sublimation process. Essence and matter must be aligned, sort of like when planets, suns, or moons align to produce an eclipse. That's the Quantum, or Karmic, aspect that determines why some individuals, despite proper guidance and all-out effort, are unable activate kundalini.

When I left for Europe, I was stuck at the No Game -> no aim level, one of the deadliest of all games. This book opened me to the Meta-Games.

De Ropp uses WH Shelton's work to support his theory of

---

51   The Master Game: Pathways to Higher Consciousness ~ de Ropp, Robert S., Gateways Books & Tapes. Kindle Edition, p. 14.

classification and it connects with Gopi Krishna's understanding of physiology:

> "Can we deny the fact that whether a fortuitous gift, divine grace, or the fruit of Karma, in every case there is close link between the talent and beauty exhibited and the organic structure of the individual?"

~ Gopi Krishna - *The Awakening of Kundalini*

The Master Game is largely informed by Gurdjieff's and Ouspensky's Self-Remembering, a system De Ropp dubbed Creative Psychology — known today as Mindfulness. There is not one mention of kundalini in his book; there is, however, the recognition (quoted previously) that sexual energy plays an important role in the Master Game: an irreparable depletion of the substances needed for real inner work and a total loss of the individual's capacity to develop. Which, once again, echoes Gopi Krishna:

> "The whole of our body is filled with a very fine biochemical essence which I call the biological Prana. Prana has two aspects, the universal and the individual. In the individual aspect it is composed of the subtlest elements. I should say some radiation from the various elements on a subatomic level. This Prana is concentrated in the sex-energy. Normally the sex energy is used for procreative purposes, but nature has designed it for evolutionary purposes also.
>
> "We are all familiar with the word sublimation, or refinement and purification. Most people believe that artistic talent, and genius to a large extent, depend on the sublimation of the sex-energy. Even psychologists like Freud and Jung ascribe it to libido. Now libido is sex-energy, life-energy in other words. So, according to the view of those who believe in kundalini — according to the views of ancient masters — the human reproductive system functions in two ways, both as the evolutionary and the reproductive mechanism. As the evolutionary mechanism, it sends a fine stream of a very potent nerve-energy into the brain and another stream into the sexual region, the cause of reproduction.
>
> "By the arousal of kundalini we mean the reversal of the repro-

ductive system and its functioning more as an evolutionary than as a reproductive mechanism."

~ Gopi Krishna - *The Awakening of Kundalini*

I have concluded, therefore, that the rules which apply to Gurdjieff's and Ouspensky's Self-Remembering system also apply to energy cultivation techniques, such as kundalini meditation, in that the aptitude for success in the practice of these systems depends a great deal on the physiological and temperamental characteristics of the individual. Whether kundalini is a prerequisite for attaining higher consciousness, or playing the Master Game, is purely an individual matter and cannot be determined in advance. On the other hand, a method such as Golden Flower Meditation (GFM), whose purpose is raising kundalini, holds the brightest chances of success because it induces permanent, deliberate safe awakenings, commensurate with an individual's Karmic state, as well as his/her physical and temperamental endowments.

> "Here it is sufficient to say that the Master Game can never be made easy to play. It demands all that a man has, all his feelings, all his thoughts, his entire resources, physical and spiritual. If he tries to play it in a halfhearted way or tries to get results by unlawful means, he runs the risk of destroying his own potential. For this reason it is better not to embark on the game at all than to play it halfheartedly."[52]

If you're wondering, "Am I a fit for the Master Game — with or without the release of kundalini?" You might very well find some answers in this prescient book first published in 1968.

Holistic Kundalini

What is Holistic Kundalini? Is it a better way of activating kundalini? Hardly. There are many ways of activating kundalini, some better than others — "better," in this instance, is defined as tailored to your specific needs, a method that suits you as opposed to the ones that

---

52 *The Master Game: Pathways to Higher Consciousness* ~ de Ropp, Robert S., Gateways Books & Tapes. Kindle Edition, p. 24.

don't. That's right, not all methods work for all people. Moreover, some people, no matter how much they want it or how hard they try, will never be able to activate kundalini by any method. That's the Karmic reality. If you're doing it via meditation, it's a lifetime commitment.

> "One thing has to be remembered about meditation; it is a long journey and there is no shortcut. Anyone who says there is a shortcut is befooling you. It is a long journey because the change is very deep and is achieved after many lives — many lives of routine habits, thinking, desiring. And the mind structure; that you have to drop through meditation. In fact, it is almost impossible — but it happens. A man becoming a meditator is a great responsibility in this world. It is not easy. It cannot be instant. So from the beginning never start expecting too much and then you will never be frustrated. You will always be happy because things will grow very slowly.
>
> "Meditation is not a seasonal flower which within six weeks is there. It is a very, very big tree. It needs time to spread its roots."
>
> ~ OSHO

Holistic Kundalini is a term I apply to the all around kundalini life experience: Seeking a method, practicing the method, activating kundalini, undergoing the awakening experience, living with kundalini, and finally helping others to understand kundalini, perhaps even awaken it. This may seem pretty mundane. "Oh, I know all about that; I've read about it," some initiates tell me. Yes, I've heard it all: Individuals who have not yet even begun a well-founded practice telling me what it is like after reading about it in books. I don't tell them I've lived with kundalini for over forty years. What's the use? These novices purporting to be experts already know more than I do. I'm not being facetious; I agree with them. Early on in my practice, I realized I knew nothing.

All the myriad of separate, yet overlapping slices of information available to today's seeker form a gigantic pie. That's the blessing of the New Age. But the overabundance of information is also its curse. Which slice is for me? Some of this information is good and some of it isn't. I'm not competent to judge all content, only wonder if it's been vetted or peer reviewed?

Still, I inform people on what to watch out for and how to set expectations. That's Holistic Kundalini — coming full circle, back to the beginning in order to help others understand the process and the stakes.

So I listen to the chatter of novices and move on. When I see them again years later, they're still turning in circles. Why? Simply and succinctly because they weren't grounded in the first place. They didn't have a goal, and you need one. They didn't have a plan, and you need one of those, too. Why? Because just as Osho says, when you expect too much, you're bound to fail. It's built-in into the process, like a sense of entitlement. I've never known it not to fail, never seen it succeed. Strut into this work with a sense of privilege and overarching confidence and you will end up turning in circles.

From the discussions I've had, most people don't have any idea what I mean when I tell them they need a goal and a plan. Yet, if they were building a house, they'd have one of each. Activating and living with kundalini are similar undertakings. You must know what you're doing, as well as the why and how of it. You need a vision.

Let's think for a moment about setting goals. How should I approach it, you ask? In the first place the goal shouldn't be all about your ego, as if you were just going to the gym to add some more muscle to impress the opposite sex. You should have something you want to accomplish that can only be accomplished by a change of being, a change of consciousness. What might that be? Gopi Krishna defined that change as, "becoming conscious of consciousness." Think about it and you'll see most people aren't.

In my case, I was looking for a way to reverse the effects of a childhood accident. At the time I wasn't able to clearly formulate it, but it was on my mind — a vision really — that eventually came to the fore. All I needed then was a plan and that was delivered to me. It took me a while to recognize it, but I finally did. What plan? To decipher and practice the method of meditation in *The Secret of the Golden Flower* — Golden Flower Meditation (GFM). The book was given to me unexpectedly. After a year of avoiding it, I realized I was supposed to do something with it.

To formulate a plan, you must think about your life. Take inventory. How old are you? Is it reasonable to undertake this work now? Who will support you? How will your kundalini practice resonate with the others in your life? Can you hold a job and do it? Why do you want to change your being, your consciousness? For selfish purposes? To heal yourself and others? To overcome addiction? What's the point of having a goal if you don't have some sort of vision?

Does a non-goal, or absence of a goal, constitute a goal? It could. It's better than doing it to acquire occult powers or to make yourself more attractive. And what about a plan? Once you have a vision, it's easy to work out a plan. Just like building a house, once you know what you want to do, it's easy. You take stock of existing tools and techniques. You examine cost, scheduling, strengths and weaknesses, benefits and inconveniences. You make tests. One approach is going to stand out, appear more suited to your person. You won't succeed if you wake up one morning telling yourself you're going to raise kundalini because you want to be Governor of Iowa. The two operate in different spheres. You need compatibility, goals and plans suited to your style of living and to YOU.

You also need to think about living with kundalini. Let's say you're twenty years old, and you've caught the kundalini bug. You practice, and you're successful. At the age of 21, you're living with a permanently active kundalini for the rest of your life. Are you prepared for this? What kind of person are you? Introvert? Extrovert? Secretive? Outgoing? Fun-loving? Although kundalini starts to remake your being and change your consciousness, personality tendencies don't change overnight. In fact, you may take on new tendencies temporarily. Negative emotions, dietary changes, sexual dysfunction. Are you prepared to handle these challenges? And what about those around you? Can they cope with this new you? It took me a long time to learn to live with kundalini, to understand what it was doing.

I knew I wanted to write about my experience, but at the beginning I couldn't. It took me thirty years before I was ready. Yet, not one day in those thirty years went by without my thinking about and experiencing the effects of kundalini. Perhaps, with a little pre-thought, a little discussion, you can do better.

Everything You Need To Know About Kundalini

Can one person know everything there is to know about kundalini? And if so, is there such a person? For instance, the other day I ran across some Online wondering about the use of kundalini in provoking and treating abdominal pain. Of course, all aspects of kundalini interest me, but here was one aspect I had never encountered and had to admit I knew nothing about.

I realized there are other kundalini-related topics that I know nothing about because they are not part of my experience, all of which points out the danger of offering advice about specific kundalini topics outside the ken of the "advisor."

I know a lot about kundalini. Most is specific to my own personal experience, which, although it shares many similarities with the experiences of others, is unique to me. I also know about a sundry and varied list of effects that my awakening has set in motion over the last 40 years. Many effects have to do with the physiological changes in my body that kundalini has induced since my awakening. Because of the variance in the state and condition of individual bodies, these effects are rarely shared. I have never met anyone who said that kundalini affected his/her body the same way it affected mine.

I also know a lot about Golden Flower Meditation (GFM), the method I used to activate kundalini; I've taught for 20 years. Yet, each time I teach this method, I am confronted by new challenges, participants' questions that were never raised before, questions I'd never encountered or thought about. And I've had to find new ways of describing a certain technique, either because someone raised the question or a better way of explaining the technique suddenly became clear to me during the explaining.

So, to sum it up, I know about my experience, the effects I've experienced, and about teaching GFM. Even among these topics, there are various degrees of knowledge — things I absolutely know by way of experience, things that are almost impossible to communicate to others, things that I've learned empirically or inductively, a posteriori and a priori. Things I learned deductively. Things I can extrapolate on —usually matters picked up in conversations with other kundalini novices, practitioners, and/or adepts. Hypotheses derived from the various changes kundalini has effected on my body. Some are hypotheses related to visions or intuitive discoveries that kundalini has brought to the attention of my rational mind.

Yes, kundalini is always working in the background, moving thoughts, emotional states, and physical conditions around, toying with consciousness, allowing me to realize things that, in my pre-kundalini days, I never could have imagined — the possibilities and opportunities kundalini made me aware of. Things already passed, and things that will come to pass. Creative things. Positive, inspired and inspiring things. Evolution hard at work, striving to avoid an imminent world collapse, as we veer — no, rush headlong — toward collective self-destruction.

So, why is kundalini important? Because kundalini is a biological expression of what Gopi Krishna termed the "evolutionary impulse." It is a subject so large that it cannot be "known" by just one person. It is also a means of changing the negative aspects of human nature and of jump-starting evolution. Its purpose is not to be trifled with.

Just as one engineer knows electronics, another knows construction, still another knows computers, kundalini has its compartments, its specializations, its specific phenomenal properties. Whether this becomes a research track worthy of further academic investigation is too early to tell. One thing is certain: each day I realize how little I know, and in so realizing I learn something new, not only about kundalini, but about myself.

Death

> And death shall have no dominion.
> Dead men naked they shall be one
> With the man in the wind and the west moon;
> When their bones are picked clean and the clean bones gone,
> They shall have stars at elbow and foot;
> Though they go mad they shall be sane,
> Though they sink through the sea they shall rise again;
> Though lovers be lost love shall not;
> And death shall have no dominion.
> ~ Dylan Thomas - *And Death Shall Have No Dominion*

A macabre presence hovered over me during a recent European trip — from city to city: London, Paris, Hamburg — the Grim Reaper, Death. Everywhere I went, old friends brought up the subject of dying, as in, "Once I consolidate... sell off all our stuff... prepare my will... settle up... let the children make their choices... convert everything to cash, I'm ready to go."

I didn't take these utterances as signs of morbidity. It seemed like an honest approach to the matter. What's the point in complicating your final years by holding onto to a lot of material things you no longer have any use for or derive any pleasure from? Seems reasonable to wind things down, no?

So if it wasn't morbidity, what bothered me then? I suppose it was the finality with which they spoke about the process —its utter end-game futility, the closing of the final chapter, for now and for all time. Not that I went into detail on The Tibetan Book of the Dead or elaborated on the Bardos. Like most of your friends probably, these aren't people you can talk to about reincarnation. They aren't easily convinced that death is only a stage in the development of the energy concentration known as I.

They're highly educated, which makes it all the harder because they believe in the power of the rational mind and are therefore constrained by its limits. The mind is a wonderful tool, but by definition also a barrier if it's conditioned to place limits on the extent to which man is capable of evolving. And if those limits are dictated by the scientific method, then they become a barrier beyond which the individual cannot penetrate because he/she has neither the spiritual practice nor the flexibility of spirit of an Einstein, who once exclaimed, "I didn't come to any of my great discoveries through use of the rational mind."

My friends maintain that there is nothing beyond the life of the brain. They are like the skeptics who believed Columbus and the other early explorers would simply sail off the edge of the Earth.

They believe that once death occurs, the brain is as useless as a broken-down motherboard. And that's true, as far as brain tissue is concerned. But there's more to the mind than brain tissue; the mind is connected to an Energy Continuum. It feeds from its inexhaustible reservoir of consciousness and contributes to that source in its own right. Yes, the physical brain dies, but the pulsating energy that animated it lives on, thereby extending the boundaries of today's known physical science, and by extension the very definition of science.

Many of my friends were exposed to fundamentalism in their youth and did not enjoy the experience. So they took refuge in the mind/brain duality, and in so doing, created a bulwark against religiosity. Nothing wrong with that except they lumped everything in together: no difference between the doctrine/dogma of organized religion and the solitary pursuit of truth through meditation/yoga.

As far as they are concerned, all of it is superstition and humbug.

> "Quite apart from the charm of the new and the fascination of the half-understood, there is good cause for yoga to have many adherents. It offers the possibility of controllable experience and thus satisfies the need for facts, and, besides this, by reason of its breadth and depth, its venerable age, its doctrine and method, which include every phase of life, it promises undreamed of possibilities."
>
> ~Carl Gustav Jung

I understand the desire to tie up loose ends, but it seems to me that once it's accomplished, the only remaining item would be to begin asking the basic questions so frequently pushed aside during lifetimes of activity and achievement.

- What was I here for?
- Who am I?
- What happens next?
- What is the purpose of life?

To start doing some original thinking on the meaning of life instead of accepting the mantra-like orthodoxy of either organized religion or the scientific method. Yes, the scientific method can be as constraining as Catholic dogma, especially if it proscribes "undreamed of possibilities."

I recognize that questioning one's existence is hard to do once old age closes in. It takes a reorientation of Being — an occasion I met with in the person of an elderly Swiss lady who sat next to me during the final leg of my journey from Zürich to San Francisco.

I didn't talk to her at first because I thought she only spoke German. But when, in the course of the flight — getting up to go to the toilet, passing trays back and forth, commenting on the vegetarian meal we'd both consumed — I learned she spoke English, and I got to hear her story: A widow in her 80s, she visits her son in San Diego twice a year for a month, but only stays a week with him because his wife is domineering and doesn't like her.

The rest of the time she stays at Yogananda's nearby Encinitas

Self-Realization Fellowship, an interest in which she developed after realizing that spending extensive time with her family was unrewarding. I was impressed by her ability to change course, to make her life over at a ripe old age. She told me it wasn't a product of "thinking things over;" it was the result of practice — through which, metaphysical actuality became as clear to her as staring at a tree or as palpable as touching the grass with bare feet.

She enumerated the program of study she'd undertaken over the six-year period she'd been going to the fellowship:
- Quickening Human Evolution
- How to Meditate
- Finding your True Vocation in Life
- Developing Creative Ability
- Overcoming Fear of Death
- Correct Breathing
- Diet and Fasting
- States of Consciousness
- The Laws of Healing
- And last, but not least:
- Life After Death
- Reincarnation

To which she added with a twinkle of the eye as we stood up to deplane, "You do know we are incarnated again in a new body, over and over?"

"Yes," I replied, "I've worked my way to the same conclusion, not by use of the rational mind, but by practicing energy cultivation techniques, albeit served up in a different tradition with some discoveries of my own along the way."

"I'm looking forward to that new body," she said, "I'm tired of dragging this one around for such a long time. There is no death, something I learned just in time to prepare myself."

And it appears this notion is taking hold. Witness this interview in The Guardian with rock star Tricky:

Q: You've got a new song called We Don't Die. Where do we go if we don't die?

A: The weird thing with me is I've had close people die, like my Mum, but I don't get sad at death. I miss them, obviously, but move on. That's not because I'm a bad person or emotionally numb, but there must be a reason it don't affect me. I think it's because death doesn't really exist. I don't believe in it. In some ways I was lucky my Mum died when I was that young. I've seen friends lose people as adults and be so traumatized they can't eat or go off the rails and into prison. But I've never had a conversation with her. I'd love to sit down with her for one hour to see what she was like.

And death have shall no dominion!

More About Death

"One other liberating experience related to OBE is that in fraternizing with death I discovered that it is only another aspect of life, another state of existence. For each one of us, death awaits, and this fact is an incitement to ask profound questions, relating to the unknown — paradise, hell, separation, or extinction. How can we find answers? OBE gives us answers through direct experience since I can enter and leave my own body, I can exist without my body. The death of my physical body therefore does not signify my end. I am able to think, feel, desire and act in other contexts than that of the physical world."

~ Akhena - *Astral Consciousness: Out of Body Explorations*

I second the emotion. Not only did I experience the same ah-ha realization during an OBE (Out of Body Experience) at the age of 20, I encountered the same extra-corporal effect 15 years later after raising kundalini. I was able to see inside my physical body, which led me to realize my being was more than my body — a series of ethereal body sheaths enveloped it.

These ethereal bodies are part of an invisible Energy Continuum (consciousness), which contains the past, present, and future of time and space, of which our biological form is only a limited expression.

At this point in the history of our sciences, we do not understand how the consciousness we deem a part of everyday life works, much less are we able to scientifically comprehend its metaphysical nature. But thanks to OBE, NDE, and kundalini, we can experience it. Verify it, no; experience it, yes.

In our present state, we talk of "losing and regaining consciousness" after getting knocked on the head or going into the operating room for a medical procedure. Mostly, we don't look beyond a very limited sense of consciousness. That is, up till now.

Meditation, yoga, mindfulness are changing this. As we pursue these various pastimes, disciplines, and practices and connect to a vaster sense of consciousness, we realize that death, like life, is a transitory state, and we are less afraid.

In 1947, when the poet, Dylan Thomas, wrote:
"Do not go gentle into that good night.
Rage, rage against the dying of the light."
Didn't he realize that the light doesn't die? The clear light that shines at the moment of death is a beacon leading you toward the Energy Continuum, the entry into a recycling process and your next incarnation.

Was it this light that beckoned John Coltrane to knowingly record a tune on his last album, *Expression*, entitled *To Be* just days before his death? What a querulous, introspective title for the usually high-octane saxophonist! A mournful tempo, featuring unusual instrumentation — Coltrane on flute (an instrument he only played once) and Pharaoh Sanders on piccolo, not sure he ever played it again — the tune was mostly ignored by Coltrane fans, who were more engaged by his fascination with the innovative and frenzied Free Jazz trend at that time.

To Be is a long, slow, introspective piece that, for me, signifies the passing of the torch or the changing of the guard, a realization by the composer (Coltrane) that "Being" has metaphysical overtones — we come and go, pass and re-pass on this earth.

The head, featuring the flute and piccolo, is followed by a

long Alice Coltrane piano solo; a Sanders, then a Coltrane solo. As Coltrane's line trails out — sort of expires — Sanders injects a lilting, melancholy phrase that reminds me of a warbling bird and has me visualizing the following scene in my mind's eye.

Personnel in Expression: Pharaoh Sanders, John Coltrane, Alice Coltrane, Jimmy Garrison, Rashied Ali

I see a man sitting in a wooden garden chair, holding a cold drink on the armrest. The camera explores his face and his surroundings. The flowers, trees. His shoes. The back of his head and neck. Over his shoulder, the armrest and the drink. The arm goes limp, the drink topples over, and his arm drops. We hear a bird, the camera finds it and we listen. Cut to the dead man's face.

From this vision, while re-listening to this tune (To Be, the bird in the above scene), I imagine the death process and know that although the body dies, the metaphysical essence that animates the body does not.

And death have shall no dominion!

Religion And Kundalini

The findings of a 2012 Pew Forum on Religion and Public Life, suggesting that religious "nones" are "on the rise" and are "less religious than the public at large," has loomed large in public discussion of the changing face of religion. But this focus on the so-called rise of the nones misses much of what is significant about the direction of religion as it is done, as people do religion.

Failings of the Pew report—for example, asking respondents to define their religiosity in negative terms ("none"), suggesting they are in no way religious, or defining religious community in terms of "shared values and beliefs"—suggest that these increasingly frequent efforts to quantify religion distract from more nuanced understandings. Respondents were asked, for example, not whether they do yoga and to what religious or spiritual effect, but rather whether they "believe in yoga." This fixation on shared belief obscures what is in fact the diverse religious landscape of the yoga industry and the "spiritual but not religious movement" at large. Many yoga practitioners, although they probably would not describe themselves as "believers in yoga," do in fact hold religious beliefs and engage in a range of religious practices.

The Case of Bikram Yoga, Andrea Jain – Tricycle, Spring 2017

We Prefer Listening to Doing

Jesus, Lao Tse, and Buddha didn't aim to start the religions they're associated with. That phenomenon was the by-product of their personal search for truth. The fact that, at one point in their lives, each of them went on a lonely quest for knowledge, using the tools available at the time, i.e., using their bodies as laboratories. They weren't thinking about religion or about science. Yet, the discoveries they made during their fateful retreats turned out to be the precursors of both religion and science.

Each of them had absented themselves for a time from their worldly preoccupations to practice a solitary meditation, and it was through this practice that they awakened kundalini, that placeholder term we use to denote the evolutionary energy in man. Similar traditions have other names for it: Chi, orgone, or life force. The names aren't important; they are interchangeable.

As Thomas Cleary says in his translation of *The Secret of the*

Golden Flower:

> "From the point of view of that central experience, it makes no difference whether one calls the golden flower awakening a relationship to God or to the Way, or whether one calls it the holy spirit or the Buddha nature or the real self. The Tao Te Ching says, 'Names can be designated, but they are not fixed terms.'"

What did these men discover? They discovered a hidden sub-system inside their bodies which, properly aroused, opened the door to higher consciousness and led them to infer an ontology for human potential beyond anything science knows today. They were doers, not talkers, impelled by what Gopi Krishna called the evolutionary impulse. An impulse to self-realization written into our DNA. What is the mechanism behind self-realization that they shared? According to historical research, they shared the practice of meditation. It was through meditation that they came to the discovery of the evolutionary energy in every human body.

Only after making their discoveries did they begin talking about them. First they practiced, then they talked. It was as if they were saying: Do before talking, and when you do talk, talk about doing.

These men didn't talk about religion; they talked about doing. They realized that talking was an excuse for not doing. Unfortunately, the doing part has become lost, especially here in the West.

As for the religious teachings surrounding their discoveries, if you boil them down to their barest denominators, they amount to not much more than the Golden Rule: do unto others as you would have them do unto you. A simple enough maxim to enunciate, but quite difficult to adhere to in practice. The very fact we in the West call our religions faiths, not practices should give some indication of what we're dealing with. In other words, traditional religion means: I'm going to talk, and you're going to listen. I'm going to give you my opinion on what you should think and believe. Never mind about verifying; shut up, listen, and believe.

Don't blame the progenitors. They didn't actually start the various religions named after them. In fact, Jesus Christ wasn't a Christian; Lao Tse wasn't a Taoist, and Buddha wasn't a Buddhist. The recruiting, party-member stuff came later, after camp followers, sycophants, and spin-doctors began politicizing and formalizing their teachings, turning them into money-making organizations. It was after the fact that these religions were named for their progenitors.

Yes, there is still a residue of legitimate devotion to the initial discoveries those pioneers made about human evolution and how we might speed it up in order to avoid the pitfalls of negative emotion, greed, war, racial hatred, wanton violence. But much of their teaching about meditation has been lost over the centuries and we are left with the man-made dogmas and doctrines that have nothing to do with doing.

Yes, we love to listen; we hate to do. In the first place, DO WHAT? What is it I should do? How do I know WHAT to do? In the second place, I don't have time. In the third place, I don't have any guarantee it would work. In the fourth place, it can't be any good if I don't have to pay a lot for it. In the fifth place, it can't be very helpful if Oprah hasn't mentioned it. And so on...

Waiting for the Next Messiah

Well, the meditation methods they practiced still work and are still doable today. That's right, whether for spiritual, religious, or scientific purposes, individuals are still using their bodies as laboratories, pushing the evolutionary envelope. One thing you need to know: in this long evolutionary journey we have not yet accomplished very much. There's still much distance to cover. We are but mere outlines of our potential. Enlightenment, self-actualization, self-realization are not carved-in-stone achievements; they are milestones in an on-going process that is never completed, but keeps us continually reaching for completion.

A Taoist Doubts My Kundalini Experience

The following is a reply to a criticism of my experience as documented in *The Backward-Flowing Method: The Secret of Life and Death*. I include it merely to show how someone on the outside looking in is not qualified to comment unless they have had the same or similar experience. Doubting is fine, but insisting that a person's experience could not have happened the way it is described — without any empirical facts — is reckless to say the least. This critic's take was based solely on a comparison of my account with the Taoist books he'd read on various subjects related to orthodox Taoist scripture. Here the critic's take:

> First, I'm giving two stars for the philosophical discussions presented. I actually liked the discussions about the early life of Christ and the conjecture of what Arius may have espoused. That Christ may have had Eastern training is wildly compelling. I think other reviewers were turned off by the extraneous information presented.
>
> Now I want to just throw down exactly why I docked three stars.
>
> Do you believe that it is possible to send seminal fluid up the back of your spine and into your brain? Neither do I. And while it is true that the Taoists associate jing with seminal fluid they are not one in the same. This book aims to help you get seminal fluid into your brain.
>
> I think the author completely missed the mark. I am a Taoist and am relatively versed in the theory of meditation. After reading 'The Secret of the Golden Flower' I truly believe that it is giving guidance for the microcosmic orbit meditation. It is obvious that it is calling out the connection of the du mai and ren mai channels and the circulation of qi in this closed loop. The author did not reach the same conclusion.
>
> The author is obsessed with the idea of giving breath direction. I think this is where knowledge in qigong would benefit him greatly. In qigong breath is used in the command of qi but again it is the circulation of qi that matters, not the circulation of breath.
>
> Okay. Here is the issue as I see it. I think it's good that you put here that you are not following a 'dogma' or an orthodox religion. The problem is that you are deciphering a book that belongs to at least two orthodox religions that interpret it very differently than yourself. So I think there was an assumption on the part of the reader (me in this instance).
>
> Allow me to illustrate. If I pick up a book titled, 'Interpreting the

Quran' I would be reasonably certain that the person interpreting is an Islamic scholar. Or perhaps at the very least someone of the Islamic faith.

As for your reference to the immortals it was noticeably disrespectful. 'The Secret of The Golden Flower', along with the tao te ching, and the chung tzu, belong to their religion and their 'dogma' as you say. That is why I reference them. You don't want to believe what is written of them then do not believe the secret of the golden flower either. You needn't trouble yourself further.

You have more or less stated above that all conclusions you have drawn and all of your thoughts on symmetry are your own and not backed by any orthodox religion. I guess I'm a simple man of observation. And to my eye nature abhors symmetry. I'll agree with you as soon as you have your heart centered in your chest. I'm afraid I cannot relate to whatever you have going on in that last paragraph.

I'm certain that you feel attacked by my review and for that I must apologize. You must understand that I was expecting an orthodox discussion so you could imagine my disappointment? I still feel my review is helpful for those in my situation. Think of it like this; I am keeping away the audience you do not want.

My reply:

"What starts out as seminal fluid is distilled into Prana, which is then 'drawn' up the spinal column into the brain. How do I know? I followed the meditation method in *The Secret of the Golden Flower. Deciphering the Golden Flower One Secret at a Time* contains the details on my experience and my first-hand discoveries on Golden Flower Meditation. My experience happened as I described it, pretty much as your Taoist tradition describes it, give or take differences in terminology. If I did not say it exactly as you believe it should be, I apologize."

"Nevertheless, I believe we're talking about the same thing. That I didn't follow a strict formula, imposed by any orthodox religion or belief system is accurate. I went out on my own. If you think about it, that's not necessarily wrong because orthodoxies tend to get stuck in dogma after a couple of centuries of doing things the same way. No new discoveries are made or accepted. But kundalini is a living biological process, not a belief system. Methods are not written in stone, they evolve. They should evolve. That's when real progress happens. Today's methods and means for activating kundalini may be unrecognizable in the future because we will have made so many advances, so many seekers trying new approaches. Searching, seeking.

"Many will fail, some will succeed, others will discover unexplored byways. Take the part on symmetry that you dispute. The reason you dismiss it is because you have not experienced in your body what I have experienced in mine. You simply have no data on the subject to report or analyze. Again, if you want to understand it from my perspective, see how symmetry (and loss of it) played a role in the development of my morphology and persona, read *Deciphering the Golden Flower One Secret at a Time*. My take on symmetry has nothing to do with the doctrine on Taoist immortals. That's second hand information you're taking on hearsay. I don't know any of these gentlemen, so I don't feel qualified to talk about them. In any case, I'm not criticizing them; I'm merely disputing your use of them to support your comments when you yourself have no first-hand experience with either theirs or my meditation or kundalini practices."

"My account is a summary of what took place in the laboratory of my own body. Did you witness the transformation of any of those Taoist immortals? Were you there? Do you know for sure the exact morphology, somatic or metabolic structure of any of the Taoist immortals you cite? What do you know about their specific symmetry or asymmetry? I write about what I know, perhaps poorly in some instances. I'll try to do better the next time. I'd love to have someone like yourself as a reviewer to go back and forth with before publication.

"Ouspensky said, 'You must verify everything you see, hear, or feel.' Good advice for all of us doing this work. That we don't get the descriptions right the first time is understandable. After all, we're using language of the physical world to explain phenomenon of the metaphysical world. We work through a series of approximations on the way to expressing our experiences as clearly as possible. That's the beauty of the Internet: we write something; we reread it; we add in new material; we find better ways of expressing our experiences; we rewrite it. As for what should be written about and what's 'in the weeds,' I wrote about symmetry and asymmetry because I uncovered information about how our bodies are constructed, how certain stimuli (exterior or interior) affect our physical maturation and growth. This is taking human ontology down to the egg-sperm —embryo, fetus — level, what happens at insemination and even before it, albeit theorizing that there is a 'controlling field,' a blueprint that determines our form and substance, and how stimuli of all sorts can interrupt the plans for our embodiment, which is then outwardly manifested by our symmetry, which in turn influences our person-alities. "Please note that I'm not the only person who has lived this, or the only person investigating this. *The Biology of Consciousness: Case Studies in Kundalini* explores this material in depth, citing, I might add, the work of others on the notion of the controlling field, a phenomenon that is also present during a kundalini awakening in that it facilitates the collision/fusion of energy (distilled seminal fluid) and matter (cranial lobes, cortex, and neurons) in a kind of Quantum event.

"Do I believe that every reader will accept my findings and my accounts? No. I know there will be objections that arise on account of terminology, differences in background and experience. Worse than these reasons, however, are the ones derived from blind adherence to a belief-system offered by self-appointed keepers of doctrinal purity, usually individuals who have never practiced or used their bodies as a laboratory."

The God vs. No God Argument

Sad is watching someone thump his chest because he believes he's won an argument that's unwinnable. That's what the God vs. No God is, an unwinnable argument,[53] an endless polemic.

In polemics the winner is the one most skilled in argumentation. Evidence, empirical or anecdotal, is not to be found, while shouting and obfuscation are ubiquitous and omnipresent. Invective, rant, tirade, broadside, diatribe, attack, harangue, condemnation, criticism, stricture, admonition, rebuke are its hallmarks. Ted Cruz is a master of polemics.

I didn't have to read *Cold-Case Christianity* (CCC) written by LA cold-case homicide detective, J. Warner Wallace to realize that it was based on customer profiling and psychographic targeting with a liberal dose of the agent's and the author's crafting a clever non-fiction book proposal, i.e. that a veteran homicide detective could apply the principles and techniques used in solving cold cases to prove the veracity of the Bible. Trouble is, the author doesn't start from scratch; he has a foregone conclusion to which he is determined to fit his so-called researched facts. I downloaded the sample pages, read them, saw where he was headed, and decided to pass on the rest. Nevertheless, the book is a big seller, which says more about the public's general lack of analytical skills than it does about the book's content. It tells us that people need constant reinforcements of their beliefs, and they are ready to accept them blindly, in whatever form they are offered — film, article, web page, book.

Bart Ehrman's book *Jesus, Interrupted: Revealing the Hidden Contradictions in the Bible*[54] offers a more coherent appraisal of the Bible's content than CCC does, but whether you accept Ehrman's or Wallace's version of the facts is not the real issue. Both are best sellers. And both put forth arguments that are mere stand-ins or

---

53 Kundalini & God - http://www.kundaliniconsortium.
    org/2013/08/kundalini-and-god.html
54 http://amzn.to/2BKVJMu

straw men for the real issue: the God vs. No God argument. One side argues that, if they can verify evidentially the accuracy of the Bible, it then follows that God must exist; the other side argues that if they can disprove the assorted "facts" in the Bible, it proves that God does not exist. This is the straw man fallacy, which Wikipedia summarizes thusly, "The so-called typical 'attacking a straw man' argument creates the illusion of having completely refuted or defeated an opponent's proposition by covertly replacing it with a different proposition." Whether the information in the Bible is accurate or not does not prove or refute the existence of God.

This straw man approach is a new wrinkle to the old "There is a God" argument, the one which urged you to accept the existence of God on faith. But like that approach, it's beside the point. Whether you argue "Bible facts" or "faith," there's no proof that God does or doesn't exist. I'm not saying He doesn't; I'm saying I don't know. No one knows, and no one can prove otherwise.

The "faith" approach is more of a movement than a proof, a political groundswell with no rational basis. The "Bible facts" argument is moot because — even though it's a diversionary straw man tactic meant to bolster the less reasoned "faith" argument — it boils down to using the intellect in trying to prove, or disprove, the existence of God. I call this the outside-in approach. It is not possible to apprehend the supernatural — I prefer the term metaphysical — with the rational mind, from the outside-in. Not possible to use intellectual pyrotechnics or polemics to authenticate the supernatural or metaphysical. Authentication must be lived and experienced first hand.

There is an alternative: the inside-out approach, which uses Eastern energy cultivation techniques such as meditation, yoga, etc. to actually awaken the hidden subsystems of the human body, allowing the individual to experience metaphysical reality directly, i.e., to pass from the physical to metaphysical planes, and thereby bear witness to what I call the energy continuum — an expanded reality beyond the material world that contains that world and the worlds beyond all cosmological worlds. How far an individual goes with this type of practice depends on his volition and dedication. Let me add here one insight it has given me: the ultimate aim of meditation is to become more and more conscious. Enlightenment, therefore, is becoming fully conscious.

How did I arrive at this? Through a kundalini meditation that projected me into a vibratory state of such profound consciousness that I realized, not because someone asked me to take it on faith, but because I experienced it, that a hidden metaphysical reality does exist, and that death is only an intermediate state — which showed me how unconscious I had been all of my life!

What sort of mechanism did this meditation trigger in order to accomplish this? It used the body's most powerful source — sexual energy. Quite simply, the energy source which creates life was rerouted and drawn up the spinal column into the brain. Since kundalini is a biological phenomenon, it needs to draw energy from a biological source in order to awaken kundalini and accomplish its purpose. This source happens to be sexual, the same energy source involved in procreation. How could it be otherwise? The energy used to create life is the same energy used in spiritual re-birth. What other source in the human body has the requisite energy to accomplish such a task?

Luckily, I was in my early thirties when this happened. Plenty of time to learn from this process and to restore my body to its optimal condition. At first, the effects were physical; my brain and its casing were reshaped (strange how the physical awakens the metaphysical which in turn kick off a reconditioning of the physical). Gradually, as these metaphysical experiences deepened, I became more conscious, until I realized I was using only a portion of my potential, that full consciousness might somehow remove me from the physical world. As I said, becoming conscious is gradual; there may be no existential leaps, only gradual illumination and insight.

But whether it boils down to what Christians refer to as a super-natural experience or to the term I prefer, a metaphysical experience, my aroused kundalini showed me that while we can't prove the existence, or non-existence, of God, we have at our disposal a vast range of experiential phenomena, such as OBE, NDE, kundalini awakenings, etc., all of which are triggered by a voluntary or an unexpected summoning of biological energy.

With this type of experience, there's no need to thump the chest; winning the argument is not the goal here. Scientific evaluation is. These cases don't depend on polemics; they occur irrespective of cultural, language, religious, educational, or geographical differences — and they share many of the same symptoms and effects. For the individual, it's a take-it-as-it-comes succession of phenomena in the laboratory of his or her own body, which, over time, also quiets the ego as it renews the being. For society, it's a piecemeal compilation of metaphysical accounts, which, as each anecdote is added, becomes an avalanche begging for a suitable means of scientific authentica-tion.

The inside-out approach jettisons the whole baggage of con-ventional wisdom, polemics, and traditional religion. Christianity, which was turned into a political party by Augustine of Hippo, whose proponents/apologists and critics/detractors have argued God vs. No God back-and-forth for over two thousand years without making any progress, is an especially sad case.

Influential early Christians like Arius and Origen, who encouraged the direct experience of the inside-out approach — much in the mode of Buddha, Gurdjieff, Krishnamurti, Milarepa, and Lao Tse — were systematically rooted out and persecuted by pro-Augustine spin doctors, a case well-documented in the Elizabeth Clare Prophet book on Reincarnation and Christianity. Yes, there are unproven hypotheses in her book, but the idea that Jesus was on a Buddha-like trip during his lost years supports the notion that the major historical spiritual figures used the inside-out approach to arrive at the insights and fundamental practices that the religions named after them are based on. The outside-in approach didn't appear until much later when the various spin doctors began arguing over the endless stream of dogma/doctrine, much to the chagrin of the real authorities on religious experience.

In fact, the supernatural yearnings Christians feel are a positive element; they need to join with metaphysicians to practice and pursue the inside-out approach that values energy cultivation and direct experience over polemics and the dictates of intermediaries, i.e. priests, spin doctors, theologians, and ecclesiastics.

Those who take the inside-out approach have made, and will continue to make, measurable progress in the practice and discovery of energy cultivation techniques which lead to direct metaphysical experience, the multiplicity of which is just beginning to be cataloged and authenticated, à la Michael Murphy's The Future of the Body, a survey of consciousness and meta-normal experience.

It doesn't only apply to spiritual questing or metaphysics; it applies to all human endeavor:

> "There are things that even though people tell you about it, you really won't understand and have a feel for it until you experience it."
>
> ~ Hideki Matsui, former New York Yankees' outfielder

Finding God — Within or Without

> "The Arian controversy was really about the nature of man and how we are saved. It involved two pictures of Jesus Christ: either he was a God who had always been God or he was a man who became God's Son. The Church's theological position was, in part, dictated by its political needs. The Arian position had the potential to erode the authority of the Church since it implied that the soul did not need the Church to achieve salvation."
>
> ~ *Reincarnation: The Missing Link in Christianity* – Elizabeth Clare Prophet

The unanswered question, not only in Christianity, but in all religions, is: how does an individual experience — Oneness with the Universal Spirit — come to pass?

Is it achieved through the practice of energy cultivation techniques that seek to awaken kundalini, thereby ushering in enlightenment? Or is it by salvation, through the intervention of some orthodox religion with its doctrines and dogmas? It's a discussion that hangs over all spiritual exploration, dramatically hi-lighted in Christianity by the 4th. Century struggle between the dissident followers of Arius and the orthodox followers of St. Augustine.

Let's turn to the Internet, that source of information elitists looks down on, but readily use. And why not? Who says the people can't manage knowledge in a rigorous fashion, can't come up with valid definitions and explanations? Let's see what the WikiNet has to say about Oneness, salvation, and religious cosmology.

In Hinduism we run across the concept of Moksha. "Moksha is a final release from one's worldly conception of self, the loosening of the shackles of experiential duality and a re-establishment of one's own fundamental nature, though this nature is seen as ineffable and beyond sensation. Moksha is achieved when the individual Atman unites with Brahman, the source of all phenomenal existence — through practice of yoga."

Here we have a framework to work within. At the same time, we have an empirically proven system — yoga — which, if successfully practiced, allows you to attain the Oneness state.

As for Sikhism, pretty much the same approach: "According to Guru Nanak, the founder of Sikhism, the goal of the human is to unite with God and for this the Sikh must conquer the ego, thus realizing his true nature, which is the same as God."

According to Buddhism, "the whole universe is a single, dynamic web of energy. There is no almighty God in Buddhism. There is no one to hand out rewards or punishments on a supposed Judgment Day. Buddhism is not strictly a religion in the context of 'owing allegiance to a supernatural being.' There is no savior concept in Buddhism. Although a Buddhist seeks refuge in the Buddha as his incomparable guide who indicates the path of purity, he makes no servile surrender. The Buddha is not an incarnation of God. The relationship between the Buddha and his disciples and followers is that of a teacher and student. The liberation of self is the responsibility of one's own self. Buddhism does not call for an unquestionable blind faith by all Buddhist followers. It places heavy emphasis on self-reliance, self-discipline and individual striving."

As concerns Christianity, "Creation now has its end and purpose in Christ. Therefore, and not surprisingly so, Christian interest in cosmology and creation has changed from being concerned with matter or technique to one of relationship, that is, a dependency on the creator not only for his creation but also for subsistence." Interesting that the author here uses the word "changed," as in the Christian interest in cosmology and creation has changed from being concerned with matter or technique to one of relationship. What does this mean? It simply highlights the evolutionary aspect of Christian doctrine, how it changed course as a result of the Arian controversy, how it demoted the idea of self-realization in favor of a process that featured the intervention of Church authority.

Again, Elizabeth Clare Prophet: "If Jesus was a man who became God's Son, it implied that other men could also become Sons of God." Sound familiar? It should, because it sums up the ontology of most of the other major religions. However, "this idea was unacceptable to the orthodox, hence their insistence the Jesus had always been God and was entirely different from all created beings. The Church's theological position was, in part, dictated by its political needs. The Arian position had the potential to erode the authority of the Church since it implied that the soul did not need the Church to achieve salvation."

In contrast to Eastern religions that encourage their followers to self-realize, Christianity veered away from the practice of certain techniques (yoga, meditation, etc.) to attain a state of Oneness. Its stated purpose urges followers to conform.

As far as righteous living goes — a set of moral standards for daily life — what more do you need than the Golden Rule? "Treat others as you would like to be treated" or its Judaic counterpart, "What is hateful to you, do not do to your neighbor." Most religions share this ethic of reciprocity. If the world's population observed these pronouncements, it's hard to imagine crime or war existing. But that's another issue.

If the goal of religion is enlightenment or salvation, above and beyond a moral code for leading a good life, then the various religions have done a poor job. Wars, pogroms, crusades, jihads, persecutions, sexual molestations, inquisitions, witch hunts are only some of their failings.

Religions are touchy, they don't like criticism. Ever hear of confession? Sounds like 1984. Big Brother, permanent inquisition. Ferreting out heresy: doubt, individual initiative, the inquisitive mind. Not only in the Christian religion, but in other religions as well. And let's not forget how orthodoxies such as Education, Medicine, Politics frown on originality and individuality. The Church of Scientology uses the term "squirreling" to denote its heretics.

Better to accept the governing teachings of one's chosen religion without questioning. But what are the governing teachings? According to a NY Times article about a test on basic religious knowledge, most true believers don't know very much about the teachings they, as members of their given faith, are supposed to know. In fact according to the test, they know less than non-believers about their chosen faith. It's almost as if people don't care what they believe in. Instead of, *Let me explore and find the answer for myself, they say, It's too much trouble, just tell me what to believe in.*

So if the majority doesn't really understand what they believe in, why should you bow to pressure from those who don't know have a clear idea of what they believe in? According to Bill Maher, 15% of the American populace are atheists-agnostics, non-believers. Yet, according the poll cited in the NY Times article these non-believers know more about the various religions than their own adherents do;

they scored better on the test.

How is that possible? Most non-believers were once believers, or were at least exposed to certain beliefs by their parents. Once they began to doubt, they ran the precepts and doctrines they were taught through logic and fact checks. That means they studied the various religions in order to substantiate their claims and found inconsistencies and anomalies along the way. Which was enough to turn them into non-believers. That doesn't mean they've stopped looking for something to believe in; it means they have applied Ouspensky's dictum of questioning everything you see, hear, or feel. Not a bad credo to live by.

So what about the believers who scored poorly? What does that say about them? Must they know a lot to be saved or awakened? Or is fervor and zeal enough? It depends on what you're trying to do. If you're trying to speak in tongues or become carried away by Pentecostal practices, then you probably don't need to know all that much. You do what you do on faith and you try to enter into the spirit of the moment; exhaustive doctrinal knowledge is not necessary. If on the other hand, you are interested in the mystical proposition, that of "merging with the creator" or spiritual awakening through meditation practice, then you have to find the path that suits you, and that demands study, not the least of which is the study of the self.

Where does that leave traditional religion? Somewhere in a vast, yet vague, middle ground with nothing much to do except debate points of dogma, lording it over the rest of us — non-believers, mystics, and Pentecostals alike — who tackle spiritual practice head-on. Yes, they probably know more that we do. But without a true spiritual practice to follow, they have a lot of time on their hands, so they set themselves up as bodies of judgment, judging you and your dedication. Are you truly dedicated? Are your thoughts pure enough? Are you a doubter? Are you squirrelly?

Do you really need someone examining your thoughts, judging

you for them? Not if you obey the Golden Rule, you don't. That's all the religion you need.

Traditional religion has failed. Why? Because it's largely a political creation; the people involved in actual religious practices are few and far between. Like the army or big business, only 20% are down in the trenches doing the work; the rest — the 80% — are politicking your future, deciding whether to include your name in this months "to be downsized" list, checking on the purity of your commitment. Yet you cling to the mainstream, in hopes of escaping immanent danger. What danger? That is never revealed, all the better to keep you afraid of the future. Shouldn't this spur you to take it upon yourself to discover the truth?

Contrast the traditional approach with the Arian[55] notion that teaches men can transform themselves into Sons of God. What's the common sense difference between the traditional and the mystic path? Well, for one, to follow the Arian path you don't need an army of supporters, supernumeraries, spinmeisters, and sycophants. By and large this work must be done alone — with you, yourself, at the helm. Two, since you're on your own, there's no one challenging your approach; no one calling you a heretic, no one blaming you because you doubt. You don't have to conform. So, adapt a pragmatic, empirically scientific approach to finding the truth. Challenge everything you see, hear, or feel. Refuse to take the word of some institution or individual many times removed from the source. Armed with an ethic of reciprocity and a meditation method like GFM, and perhaps, a touch of yoga or Tai Chi, seek and find the truth by yourself. If you do, your path might look

---

55 Arian, used inclusively. Encompasses early Christians and others who believed through spiritual practice men could attain union with God, much the same way they believed Jesus and other adepts had done. Gnostics, Siddhartha Gautama, Pathagorians, Neoplatonists, Catharists. Sure there are differences among these groups, but by and large they sought awakening or union with God through personal practice. I call it Merging with the Creative Superstructure of Life, or the Energy Continuum.

something like this:

You don't have to feel guilt and you don't have to contribute money. No one's going to get burned at the stake because you meditate in the quiet of your own room.

Look at the growing numbers of those striking out on their own path. Compare them to the numbers of those leaving conventional religions. And not just for reasons of disillusionment, sexual molestation and the lot. People are tired of top-down, people are reading and thinking more. People are experimenting with everything from tattoos to the personalization of religion – the self-awakening process, self-realization. Can the truth — the Way, the Path, whatever you want to call it — only be handed to you by some authorized representative of orthodox religion or can you find it within by using your wits and trusting your eternal nature?

Spiritual But Not Religious (SBNR)

Spiritual but Not Religious (SBNR) is the title of a current Tricycle Magazine article, which I glimpsed passing through the checkout line at my local CO-OP. Before reading the article, I immediately started to ruminate on its theme and thesis, thinking I'd take a whack at it on this blog, not so much as a rebuttal — I hadn't yet read the article — but as an alternate take on the topic, which most people agree has become a mantra, if not a bromide.

Its ever-evolving course shows up in the following Google Ngram query as a narrowing of, and also a decline in, the usage frequency of Religion, as well as a rapprochement of the two, spearheaded by an uptick in the Spiritual.

I n this special section from the Spring 2017 issue of *Tricycle*, religion scholars, journalists, and laypeople share their thoughts on a phenomenon that is here to stay: the rising number of people who identify as spiritual, but not religious.

As Professor of Religious Studies at Rice University William B. Parsons says in his introduction:

"During a year of research among the religiously unaffiliated, for example,

Rapprochement of Religion and Science

My guess is the thesis of the Tricycle article is that interest in formal religion has decreased significantly over the past 100 years, but of all religions, Buddhism is the least "religious" and the most "spiritual." Which may be true. True or false, could you imagine the Pope bragging about how spiritual, as opposed to religious, Catholicism is? I can't; it's not in their DNA.

And yet, I don't know if my guess is accurate, nevertheless here's an explanation for why people have become more "spiritual:"

1) It's a sign of the times. It's hip to be different; it's hip to explore the latest. Due diligence be damned, if it's first in the Google rankings, go for it. Choose ideas from various methods and persuasions. No rules, make your own.

2) There are so many new religions, sects, new-age persuasions. Sects, based around the worship or teachings of a single person, abound. Many pay only lip service to established religion.

3) The Internet allows access to thousands of competing ideas. Someone mentions a new trend, look it up on your iPhone. Google yourself into a new set of beliefs, after all there's a stodgy aspect to your parents' established religion.

4) From sex scandals to embezzlement, the frightful corruption surrounding religion has not only driven church members away from their traditional religion, it has driven them away from organized

religion altogether.

Being spiritual is an inclination, like becoming a baseball fan or a lawyer. You're drawn towards it. Heaven knows why. If someone asked you why, you'd be hard pressed to give a cogently coherent reason. Religion is also an inclination, mixed in with a dose of environmental and social programming passed from generation to generation. The programming and societal indoctrination obliges you to pass along adherence to your offspring and even, in some families, pressure your child to become a priest or minister.

One hundred years ago, you'd stick to your parents' religion. Today, they may not even have a religion. Whether they do or not, you're no longer expected to stick with the religion you inherited from your parents. You're free to follow your own inclinations.

Is it reasonable to assume that a child born into a religion, say in China, were he to be born in Afghanistan, would not adhere to the religion of his alternate place of birth?

As the new age progressed, SBNRs seem to be looking for more radical practices, often acting like thrill seekers. Many are now focusing on kundalini, much to the occasional chagrin of some seekers, as things don't always turn out the way one wants. It's a solitary endeavor; there are dangers attached.

Kundalini is not an inclination; it's a biological process, an expression of consciousness, and as such, an instrument of great power and energy. That you might be interested in activating kundalini does not guarantee you'll be able to. Yes, there are methods, but success is never certain. The likelihood of its randomly striking someone who's never heard of it and is totally unprepared appears to be greater than the likelihood of your willfully activating it.

Consciousness envelops and drives the universe, its biological processes and evolutionary impulses. Kundalini acts like psychic fuel, driving evolution forward.

At this point (see image below), I realized Tricycle wasn't posting the full article, only a come-on, to the their website, so I headed back to the store to purchase it:

I n this special section from the Spring 2017 issue of *Tricycle*, religion scholars, journalists, and laypeople share their thoughts on a phenomenon that is here to stay: the rising number of people who identify as spiritual, but not religious.

As Professor of Religious Studies at Rice University William B. Parsons says in his introduction:

"During a year of research among the religiously unaffiliated, for example, the American writer Kaya Oakes encountered many more people who dip in and out of various Buddhist traditions than people who actually identify as Buddhists. To help with background, historian Matt Hedstrom sheds some light on little-known Protestant educational trends that may have paved the way for contemporary mindfulness. Religious studies scholar Andrea Jain offers an example from the world of yoga that parallels some of the strongest critiques—familiar to *Tricycle* readers—of spirituality as a consumer product. And finally, Diane Winston, a journalist and historian of religion, relates her experience teaching an undergraduate class in which students seem neither religious *nor* spiritual."

Spiritual but not Religious

The article, I discovered, is not one, but a series, of which I've read the first two. Here are some quotes from the introduction by William B. Parsons.[56]

"Walt Whitman announced this shift in 1871 when he observed that the 'spirituality of religion' would issue forth only in the 'perfect uncontamination' and 'solitariness of individuality' — an utterance that signaled the move to an unchurched, nontradition-al, even anti-institutional orientation towards the divine."

"Carl Jung proposed that religion was not outside us, in insti-tutions, but inside, in the very deepest part of our unconscious. In fact, the essential truths at the heart of organized religion can be known by diving deeply into the self. Terms like 'peak

56 https://tricycle.org/magazine/spiritual-not-religious-table-contents/

experience,' 'self-realization,' and 'individuation' are all legacies of this approach."

The articles endorse my thesis that 'direct experience' is what SBNRs are searching for.

Perhaps, the writer also remembers that Carl Jung was one of the driving forces behind the rediscovery and legitimization of *The Secret of the Golden Flower*, one of the first books to bring the theory and practice of 'energy cultivation' and 'direct experience' to the West — a book with a roadmap for activating kundalini.

Kundalini and God

Back in the 50s when I was young, bars and taverns featured philosophical discussions in which showing off your vocabulary and your syntactical prowess played a large part. Mastery of debating and spoken language was important. Perhaps we had fewer distractions — no iPads, no Internet, no Netflix, no Kindle Fire, no TV remotes. You had to get up and walk across the room to change the channel. Pretty much a linear world. Books opened on page one and proceeded to the last page, cumbersome LP records loaded, then played from track one to the end. No hopping around, no random channel zapping.

Did this paradigm affect our train of thought, our self-expression? Probably. I remember formal discussions, often centered on theology — God vs. no God, free will vs. predetermination, life and afterlife, — often quoting Aristotle, Thomas Aquinas, Voltaire, Bertrand Russell, and other sources, many of whom had been dead for hundreds of years. We were closer to classical literature then, closer to formal expression and grammar. For example, we took pains to use "few" correctly, instead of lumping paucity under the all-inclusive "less." Not only did we discuss in bars, impromptu forums were everywhere: around campfires, on trains, in schoolyards and campuses, even in Army barracks.

During one discussion I remember fading into a kind of

beer-soaked reverie, a moment of clairvoyance in which I was a separate entity outside myself, watching the words come out of my mouth, people's arms waving, beer being swigged. It was as if I was a ventriloquist's dummy someone else was manipulating. Yes, it was me talking, but the words weren't really mine; I was a mouthpiece for something I'd heard or read. I felt a shudder, as if I was, and had always been, involved in a vain search for recognition, a desire to be taken seriously, in spite of the second-hand nature of my words.

I wondered if anyone had answers. Or were we simply verbal shadow boxers, some more eloquent than others, aimlessly repeating without any empirical basis to our thoughts? Were we merely casting opinions, hoping others would somehow fall under the spell of our words?

There had to be another way of exploring these issues. Endless discussion around beer-laden tables was not it. Quoting the cognoscenti led to nothing. But what way was there? And if there was a way, was it worth pursuing?

Whatever it was, instinctively I knew I would have to find it myself, go it alone. I would have to step outside groupthink and conventional wisdom, stop repeating what someone else thought or how someone else had rationalized the existence or non-existence of God.

My search led me to yoga and kundalini, and back to the very essence of my Being, like the following Tagore poem suggests, coming back to where I started:

The time that my journey takes is long and the way of it long.
I came out on the chariot at the first gleam of light, and pursued my voyage through the wildernesses of worlds leaving my track on many a star and planet.
It is the most distant course that comes nearest to thyself, and that training is the most intricate which leads to the utter simplicity of a tune.
The traveler has to knock at every alien door to come to his own, and one has to wander through all the outer worlds to reach the

innermost shrine at the end.
My eyes strayed far and wide before I shut them and said 'Here
art thou!"
The question and the cry 'Oh, where?' melt into tears of a
thousand streams and deluge the world with the flood of the
assurance 'I am!'

Activating kundalini in 1973 was serendipitous, but unintentional,
in that, yes, I was meditating, but at the time, I had never heard of
kundalini. I stumbled into it as a result of my meditation practice. I
didn't really understand what might happen should my meditation
practice succeed. Heck, I didn't even know what 'success' might bring
or if there was such a thing as success in the work I was doing. Back
then, it wasn't like it is today; there was very little information on
kundalini and I didn't even start looking for it until my awakening
happened, mainly because I didn't know what to look for.

Forty years later I now understand the futility of polemics. The
only thing that matters is experience, and what you see, hear, and
feel during your experience. Reading won't get you there. Neither
will science, law, education, religion, money, or good works. If they
worked, we'd all be illuminated.

Kundalini takes no position on God; it merely connects you
to the energy continuum. Trouble is people (very intelligent people)
will see you as an advocate of religion, despite the fact that kundalini
is a biological process, at once agnostic and ecumenical. To activate
it you do not have to follow rituals or say prayers. No invocations, no
learning of doctrine, no chanting the names of Saints.

There are no cultural, no language, no geographical barriers to
activating kundalini. No religious prerequisites either. An individual
can do it if he/she is a Christian, a Jew, a Muslim, a Buddhist, a
Hindu. Or none of the above — a person without religious affiliation.
Once I realized this, I said to myself, Hey, this isn't religion; this is
science, albeit a kind of self-empiricized science that most people
refuse to recognize.

Unfortunately, one of the constraining factors around kundalini is that, once an experience like this (a kundalini activation) happens, one looks around for verification and support, and the only place one finds it is in Hindu, Taoist, and/or Buddhist texts. So the initiate throws in his/her lot with Eastern religions...for a while, at least. But if he/she starts to examine the issue as I have over the past 40 years since my kundalini activation, he/she sees that what happened to him/her could happen to anyone. And he/she begins to see the scientific ramifications of his/her experience, begins to realize kundalini is neurobiology with metaphysical, not religious, overtones.

The danger is getting so carried away with religious fervor that you miss the science. It leads to getting tainted with the kiss-of-death Spirituality label. There is a term that describes this work but it's not spirituality, it's Metaphysical.

What's the difference? you ask. Spirituality has become a cliché. Ask 50 people to write down a one-sentence definition of spiritual and you get 50 different, contradictory answers. The word has no meaning. Metaphysical, on the other hand, is clear: it means beyond the physical.

So be careful. Just because you feel a religious fervor on awakening kundalini, don't say you spoke with God or saw Him if you didn't. For instance, perhaps, you saw a white light accompanied by feelings of absolute bliss, but don't assume that God is somehow in the light, not an anthropomorphic representation, that is. God IS there, just as God IS everywhere. The God I'm talking about, however, is as much the consciousness of the Energy Continuum as it is You in your self-realized state.

Try to catalog your experience scientifically. Include only the realities you see and hear. Don't start with someone else's assumptions. Yes, there is an Energy Continuum, but just because you now perceive and are part of it doesn't mean that you have to embellish it. That only does a disservice to those who are trying to gain mass critical acceptance for kundalini. Yes, the Energy Continuum is wonderful, like Disneyland to a child, but place yourself in it accurately. Don't get labeled as a spiritualist. At the very least, step back from your experience to evaluate it. Is it a scientific experience or a religious one? It's got to be one or the other; it can't be spiritual, because the word has no meaning. If religious best describes it, realize you get nowhere. People will call it spiritual and lump you in with cultists and fanatics. If metaphysical best describes it, then it's scientific, because metaphysics is the science of that which lies beyond the physical. Never forget kundalini is a direct result of physical activity. A greater consciousness rising out of mechanical pieces and parts, namely your breathing apparatus and your sexuality — neurobiology at its most potent.

So, if you come out spraying a lot of new age mumbo-jumbo, everyone you talk to will be thinking it's all in his/her mind. Don't give them the satisfaction of lumping you in with religions based only on faith or spiritual cults based on accepting someone else's arbitrary opinions. Try relating it to the real world. You'll find there's no separation. They flow into one another — the physical into the metaphysical.

Just because you can't furnish empirical proof that science accepts today, doesn't mean your experience isn't real. In time it will be empirically proven, once we have the tools and/or the means to do so.

Today, we have the nouveau atheists, Stephen Hawking, Richard Dawkins, Christopher Hitchens, Sam Harris, who carry on about God and no God. More words, cleverly put together. It's still only opinion. And it's beside the point. They are talkers, not doers. And metaphysical knowledge cannot be gained by talking.

Do they have a case? Absolutely, their arguments about the limits of religion are correct; everyone should read their books. Accepting anything on faith is wrong minded. But they add no empirical evidence to the matter, just more rationalization.

Ask yourself: Why do neurobiologists ignore kundalini? If they're really investigating the neurological effects of biology, shouldn't they be investigating the most powerful means of enhancing the brain? Should they really be saying the only way to study the brain is from the outside-in, not the inside-out?

Whether it's from the side of religion or the side of science, it's only so much talk. No one knows without doing. The problem with doing is there's a tendency is to overdo. To get carried away with religious fervor when it's really a scientific experiment you've just lived through, one that took place in the laboratory of your body.

The Cosmology of Kundalini

"Until we can consider who or what started the Universe and controls it, it is probably simpler to use the term Nature to describe the creative, organizing force behind life."

~ *Design for Destiny* - Edward Russell

Self-Realization Begins At Birth

Consider the words of Indian author, Tarun J Tejpal:

"The greatest book in the world, The Mahabharata, tells us we all have to live and die by our karmic cycle. Thus works the perfect reward-and-punishment, cause-and-effect, code of the universe. We live out in our present life what we wrote out in our last. But the great moral thriller also orders us to rage against karma and its despotic dictates. It teaches us to subvert it. To change it. It tells us we also write out our next lives as we live out our present."

The Alchemy of Desire - Tarun J. Tejpal

The author insists that Karma can be "improved." Whether it actually can or not, I don't know, but because of personal experience, I lean toward believing.

I came to *The Secret of the Golden Flower* (SGF) through serendipitous happenstance. It was only after I started practicing the method that I realized its empirical value as a manual for activating kundalini. *Deciphering the Golden Flower One Secret at a Time* pays homage to those ancients: Chinese, Tibetan, and Indian, who, during solitary, self-imposed exile, developed techniques for self-realization. I believe that my journey closely parallels theirs much more than it does the more modern, feel-good, New-Age Western approach so prevalent today.

It wasn't an ability to see beyond my circumstances that led me to start meditating. It was a combination of dire straits, detective work, and luck. But something in me blazed — some spark of self-awareness allowed me to find the right, and only, means (The SGF) to restore me to my perfect body. There was also a personality component: I'm resilient.

After a childhood accident, my body slowly imploded. As a consequence, my abilities in math and music disappeared. The changes were physiological, caused by interference with vital nerve conduits — the result of my refusal to tell doctors about the splinter lodged in my ankle. This is difficult to understand because most people live their entire lives with their bodies in a single morphological state. They experience normal growth, and do not lose faculties or abilities and do not change their base morphology.

My 1977 meeting with Gopi Krishna in Kashmir was my first encounter with a confirmed kundalini practitioner/researcher. He got me thinking beyond the difficult-to-reconcile spiritual aspects of kundalini. He got me wondering about kundalini meditation as a scientific process and a kundalini awakening as the result of an experiment — one performed in the laboratory of the body. A deliberate and repeatable experiment, the techniques for which, can be passed along.

Gopi Krishna was the first person to understand my condition completely. And he provided me with practical information on living with kundalini.

Kundalini practitioners are like the people in *Close Encounters of the Third Kind* (1977) — obsessed. They undertake a great journey, and like most explorers they want to share their experiences with others. I wanted to write my story earlier, soon after it occurred in 1972. However, much like Gopi Krishna, I felt I had to wait until the experience ran its course. Little did I know I would still be experiencing the after effects some forty years later. Still, not a single day goes by without some concomitant due to kundalini.

The changes wrought by kundalini are:
- Heighten and enhance consciousness to effect a release from Karmic bondage,
- Increase psychic abilities, astral travel, OBE, as well as creativity,
- Reverse self-destructive and addictive behavior, be a better problem solver,

- Trigger autonomic self-healing, retard the aging process,
- No longer fear death.

This is a mere subset. I have experienced most of them in one form or another; I was attracted to The SGF because of its stance vis-à-vis the real world:

> "When there is a gradual success in producing the circulation of the light, a man must not give up his ordinary occupation in doing so. The ancients said, 'When occupations come to us, we must accept them; when things come to us, we must understand them from the ground up.'"

Living with kundalini is something most people don't think about while they are trying to raise it. My GFM method takes about a year, but once raised, you live with its effects for the rest of your life. There is a never-ending period of adjustment. Whether it's benign or not depends on how open you are to it. Kundalini not only changes your metabolic and somatic systems, it affects how you relate to the world and to others emotionally.

If we didn't inhabit bodies, there would be no material attachments, no negative emotions, war, greed, pride, fear, pain, etc. Kundalini makes us feel we should be rid of these things. But however petty, selfish, imperfect, or foolish the world outside may seem to you, despite living in a body primed with kundalini energy, you are still human. At the same time kundalini is developing greater consciousness, you cannot neglect real world obligations.

I have worked hard at developing a foolproof method for activating kundalini — one that works for every individual. Nevertheless, we are all different. Some people, try as they might, are not able to activate it. Not only is Prana involved (psycho-sexual fuel), it must "collide" with nodes in the brain that govern essence (primal consciousness), and the collision must take place in a kind of Quantum event which determines success.

It may take critical mass to vet Golden Flower Meditation, or any other method for that matter. Are we on the right track to achieving critical mass? I think the numbers show we are. Unfortunately, there are also indications that we aren't.

There are many types of kundalini awakenings: deliberate, permanent, temporary, accidental, casual. Gopi Krishna's and mine were permanent, but that doesn't mean we are set for life. Kundalini only provides fertile ground for continued spiritual development. Nothing is automatically granted; the work is never done.

The aftermath is just as problematic as the actual awakening. So are the reasons and the motives for undertaking the activation process in the first place: you should have a good one. It's not a casual or frivolous undertaking.

I believe I was lucky in that respect. Forty years ago when I activated kundalini, I had never even heard the term. Unlike many today, I wasn't looking for extraordinary powers; I was practicing a breathing method, hoping it would repair my body and help me center myself.

Once activated, everything came together. It's been that way ever since; it's the gift that keeps on giving — once you realize you have to surrender to its power.

I don't regret my past. I was lost and now I am found. In fact, living a self-destructive life taught me to be empathetic, to put myself in the place of others. In this era of narcissistic self-aggrandizement and self-absorption, empathy is an indispensable human quality.

When I started, I didn't know what I was doing. Headstrong trailblazing, perhaps, but my ignorance allowed me to press forward without second-guessing myself. And it just so happened that the method I discovered — the backward-flowing method — doesn't allow the energy to travel up the wrong channel in the spine.

If you think about it, there's always a first time, always someone out on a limb, doing it on their own. I am one of them. I didn't realize until later that I was using my body as a laboratory. Yes, there are pitfalls, but as Gopi Krishna pointed out there are very few people — even in India — who could answer his questions about kundalini with empirical authority. Yes, you can do it with supervision, but how do you know the person supervising you knows more than you do? And suppose you do encounter problems, how can another person really help? Are they expert enough to channel your kundalini energy correctly or will they simply comfort you by talking common sense? In the end, each person has to find the techniques that work best for him/her. It's not like dancing or cricket where coaches can correct improper form or posture. We're working with inner space where self-observation plays an all-important role.

There are systems that work and systems that don't. There are systems that work for certain people, but not for others. At the beginning supervision is useful, but there are Gurus who tend to have something else going on. If that something else involves the cult of personality or money grubbing, then it's not useful.

The SGF talks about sexual sublimation, Gopi Krishna talks about it. So do I, and many others. As for my process, I didn't say, "I'm going to sexually sublimate." I simply learned to breath correctly. The sexual sublimation process was a seamless by-product of correct breathing. Once you master Diaphragmatic Deep Breathing, you should feel an energy build up in the lower belly. At this point, you command the energy to change direction, which draws distilled sexual energy (Prana) up the spine to the brain. My book, *The Backward-Flowing Method: The Secret of Life and Death* explains the process in depth.

As for why Gopi Krishna found the topic so hush-hush in India, Indian friends of mine tell me that Gurus talked about kundalini in terms of religious doctrine, thereby excluding those practices that are inconsistent with their doctrines.

Americans are caught up in an opposite paradigm. To raise kundalini, there are thousands trying everything from harmful drugs to intensive yoga to drinking exotic tinctures to questionable Tantric practices. Gurus/Teachers, whatever their origin, are territorial, out to protect their own domains. Sadly, there's very little collaboration, very little sharing of information as challenges are encountered and new techniques come to the fore.

"Self-realization begins at birth; it is the journey as much as the destination."

The Energy Continuum

I don't know if the phrase Energy Continuum originated with me; I don't care. What I do know is it's the closest I can come to expressing what I perceive to be the reality of what can only be termed consciousness that extends beyond the physical, material dimension we like to believe is all there is. I use it because it applies to my observations and experience. It's what I have observed since my kundalini activation provided me access to the metaphysical dimension, allowing me not only to see beyond the material world, but also into the inner workings of a metaphysical subsystem within my own body.

At present, my accounts cannot be disproved or proven by the scientific community, only discounted as anecdotal. The fact that thousands of kundalini adepts and near death experiencers (NDEs) have witnessed and merged with the Energy Continuum holds no sway with scientists. That's fine. Nevertheless, these accounts, though anecdotal, are the first wave in what will ultimately become a tidal wave of scientific exploration on the Energy Continuum, and on Consciousness with a capital C.

Discounting the existence of the Energy Continuum is actually silly. Why? Because so much energy is spent by scientists/atheists and their religionist counterparts in proving/disproving God/No God theories — theories that cannot be proven or disproved.

As stated previously, there is no evidence for, or against, either of the two positions: God or No God. None. But there is evidence, albeit anecdotal, for the Energy Continuum.

This should actually please the respective sides of the God/No God argument. Sadly, it doesn't. They've been at it so long, they can't foresee an end to the argument, even though, if they'd settle for what we do know, thanks to mountains of first person kundalini and NDE accounts, they might drop all the posturing about a notion (God or No God) which, at this time, is neither provable nor disprovable. Drop it and do what, you ask. How about trying to piece together the various accounts of the Energy Continuum and extended Consciousness?

What kind of accounts? We're talking about out-of-body, kundalini meditation, Near Death, astral travel, kundalini experience, Energy Healing, consciousness, and psychic prescience. I'm sure I've left someone or something out. I'm sorry. But there are so many firsthand accounts that metaphysics (that which exists beyond the physical) has got to be more than coincidence, more than synchronicity. It has to have some foundation, or one out of four people are crazy. I'm not crazy. I have seen the other side and it is continuous (as in everlasting) and full of intelligent energy (as in conscious energy). Others — too many to ignore — have also witnessed or become immersed in the Energy Continuum, each in his/her own individual way. Each has his/her story to tell. Why not join forces to study these experiences?

Yes, there is resistance. It comes in many forms, people who say things like:

- It's all in you mind.
- There's no proof.
- Science does not accept anecdotal evidence.
- Death is like the crash of a motherboard.
- It's not a question of belief; it's a question of faith.
- There is no heaven or afterlife for broken down computers.

Why should this discussion matter to someone pursuing self-realization or metaphysical truth? Why should you care if no one believes in your experience? Is it worth trying to convince closed minds to open and to remain open?

Think about it. When you choose the path of faith and belief, you give up your power. You become subservient to the argument you support; you become subservient to someone else's opinions; you become subservient to polemics, useless discussion of something that cannot and does not affect your life, your health, your conscious refinement, or your being. What do I mean?

If you are truly interested in self-realization, you will forget polemics; you will concentrate on practice, secure in the knowledge that there is an Energy Continuum. Why should you take my word for it? You shouldn't. But the fact that you are reading these words means that something has piqued your interest in the subject. Most likely it wasn't a discussion in a bar about the non-existence of God or a sermon in church about the existence of God; it was an actual physical sensation or an energetic experience. Something inexplicable happened in your life: a feeling of weakness followed by a renewal of strength, a moment when you felt great clarity, the ability to heal yourself and others, an instant of energy surging up your spine, an out-of-body experience, clairvoyance, some unusual feat of dexterity, a precognitive vision, the capability to control heart rate or body temperature, extraordinary somatic awareness, scientific or artistic inspiration, and so on. In short, a metanormal experience.

What mattered most to you was the certainty that your sensation or experience was real, not a figment. So what do you do when someone attributes your sensation or experience to mania, madness, mental illness or aberration? What can you learn from this sort of criticism? Simply, that it's better not to talk with close-minded people. You can't get anywhere by arguing. So don't. Redouble your efforts and continue to practice, knowing that many are doing the same. They may not be using the same techniques or the same method, or even the same terminology. Respect that, knowing that they were probably "piqued" by a metanormal experience in much the same way you were.

There's an energy revolution on this planet. I'm not talking about the energy we extract from the ground. This revolution is taking place in the bodies and souls of men and women. This is the millennium of the Energy Continuum, man's last greatest frontier. If we are to survive on this planet and in this universe, we must find a way to master the negative aspects of our Beings, to change our consciousness as we move forward in a complex, unforgiving, technological world.

Metaphysics - The World Beyond the Visible World

Kundalini, Out of Body Experience (OBE), and Near Death Experience (NDE) are related. Each begins as a physical experience that ultimately triggers a variety of metaphysical phenomena, yet only NDE is studied in the Psychology Departments of large universities and in medical schools, in spite of the fact that strict corroboration by the scientific method has not yet happened. But like so many discoveries in science, just because they are not corroborated until the moment they are discovered and verified doesn't mean they do not exist. No one knew about the endocrine system, DNA, atomic power, or genetic code before they were discovered. Doesn't mean they did not exist.

OBE, NDE, and kundalini are brought about by physiological conditions (breathing exercises and arousal of sexual energy in the case of kundalini), which almost immediately induce metaphysical (beyond the physical) experiences, and that's where scientists balk. At least many of them do, however...

Dr. Sam Parnia, a critical care doctor and director of resuscitation research at the Stony Brook University School of Medicine, studies what people experience in that period after their heart stops and before they're resuscitated.

> "The experience that people have is very personal and it's very real to them. So, for most people who've gone through these experiences, as far as they're concerned, what they've experienced is absolutely real. They've described and seen something of the other side. Now, for those of us who haven't had the experience, it's impossible to verify that, but in the same way that, for

instance, if a patient comes to me and says, 'I have depression,' it would be completely unacceptable for me as a physician to simply discard that experience and say, 'Well, I don't think [so]. You may feel that you're depressed, but actually it's an illusion of having depression or you're hallucinating. Your depression, it's not really real.' So we have to remember that to the people who've had the experience, it's real to them."

"In his new book *Erasing Death: The Science That Is Rewriting the Boundaries Between Life and Death*, Parnia examines the experiences patients describe, but whereas much discussion around the experience of death has been philosophical or personal, Parnia is looking at the subject scientifically."[57]

Although many people feel that NDE stories are too far out, many others do not. Obviously, one's upbringing, lifestyle, and convictions influence acceptance of these accounts.

Why is NDE Being Studied?

For two reasons. One, there are corroborated accounts of NDEers, who have been declared clinically dead, being able to cite observations, identifying certain factual information only occurring during the time they were certifiably dead. For instance, a nurse wearing a yellow dress comes into the hospital room of a "dead person." Later, after the dead person is revived and he/she sees the nurse who wore the yellow dress a few days later, he/she complements the nurse about the "yellow dress," even though the nurse is now wearing a green dress and only wore the yellow one once, during the time the patient was declared clinically dead.

Two, because, even though the accounts of individuals who have undergone an NDE cannot be completely verified by present means of physical science, they are plentiful, common, and ubiquitous, and that means critical mass.

And what is science all about if it's not critical mass? Think about it. If one elephant talked, it'd probably be called witchcraft.

---

57 *Erasing Death: The Science That Is Rewriting the Boundaries Between Life and Death* - Sam Parnia, http://amzn.to/2C6gW3K

But if elephants all over the world started talking, scientists would investigate and it would be considered worthy of study. And the graduate research students they use as cheap labor would be begging for a chance to work on the phenomenon to get recognized. Energetic young people able and willing to undertake the work of testing, discovery, and data classification. That's the difference between kundalini and the NDE — critical mass and the fact that kundalini experiences vary so much from one individual to another. Nevertheless, kundalini is a physiological, and as it progresses, a metaphysical, reality. A biological actuality. Yet, so far, scientists have not recognized its study value. But if the NDE is worthy of scientific investigation, so is kundalini. NDE and Kundalini induce the same effects, exhibit the same characteristics, use the same biological subsystem to effectuate the transition from physical to metaphysical.

Why Have Scientists Neglected Kundalini?

Why not investigate the links between 'L-Field' research, OBEs, NDEs, Kundalini, and *The Tibetan Book of the Dead*? A body of information at the very interface of physical and metaphysical.

The reason kundalini has not attracted scientific research is money. The same reason that science in the 1940s turned away from the startling discoveries of Royal Raymond Rife, who, like myself delved into the sub-molecular structure of life — each one of us from different angles.

"After activating the kundalini-life force energy, I was able to see the blueprint of my perfect body..."[58]

My empirical research in the laboratory of my own body resonates with Russell, Rife, and Tesla among others.

"That is an extremely crude illustration of the way in which the 'fields of life' keep the changing atoms, molecules, and cells in the same pattern. The human electromagnetic field, of course,

---

58 *Deciphering the Golden Flower One Secret at a Time*
   - JJ Semple, Life Force Books, 2007

is infinitely more complicated than an ordinary magnetic field because it contains many local or 'sub-fields' of the atoms, molecules, cell and organs which, to some extent, interact with it. Despite this 'feed-back' from the subfields there is plenty of evidence that the overall field of the body is primary and controls its component fields."[59]

Belief Systems and Kundalini

"In meditation, we practice observing our thoughts, seeing them come, seeing them change, seeing them go. They are a phenomenon of the mind, empty of any permanence. We discover that we are not our thoughts. Our inner witness or observer bears testimony to this. In the same manner, we must practice observing our beliefs. They come, they change, they go. They also are a phenomenon of the mind, empty of permanence. In this manner, our inner witness can become an instrument of compassion, not of judgment, with those who do not share our particular beliefs."[60]

~ *"Being Overly Identified With Our Beliefs"* - Mehru Danda

Beliefs are like being slowly poisoned. You don't know it's happening until you're half dead — in this case brain dead.

Not all beliefs are harmful: believing that your dog has a spiritual connection with you harms no one. But believing that your religion is the one and only truth is largely the result of cultural indoctrination and social conditioning accompanied by harmful — sometimes even militant — proselytizing. But I'm not out to generalize; I'd rather look at my own case as honestly as possible — a survey of my beliefs over the decades, what I've done with them, how they influenced me, or not.

First, let's remove facts from the discussion; facts are not beliefs.

Beliefs are like hypotheses with emotional baggage. Instead of trying to validate a belief, like we would a hypothesis, we accept them for a variety of reasons, usually because of social or cultural pressures. When young, everyone is exposed to a variety of beliefs.

---

59 *Design for Destiny: Science Reveals the Soul* - Edward Russell, (1970)
60 The Kundalini Consortium, http://www.kundaliniconsortium. org/2015/12/being-overly-identified-with-our-beliefs.html

If they take hold, they're hard to get rid of, even subsequently, when doubts surface. And when people construct political systems around beliefs they become doubly dangerous.

Beliefs are relative, not absolute. Relative, that is, to surrounding environmental factors. They are not an inherited byproduct. In other words, beliefs are not the result of heredity or some sort of ontological programming passed on through DNA. They are derivative.

Luckily, I was moved around so much as a child that I was mostly confused, rather than zealous or devout. Prejudice never took hold. As for religion, I admired some of the liturgy and literature of the Episcopal Church, but the doctrines left me thinking: there must be something else — something that didn't involve an anthropomorphic being somewhere in the sky. Something more tangible. I didn't stop to think what it might be; that was way beyond my ken. How could there be something that bridged the seemingly unbridgeable gap between myself and some sort of God? As an entity, I felt limited. It didn't occur to me that religion had probably sprung up as a result of man's feeling just that way — small and insignificant.

Well, after many hardships I found the bridge. I won't go into the details; my books do that. They're all about my discovery and practice of kundalini meditation, which is not a belief system but a physical-to-metaphysical transformation process, one that involves the body as much as it does the spirit.

I should like, however, to point out that kundalini reinforced my inherent skepticism. It reengineered my cognitive essence so I would question everything I saw, heard, or felt. Does it do this to every person it touches? From what I've observed, the answer is no. Some people are so dependent on set beliefs that they keep replacing outmoded or debunked beliefs with new ones in spite of the fact that they have already discarded many sets already. Is this harmful? Unless what they believe in concerns violent political or religious opinions, I can't say for sure. I just wonder why kundalini was able to wipe my psyche clean while other kundalini adepts still adhere to beliefs that are, at best, unproven hypotheses. My reality filters are gone.

If kundalini can't consistently expunge unverifiable beliefs, what can? Once again, science comes to the rescue:

"New research involving a psychologist from the University of York has revealed for the first time that both belief in God and prejudice towards immigrants can be reduced by directing magnetic energy into the brain.

"Dr. Keise Izuma collaborated with a team from the University of California, Los Angeles (UCLA), to carry out an innovative experiment using transcranial magnetic stimulation, a safe way of temporarily shutting down specific regions of the brain.

"The researchers targeted the posterior medial frontal cortex, a part of the brain located near the surface and roughly a few inches up from the forehead that is associated with detecting problems and triggering responses that address them. In the study, half of the participants received a low-level "sham" procedure that did not affect their brains, and half received enough energy to lower activity in the target brain area. Next, all of the participants were first asked to think about death, and then were asked questions about their religious beliefs and their feelings about immigrants.

"The findings, published in the journal Social Cognitive and Affective Neuroscience, reveal that people in whom the targeted brain region was temporarily shut down reported 32.8% less belief in God, angels, or heaven. They were also 28.5% more positive in their feelings toward an immigrant who criticized their country. Dr Izuma, from the University's Department of Psychology, said: "People often turn to ideology when they are confronted by problems. We wanted to find out whether a brain region that is linked with solving concrete problems, like deciding how to move one's body to overcome an obstacle, is also involved in solving abstract problems addressed by ideology." 61

What these experiments mean to me, a layman, is that there are regions of the brain that store beliefs and certain types of energy

---

61 Belief in God and prejudice reduced by directing magnetic energy into the brain – Science Daily https://www.sciencedaily.com/releases/2015/10/151014084955.htm

directed at those regions may affect the severity or degree of one's attachment to said beliefs.

Of course, some people are already saying this kind of experiment is dangerous because scientists might also be able to replace one belief system with another. Nevertheless, it appears to be one more indication that beliefs are relative, not absolute. But even though they are relative and replaceable, this research has me wondering why some people seemed to be hard-wired in their belief in opinions that are counter to proven fact, climate change, for instance. Is it because the parts of the brain that store beliefs are "walled off" from the parts of the brain that deal with skepticism and logic?

As Long As We Inhabit Bodies...

Talk about you are what you eat! When you apply it to ingrained cultural habits, it takes on a whole new meaning:

"Patriotism is the fond memory of food eaten in childhood."

~ Lin Yu T'ang

This statement is very profound. Extended to its logical conclusion it means that our national identities — as symbolized by national flags — could actually be represented thusly:

- American - The Hot Dog
- French - The Baguette
- German - Sauerkraut
- Philippines - Chicken Adobo
- Spain - Paella
- Morocco - Couscous
  and so on...

You don't have to agree with Lin Yu T'ang's statement, but you must admire his logic. He's saying that the foodstuffs we grew up with and cherish are really unifying cultural elements. They unite us — send us out as a group to do battle against the "other." They are the things that really bind us together. He's hinting it would actually be more honest to send us out under the banner of The Hot

Dog or The Cheeseburger or The BLT than any arrangement of abstract symbols of stars, crescents, stripes in assorted colors.

We identify with our cravings; we form societies around them and, as long as we inhabit bodies, we never quite get over them, to the point where the images of our favorite foods are always foremost in our minds at times of stress, boredom, or respite.

For example, in the service and required to walk a 4-hour guard duty shift on shipboard or on land late at night, what did my thoughts eventually turn to? Not... was someone going to jump out of a tree or mow me down. I kept my eyes and ears open on duty; I was vigilant, but at the end of a long shift, I always seemed to conjure up the image of a bowl of cornflakes, a peanut butter and jelly sandwich, or a cheeseburger. I asked others what they thought about during their tour on guard duty. Always the same refrain: food fantasies, some special dish. We might not — each one of us — crave the exact same dish, but the choice always came from a common taste pool: the dishes Americans identify with.

That's why it's so difficult to be a traitor; most people cannot renounce the foods they grew up with. Think about the things that tie you to your roots and food comes up big. For most people, it's in first, second, and third place. Not only do we identify with foods, we become adept at justifying their consumption, in spite of the dangers inherent in many of our favorites.

Over forty years ago my awakened kundalini displaced my exploratory relationship to drugs with something much more powerful, but it never completely purged my affection for the foods I loved as a child. For many and most, food is the final addiction.

Today, I eat completely differently — 90% raw. I haven't eaten a cheeseburger in 20 years; I couldn't digest one. Same goes for most of the foods I used to pine for on those long, lonely tours of guard duty. I no longer think about them, but I understand how dangerous they are and I do understand their attraction.

Each one of us inhabits a different body, with different tastes and different cravings. Imagine if we were bodiless beings of pure spirit. All of these cravings, all our longings would disappear. They will disappear as soon as we become pure spirit, which inevitably we will.

How do I know this? My kundalini awakening revealed it to me. It's our evolutionary path. Without bodies there are no needs, no cravings, no addictions, no negative emotions. Today, we cannot envisage such an existence. That's fine. Before we traveled to the moon, many thought it impossible, or never thought about it at all.

Is it reasonable to believe our evolution is at an end, that no further evolutionary developments can ever occur, that the form our bodies take today will be the same in 10,000 years? And if we do evolve in form, will our immaterial and metaphysical aspects not evolve as well?

So what form will future bodies assume? A second head, another arm? Or will future evolution concern mostly the brain and the up-to-now mostly esoteric capabilities associated with energetics. Given the current runaway interest in kundalini, I'd be surprised if kundalini didn't hold some surprises as to our future evolutionary development.

Bodiless beings are not for next week or next month. We must survive eons of challenges to our physical forms, but eventually we will shed those elements that bind us to our earthly limitations. Our bodies being one of them. The first step can be taken now — through meditation practice.

Finally, if it's any consolation, are not the growth and acceptance of ethnic foods already changing the visions we conjure up when famished. Fifty years ago when I walked guard duty, I had only standard American fare to excite my imagination. Today's soldier has a panoply of ethnic cravings to draw from. As we begin to accept foods from other cultures — the cooking shows on TV offer an endless array of ethnic shows — will our interest in other cultures not increase? And, as a result, gradually allay the feelings of otherness we reserve for foreigners?

Will we still be doing battle under the banner of the Hot Dog in 2518? Or will Pizza or Moo Goo Gai Pan replace it?

How Kundalini Communicates With The Rational Mind

Does kundalini communicate with the rational mind? And if it does, how does it work? Does it send mixed signals or try to trick the rational mind? Most accounts identify some kind communication between the super-conscious kundalini and the rational mind. So how does it work?

I want to address this issue because it was raised in a post by a commenter calling himself go for the gold:

"The more I read the more confused I become. My experience of kundalini is not like others'. I was a neutral observer when I first experienced my kundalini awakening, which was by accident. Even so, the Kundalini Serpent is definitely its own entity, looks exactly like a serpent or a dragon, thinks for itself, and almost constantly sends ideas of deception up and into my frontal lobe without my permission."

To address this, we must first explore the cosmology of kundalini and its relationship to the formation of our Beings, and that takes us to The SGF:

"In this part there is described the role played by the primal spirit and the conscious spirit in the making of the human body. The Master says, The life of man is like that of a mayfly: only the true human nature of the primal spirit can transcend the cycle of heaven and earth and the fate of the aeons. The true human nature proceeds from that which has no polarity [the ultimate] whereby it takes the true essence of heaven and earth into itself and becomes the conscious spirit. As primal spirit it receives its human nature from father and mother. This primal spirit is without consciousness and knowledge, but is able to regulate the formative processes of the body. The conscious spirit is very evident and very effective, and can adapt itself unceasingly. It is the ruler of the human heart. As long as it stays in the body it is

the animus. After its departure from the body it becomes spirit
While the body is entering into existence, the primal spirit has not
yet formed an embryo in which it could incorporate itself. Thus it
crystallizes itself in the non-polarized free One.

"At the time of birth the conscious spirit inhales the energy and
thus becomes the dwelling of the new-born. It lives in the heart.
From then on the heart is master, and the primal spirit loses its
place while the conscious spirit has the power.

"The primal spirit loves stillness, and the conscious spirit loves
movement. In its movement it remains bound to feelings and
desires. Day and night it wastes the primal seed till the energy
of the primal spirit is entirely used up. Then the conscious spirit
leaves the shell and goes away.

"Whoever has done good in the main has spirit-energy that is
pure and clear when death comes. It passes out by the upper
openings of mouth and nose. The pure and light energy rises
upward and floats up to heaven and becomes the fivefold present
shadow-genius, or shadow-spirit. But if, during life, the primal
spirit was used by the conscious spirit for avarice, folly, desire, and
lust, and committed all sorts of sins, then in the moment of death
the spirit-energy is turbid and confused, and the conscious spirit
passes out together with the breath, through the lower openings of
the door of the belly. For if the spirit-energy is turbid and unclean,
it crystallizes downward, sinks sown to hell, and becomes a
demon. Then not only does the primal spirit lose its nature, but
the power and wisdom of true human nature is thereby lessened.
Therefore the Master says, If it moves, that is not good.

"If one wants to maintain the primal spirit one must, without
fail, first subjugate the perceiving spirit. The way to subjugate
it is through the circulation of the light. If one practices the
circulation of the light, one must forget both body and heart. The
heart must die, the spirit live. When the spirit lives, the breath
will begin to circulate in a wonderful way. This is what the Master
called the very best. Then the spirit must be allowed to dive down
into the abdomen (solar plexus). The energy then has intercourse
with spirit, and spirit unites with the energy and crystallizes itself.

This is the method of starting the work."[62]

In simplest terms, this passage describes how the primal spirit (the term the SGF uses for kundalini):

- Plays a role in the formation of the Being,
- Works in the background after birth,
- Can be re-awakened later on in life.

Notice that the word kundalini does not appear at all in the text. So how do we know we're talking about kundalini? This irony — the fact that we are talking about a particular phenomenon in other languages — is the result of having so many different traditions using different terms for the same thing. The translators of The SGF, Richard Wilhelm and Carl Gustav Jung,[63] — use *primal spirit* to denote kundalini. They use *conscious spirit* to denote the Mind/ Senses/Ego paradigm. To further confuse the reader, Jung bullied Wilhelm into using some of his favorite psychology terms: Animus for Conscious Spirit = Mind/Body/Senses paradigm and Anima for Primal Spirit = Kundalini. And they appear throughout the text interchangeably, and are misleading.

Kundalini Plays a Role in the Formation of the Being

Kundalini (the primal spirit) is the agent of Consciousness incarnate, the pervasive energy continuum that links all existence. It is responsible for your embodiment — creating it from a blueprint of your perfect body conceived before conception, and then transforming the plan for your perfect body into flesh and blood, embryo to fetus to newborn to adult. The primal spirit doesn't know algebra, how to balance a checkbook, or do crossword puzzles. It does, however, know the human body. It does know evolution and energy. It does know DNA. It's the non-verbal intelligence of the life force, that which needs no words to execute its evolutionary mandate.

After Birth, Kundalini Works in the Background

---

62 *The Secret of the Golden Flower* - Wilhelm Translation, pp. 28-29.
63 Author/Translator Thomas Cleary populates his translation with his own terminology and cosmology.

Kundalini (the primal spirit) works in the background after birth. Doesn't mean it no longer exists; every being has this subsystem in their body. It's like a warranty — you can use it at any time to renovate and re-engineer your body. If kundalini didn't serve a purpose, evolution would have eliminated it. That's how evolution works.

Trouble is, not everyone knows that kundalini exists. And many who've heard of it, dispute its authenticity.

Kundalini Can Be Re-activated in Later Life

However, before activating it, you first have to know that it exists and is standing by, waiting for you to activate it. There are many ways of activating it (triggers) and many changes that it brings about (effects). In fact, it turns the being into a Being. I can only speak for myself, and I have through my books, providing information on my kundalini activation, the challenges along the way, and the methods I practiced.

Nevertheless, *The Biology of Consciousness: Case Studies in Kundalini* does feature nine accounts of kundalini activations with different triggers and a variety of effects. Its purpose is to help readers become aware of the vastness of kundalini interest in today's world. Obviously, these accounts are not exhaustive.

Back to how kundalini communicates with the rational mind and whether it sends mixed signals. I can only testify that signals/messages do bubble up from the non-verbal consciousness to the verbal mind. And for me they have been benign.

This is an issue I've written about extensively, for instance in a previous chapter "Is Kundalini Intelligent?" that features Jill Bolte Taylor's account of left-right brain interactivity during her stroke. It's an excellent explanation of how the primal spirit (kundalini) takes over when the left brain shuts down. Kundalini (the life force, and all its other pseudonyms) is always benign, whether it's telling you what not to eat or it's trying to save your life. It has certainly never told me to smoke a cigarette, in fact, just the opposite: It recoils from the very thought of cigarettes, has me gagging if I'm around smokers.

Kundalini communicates via the nervous system, which stimulates psycho-cognitive activity. If you fight it, the message can get distorted by filtering it through too much reflexive social conditioning. Open your heart. Don't try to control kundalini energy. Remember, after activation, IT does YOU; you no longer do it.

After living with an active kundalini for more than forty years, I've found that it (kundalini) clears away the conditioning that the rational mind and senses imposes, and I am able to receive and process messages/instructions/signals (or whatever you want to call them) from the unconditioned "energy continuum/total mind/ life force," and they are always benign. Mostly, they have to do with making right choices, such as things to avoid.

I'm not talking about delusions or messages from an anthropomorphic God. I'm talking about messages that concern health and "right living," knowledge that kundalini receives from the Energy Continuum:

- Controlling negative emotions.
- Practicing self-remembering.
- Practicing meditation and yoga.
- Avoiding material attachments.
- Avoiding addictions and harmful foods and substances.
- Taking care of the body

If it weren't for conditioning, we would all be tuned to right living — acting more in accordance with the life force and its benign, non-verbal dictates.

The Biology of Consciousness

In the New Age consciousness has become a buzz word, a mass movement. Yet consciousness is related to human biology, a fact most people are unaware of. They see the treetops, but not the roots. *Deciphering the Golden Flower One Secret at a Time* is a case study on how kundalini overhauls biology — brain cells, morphology, and metabolism, even genetic profile — to create a new human being in one lifetime. That is the power of kundalini. The potential is there

The question put forward, extrapolated from my experience, is: With the adoption of systems from other cultures, such as meditation and yoga as well as the veritable explosion of New Age "self-realization" systems could the mass experimentation with these techniques ultimately trigger an acceleration of human evolution or will we have to wait for evolution to simply take its course? Is there sufficient critical mass to allow the various self-realization techniques to push humanity over the threshold of higher consciousness or do these techniques only produce temporary change in a given individual? If we could influence evolution by the mass practice of these techniques, which ones work best?

Yes, there are many paths, many systems, many techniques; they work in different ways. Some work by improving the individual's outlook and worldview. Some actually overhaul the entire being. But how many of them alter brain chemistry in any significant fashion? Because that is where higher consciousness is forged. In my case, an activated kundalini altered my somatic, metabolic, and genetic core, rearranging me physically.

While practicing a given system, one often becomes a devoted disciple, forgetting to evaluate the results with a critical eye. Does the system I practice actually produce results? Am I changing? How? Is my brain chemistry changing? For instance, am I able to function at a higher level? Do I have a greater existential awareness? Could I possibly give up intercourse and use my distilled sexual energy for sublimation purposes? How can I prove I am changing? Can I demonstrate altered brain chemistry? Or have I only convinced myself that I must be changing because I'm an eager follower of such-and-such a system?

Is there a scientific way of confirming altered brain chemistry, a way of showing that Method A alters brain chemistry more completely than Method B?

Right now, scientists combating Alzheimer's offer solutions for increasing, or stabilizing, brain cell propagation — cognitive techniques of all sorts, from tic-tac-toe to Monopoly to crossword puzzles to attention, memory, and coordination games. There are websites devoted to these types of exercises. Websites that after a few free rounds ask you to pay. Here's how one site, Lumosity, describes their neuron rebuilding program:

> "The Human Cognition Project makes it easy for neuroscience researchers to study the questions that advance their research in ways that have not been previously possible. The ease of use and engaging nature of the Lumosity programs means that people enjoy doing the training, making it easy to recruit and retain participants in university-based studies. It also means that the database of users worldwide is growing everyday, giving researchers a new venue for exploring cognition not previously available. With over 14 million members worldwide having played hundreds of millions of games, Lumosity has the largest database of human cognition ever assembled. Researchers are actively exploring this database to understand the determinants of cognitive performance and cognitive enhancement — all in an effort to make the world a smarter place."

For all the buildup it's not really scientifically certain that cognitive exercises prevent the onslaught of dementia. So what about New Age consciousness enhancing methods? What about traditional methods, like yoga and meditation? What is their track record?

I'm not sure there is one, except for scattered, unfiltered anecdotal reports. Unfortunately, scientists don't approve of anecdotal data. Even the thousands of statements related to Near Death Experience make them uncomfortable, despite the fact that similar statements are collected from people who don't know each other, live in different places, belong to different religions, and don't share a common culture. Doesn't the notion of critical mass begin to apply here?

It's the same for kundalini, for Tai Chi, for Reiki, for meditation methods of all sorts, for all New Age proclivities and predispositions. It's up to each of us to find a means of quantifying the neural regenerative aspects of a given system and then comparing the results with, say, cognitive game therapy such as Lumosity. In the future we will have to work together, but with so many different types of awakening experiences we can start by exploring the brain chemistry altering capabilities of a science like kundalini meditation, which actually floods the brain with dementia fighting substances, derived and distilled from sex energy.

Spotlight on Consciousness Research

You've visited imaginary worlds and other dimensions in science fiction movies, in comics and in novels. Are they just the writer/director's hallucinogenic fantasies? Or are these dimensions actually KNOWABLE? If so, how can we prepare ourselves for this type of altered perception?

Jacob's Ladder. The Matrix. Memento. Altered States. Fictional worlds in which material reality suddenly melts away and the protagonist is left to fend for himself in harrowing, seemingly unreal situations. We believe these worlds to be figments of the writer's imagination. But are they?

These so-called imaginary worlds are as real the people, streets, houses, and stores we encounter in our normal daily rounds. Although we cannot see these apparitions in our current state, scientists and other investigators are finding they are real. Moreover, they are not the threatening specters moviemakers would have us believe — but simply exist beyond the reach our limited consciousness.

At a key moment in *Jacob's Ladder*, Jacob's friend, chiropractor and guardian angel Louis (Danny Aiello), cites the 14th century Christian mystic Meister Eckhart — "Eckhart saw Hell too; he said: 'the only thing that burns in Hell is the part of you that won't let go of life, your memories, your attachments. They burn them all away. But they're not punishing you,' he said. 'They're freeing your soul. So, if you're frightened of dying and... you're holding on, you'll see devils tearing your life away. But if you've made your peace, then the devils are really angels, freeing you from the earth.'"

This is straight out of *The Tibetan Book of the Dead*. In fact, this film is a fictional interpretation of a Near Death Experience (NDE). At the end we see "Jacob never made it out of Vietnam." His body is shown in an army triage tent just as he expires. Apparently, the entire series of events turns out to have been a dying reverie. Jacob's experiences appear to have been a form of purgation in which he releases himself from his earthly attachments, finally joining his dead son Gabe to ascend a staircase (Biblically known as Jacob's Ladder) toward the bright light."

The science of consciousness, or should we say the scientific investigation of it, inevitably delves into the unseen — that which lies behind the physical — the metaphysical. This investigation is now moving forward on two fronts (metaphysical investigation and physical science) toward the same objective, namely the full unfolding of consciousness, or as Gopi Krishna called it: "Knowing the Knower."

Much investigation is still outside the realm of traditional science, yet, as metaphysical exploration moves forward, we apply more scientific methods, which caused me to wonder, "Who's to say that the same scientific methods we apply in the physical realm won't someday apply to the metaphysical realm? The NDE provides palpable evidence of meta-physicality."

Again, this exploration is being conducted by two informal, loosely-knit research tendencies, not by any sanctioned organization. Nevertheless, it moves forward with a dynamic élan, prompted, I believe, by what Gopi Krishna called "the evolutionary impulse." Metaphysical investigators explore consciousness from the inside-out while physical scientists explore it from the outside-in. Instead of sniping at one another, they need to cooperate.

Group 1: Metaphysical investigators

Metaphysical investigators, those who have undergone Kundalini/NDE experiences, write about them from the inside-out, just as a 16th Century explorer might have kept a journal of his adventures during a sea voyage. This inside-out group is headlined by such researchers as Gopi Krishna, Richard Bucke, J Krishnamurti, and PD Ouspensky, who cautioned that metaphysical research in the laboratory of the body deserves a rigorous methodological approach:

> "There is no question of faith in all this. Quite the opposite, this system teaches people to believe in absolutely nothing. You must verify everything you see, hear, or feel. Only in that way can you come to something."

In *Deciphering the Golden Flower One Secret at a Time* I described the insights gained in the Energy Continuum thusly:

> "After activating the Kundalini-Life Force, I was able to see the blueprint of my perfect body and compare it to my actual state. Amazingly, the Life Force recognized my deformity and immediately began to correct it. I witnessed it slowly reshape my body to the exact proportions in the blueprint.
>
> "I could see my original design and the fact that it is perfect means that an unseen sentient entity in nature created it before my incarnated body came into this world."

These observations are alluded to in the writings of other kundalini researchers, such as Michael Bradford — already quoted in a previous chapter, repeated here for its relevance:

> "This control and guidance is also evident in the experiments done with developing animal embryos in which the removal or substitution of tissue, if done at an early enough stage, does not result in a totally deformed final form but rather in a smaller or modified, but still complete form. If the process of development were strictly a mechanical one, this would certainly not be the result. One logical explanation for this phenomenon is the

existence of a controlling field, such as the pranic spectrum, which has a predetermined form towards which it is guiding the development of the organism via the growth processes."

In *The Backward-Flowing Method: The Secret of Life and Death*:

"Where this blueprint had been stored between the time of my conception and my 35th year, I did not know. Physical scientists, geneticists, in this instance, would probably say it resides in the brain, and that is a safe assumption, for, until we can prove it resides outside the body, we must assume it is somehow connected to it, as in lines of code stored in DNA. Nevertheless, the fact that I saw the blueprint and watched the Life Force energy use it to "reengineer" my body makes me think that some sentient agency must play a role in reproduction, and in the design and formation of the body. Why had this blueprint suddenly reappeared? Where has it been for thirty-five years? Why is the Kundalini-Life Force using it? If it had no purpose, wouldn't it have ceased to exist? So then, it must have a purpose, for it is still there."

In *The Biology of Consciousness: Case Studies in Kundalini*, I continue this discussion on the controlling field (an outside the body meta-physical entity):

"As applied to my situation, the 'controlling field' referred to in the above passage used a blueprint of my perfect body to manage my embodiment. The changes in symmetry I experienced were due to neural blockages caused by the splinter — blockages causing a massive redistribution of growth energy throughout my body. Ergo, my transformation from a symmetrical to asymmetrical being. Not only did this newly awakened pranic energy (kundalini) reverse this process, it started it going in the other direction, namely from asymmetrical back to symmetrical. It healed me, and it did so intelligently, which made me realize it had access to DNA and other evolutionary information about the intended form of my being. And that is what I base my hypothesis about kundalini's ability to modify DNA on: finding a way to restore and revitalize the affected body parts, a process that included conforming my body to the blueprint for its intended embodiment. It still amazes me that 35 years after my birth, this 'controlling field' or super-consciousness went back to my 'archives,' found the blueprint, and used it to restore my body to its original, intended state and form."

Group 2: Physical scientists

Physical scientists, such as Dr. Harold Saxton Burr of Yale University, who explored field theory in the 30s.

"Physicists define a field something like this: when something occurs somewhere in space because something else happened somewhere else in space, with no visible means by which the cause produced the effect, the two events are connected by a 'field.'

"As everyone knows, when we sprinkle a card with iron filings and hold it over an ordinary magnet, the filings will arrange themselves in a pattern that represents the 'lines of force' of the magnet's field. And though we can change the filings as often as we like, each set of filings will always assume the same pattern.

"Even by the most pedantic, therefore, the 'fields of life' can be considered a scientifically-respectable phenomenon, eligible one day for the imprimatur of the hierarchy. When that will be will depend on how long it takes biochemists to lose their enthusiasm for present fashions (and perhaps for economic interests to open their focus to cost-effective natural vs. patented chemical solutions)."

If this is true, then:
- The fact that we do not perceive these states/fields means our current consciousness is inhibited,
- There is consciousness in every field/cell.

As author Sol Luckman points out:

"A salient point in the evolutionary model I am elaborating is that evolution of species ultimately is driven not by material, but by metaphysical energy, or consciousness, of a spiraling, 'meta-genetic' nature.

"If today we are to embrace a worldview in which consciousness is more important than matter, we need to base our timekeeping on the nonphysical, invisible reality (that gives rise to reality) rather than on the physical."

If both groups combine their efforts, they will uncover conditions that make the themes explored in science fiction a reality, enabling, as Gopi Krishna so aptly phrased it, "a state of perception where the invisible world of intelligent cosmic forces will be cognizable to every human being."

Happiness Influences DNA

Recently, researchers discovered that the type of "happiness" an individual experiences actually influences that individual's genetic profile.

The researchers examined the biological implications of both hedonic, pleasure seeking happiness, and eudaimonic[64] happiness, contentment from a life of purpose and meaning, through the lens of the human genome — a system of some 21,000 genes that has evolved fundamentally to help humans survive and be well.

The researchers drew blood samples from 80 healthy adults who were assessed for hedonic and eudaimonic well-being, as well as potentially confounding negative psychological and behavioral factors. The team used the CTRA gene-expression profile to map the potentially distinct biological effects of hedonic and eudaimonic well-being.

While those with eudaimonic well-being showed favorable gene-expression profiles in their immune cells and those with hedonic well-being showed an adverse gene-expression profile, "people with high levels of hedonic well-being didn't feel any worse than those with high levels of eudaimonic well-being," Cole said.

Both seemed to have the same high levels of positive emotion. However, their genomes were responding very differently even though their emotional states were similarly positive.

The study, published in the Journal Proceedings of the National Academy of Sciences, said doing good and feeling good have very different effects on the human genome, even though they generate

---

64 According to Aristotle, eudaimonia actually requires activity, action, so that it is not sufficient for a person to possess a squandered ability or disposition. Eudaimonia requires not only good character but rational activity.

similar levels of positive emotion.

Apparently, the human genome is much more sensitive to different ways of achieving happiness than are conscious minds," said Steven Cole, a University of California, Los Angeles, professor of medicine.[65]

From the above, it follows that our behaviors (such as the ability to put oneself in another's place, care for, and/or empathize with others) impacts DNA and DNA transmission. Couple this with practices (such as yoga, meditation, Reiki, Tai Chi) that actually trigger super-consciousness and you have a well-rounded recipe not only for influencing DNA, but for self-realization as well.

Imagine a feedback instrument capable of monitoring the levels of eudaimonic well-being in real-time. With this type of instrument, everyone — not just kundalini adepts — would receive continual feedback on their behavioral states and would be able to "pull themselves back" to the eudaimonic norm when tempted to act selfishly or immoderately. Likewise, kundalini adepts, especially those in the early stages of awakening when disorientation prevails, would be better able to harmonize their behavior with the energetic forces of super-consciousness.

In the early stages after kundalini activation, the initiate gets pulled in many directions at the same time. Eventually, he/she is able to recognize, accept, and integrate the various effects and phases of the kundalini experience. Having a biofeedback device to monitor behavior would help initiates integrate the pranic energy kundalini generates.

Now I realize that studies like the above may leave you scratching your head, wondering if it's for real. Is it science? Is it metaphysics? Is it gobbledygook? Does it have any real world value? Is the author citing another study and moving on, leaving me, the

65 A person's type of happiness can affect their genes - https://www.upi.com/Health_News/2013/08/01/A-persons-type-of-happiness-can-affect-their-genes/UPI-78311375412636/

reader, to derive what I can, hoping I won't question the study's authenticity?

All I can add is: I wasn't there when this study was conducted. So let me see if I can make it more relevant by relating it to my own experience.

After my kundalini activated, most of my hedonistic tendencies disappeared immediately. I didn't have to work on eradicating them, didn't have to pray to God to deliver me from temptation. Gone was the desire for drugs and alcohol. Gone was the thrill of wild parties. Chasing women: gone overnight. This happened when I was thirty five. I didn't have to grow old, watch myself continue to lust after the hedonic. I consider myself lucky. There's nothing more pitiful than watching someone of advancing age fall victim to continued dissipation. Once I comprehended the vastness of the force I had awakened, I gave thanks at no longer being motivated solely by the pursuit of pleasure.

A couple of years before this, while I was in college. I used to hang out in a bar on Pennsylvania Avenue, close to the George Washington University campus with a disparate group: students, young couples, artists, writers, professionals, quasi-criminals, recent graduates, job hunters. One day, two guys, who obviously weren't college students, showed up. At first, we thought they were attracted by the girls. But that wasn't it. It was the ambience, the camaraderie, at least at first. One guy I'll call Frank became an everyday regular. He liked being with the students, liked talking with us.

Turned out he had just retired from the US Navy at thirty-seven years old. He had a small apartment in Foggy Bottom, used to invite students for chili dinners on Saturdays. Beer and chili. No drugs, Frank didn't approve. It was in the early 60s, before drugs became a universal staple.

Frank spent more and more time in that bar, just drinking. I watched him age. His face was a journal of his condition. Day-to-day it reflected his worsening state. Not only did his whole appearance

— face, skin, hands, arms — age rapidly, he became glassy-eyed, as if he was looking through you while speaking directly to you. It was graphic, but in my hedonic state — my mid-twenties — I thought Frank just another good 'ole boy enjoying the ambience of the bar scene.

From stopping to chat with him, I began nodding and passing by quickly. Sometimes he'd be sprawled over his table, passed out. His friend would carry him home.

Having witnessed the efficacy of AA in my father's life, I tried to talk to Frank about it once. To no avail. The Frank that first walked into the bar shortly after his retirement was no more. He was an empty vessel, drained of sense and spirit. He lived to drink.

I frequently look back those early days with wonder at the person I once was. How I went one way and Frank another. Frank had his whole life in front of him. A generous retirement, a genuinely nice person, yet he drank himself to death at 38, one year after retiring. Why him and not me? I consumed as much as he did, was often drunker and more out of control. Yet, I have always been optimistic about life, believing that I would find ways to remove myself from the grip of bad habits and materialistic urges. This evolutionary impulse was very strong; it led me away from pessimism, fatalism, and negative emotion. It led me to kundalini meditation. I was able to change my nature and Frank wasn't. Thinking about Frank makes this study real for me.

By altering brain chemistry, kundalini produces an entirely new being, one much less inclined to hedonic, pleasure seeking happiness. It actually helps eudaimonic tendencies flourish.

I found meaning in my life and Frank didn't. I jumped five layers of Maslow's pyramid, from Belonging & Love Needs to the Self-Actualization layer in one do-not-pass-go leap. By the way, it wasn't me that jumped those five layers in the Maslow pyramid. It jumped me, Kundalini did. That's the way it works if you let it. Doesn't happen overnight. You have to surrender, not see it as some sort of character aberration or soul warp. Not fall victim to depression. And that's difficult because kundalini wants to erase your ego and start you over from scratch. An empty vessel that gradually integrates the wonders of super-consciousness into everyday life.

Kundalini drained me just as alcohol drained Frank. Two sorts of empty vessels: one whose ego, indoctrination, conditioning were swept away in one fell swoop by kundalini; the other a vessel whose soul was anathematized by alcohol. Kundalini tore me apart and put me back together the right way.

It's not like I went out one day to search for meaning; I didn't. I began a meditation practice that involved breathing. One thing led to another. Relatively basic breathing exercises led to the activation of a biological process that overhauled my being. Is this so unusual, something only I could accomplish? Is feeling happy the right way really so boring, so unexciting? Before kundalini, I felt the pull of hedonic living day and night, felt superior to people living normal lives. What a joke life plays on us — that the hedonistic life style our culture exalts is an illusion many discover too late. At the same time, being happy the eudaimonic way remains largely ignored.[66]

Evolutionary Biology and Kundalini

"A phenotype is an organism's observable characteristics or traits: such as its morphology, development, biochemical or physiological properties, behavior, and products of behavior (such as a bird's nest). Phenotypes result from the expression of an organism's genes as well as the influence of environmental factors and the interactions between the two."[67]

Kundalini is advanced evolutionary biology, in that it changes an individual's phenotype characteristics during a single lifetime. But since "Individual organisms do not evolve, they retain the same genes throughout their life" how is it possible to claim that kundalini

66 This material is excerpted from JJ Semple's book, *The Biology of Consciousness: Case Studies in Kundalini*, © Life Force Books and JJ Semple, 2014. All Rights Reserved.

67 Phenotype, Wikipedia - https://en.wikipedia.org/wiki/Phenotype

affects evolution?

"Populations evolve. [evolution: a change in the gene pool] In order to understand evolution, it is necessary to view populations as a collection of individuals, each harboring a different set of traits."[68] So if populations, but not individuals evolve, and yet kundalini affects Phenotype, why can't we say kundalini influences Evolution, especially at this moment in history when so many people are struggling to, or have already, awaken(ed) kundalini? If kundalini can modify phenotype, will the kundalini revolution not create a gene pool variation capable of influencing natural selection? We may not be able to quantify or analyze it today, but that doesn't mean it isn't happening. We are speeding up evolution because kundalini affects brain chemistry, and brain chemistry affects phenotype.

Then again, if it we were only talking about one, or several hundred, individual(s), it might be different, but the hundreds of thousands now practicing kundalini (energy cultivation techniques) are bound to produce genetic modifications and pass those modifications onto their progeny, thus creating suitable conditions for natural selection. We may not see it now just as we failed in the past to perceive the totality of human biology, just as we do not yet understand man's aggregate nature.

For centuries, man explored the body, gradually learning about its various sub-systems: Respiratory System, Cardiovascular System, Skeletal System, Digestive System, Muscular System, etc. The more physically "obvious to the naked eye" the sub-system, the more visible it was, the easier it was to locate. The Lymphatic and Endocrine Systems were less visible, therefore, they were "discovered" relatively recently. That doesn't mean they weren't there all along. Kundalini is an evolutionary actuality, a biological reality present in every living body. It belongs to an even more "invisible" sub-system, known as Chakras, or energy centers.

Authors like Gary Osborn describe the Chakras as "metaphys-

---

68 Evolution - http://abyss.uoregon.edu/~js/21st_century_science/lectures/lec09.html

ical counterparts to the endocrine glands." However, claims such as this are always followed by disclaimers that "these associations have never been scientifically verified." Nevertheless, kundalini, as a by-product of refined Chakra energy, is part of evolutionary biology, even though its presence — much like the Lymphatic and Endocrine Systems in the past — has not yet been detected by outside observers. Doesn't mean that it doesn't exist, only that it hasn't yet been discovered...except by the millions that have awakened it.

Passing on beneficial phenotypical characteristics through DNA — such as aptness/suitability for kundalini arousal — is greatly facilitated if the subject is symmetrical.

"Evolutionary psychologists claim that our preference for symmetry can be explained in the context of mate choice because symmetry is an honest indicator of the genetic quality of potential mates. These arguments assume that asymmetry in human faces is fluctuating asymmetry (FA), because this form of asymmetry can be revealing of developmental instability."[69]

...and also an honest indicator of the subject's aptness for a successful kundalini awakening.

Kundalini is a biological actuality, a phenotypical driver that occurs in spite of any environmental influences such as, religion, social status, political affiliation, culture, or education. These influences do not determine an individual's aptness or ability for activating kundalini. And this is its strength. It's like music. If you're a musician, you can take your music to Japan and successfully integrate with Japanese musicians, even though you don't speak Japanese.

So too with kundalini; it's trans-national, trans-cultural, and, most important trans-denominational. All of which speaks to the Oneness of life. That we are really intertwined in so many ways, in

---

69 Are human preferences for facial symmetry focused on signals
     of developmental instability? *Behavioral Ecology* - https://
     academic.oup.com/beheco/article/15/5/864/318486

spite of the self-imposed, man made barriers we erect to separate us.

Changing Human Nature

Once before a writer's forum, I thought it a good idea to read a book written by Matthew Fox, another member of the panel. I wanted to see if there was any synergy between us. The organizer suggested his book, Creativity. I'm glad I asked because I found the synergy I was looking for — a section on human nature in which he listed a series of attributes that we ideally should not exhibit:

- We are not consumers,
- We are not addicts,
- We are not passive couch potatoes,
- We are not boring,
- We are not cogs in a machine,
- We are not lazy,
- We are not destroyers.

Unfortunately, although we ought NOT to exhibit these attributes (consumer, addict, boring, cogs in the machine, lazy, destructive), we still do. At the moment, in our present state of consciousness, we are mere aberrations of the ideal human nature Matthew Fox believes us capable of.

Ouspensky said, "in our present state of consciousness we are asleep; we are machines; we are incapable of true knowing." So, how do we change our human nature? How do we stop feeling like "cogs in the machine?"

Remember *2001: A Space Odyssey*, Stanley Kubrick's masterpiece? Remember the much talked about black monolith that appears in the midst of a primitive tribe?

Walking out of the theater I had something no one else in my group of friends had. For some intuitive reason, I knew what the black monolith meant. I was certain that it signified a dramatic shift in consciousness, a symbol for man's first instance of self-awareness, a parable describing the discovery, the use, and the development of tools. Self recognizing other for the first time. Man, in effect, becoming modern man. The moment homo added sapiens to his pedigree. And if you think about it, the modern space shuttle is but a mere extension of the bone picked up by the primitive tribesman in Kubrick's film. In fact, there has been a greater lapse of time between the origin of man and the discovery of that first tool than the lapse of time between the discovery of that primitive weapon and creation of the atomic bomb.

In the intervening thousands of years since that primordial moment — the hand reaching down to grab the bone at the same instant the grabber realizes its deadly purpose — there has not been another existential leap of consciousness of the same magnitude. No new black monolith. No moment of greater self-awareness spreading like wildfire through the entire race. Sure, technology has moved ahead at a rapid pace, but outside of the development of the prefrontal cortex (the region of the brain devoted to higher cognitive functions), the development of the other lobes of the brain has been minimal. It's often said that man's decisions are still governed by his animal brain — emotions and feelings overruling rational centers.

What does this have to do with changing our human nature? In order to change our human nature we have to change our state of consciousness.

The reason human nature varies so greatly among individuals is because human nature is subordinate to the individual's current state of consciousness. The higher the state of consciousness of the individual, the nobler his nature. Unfortunately, the aggregate state of human nature at the present time has created a world of financial disparity, war, greed, illness, obesity, addiction, wide-scale sexual slavery, racial hatred.

Negative emotions, selfish habits, bleak outlook, addictions, lack of civility, aggressive behaviors, faulty cognitive processes have created a "lowest-common-denominator" societal standard. The negative behaviors we exhibit are a kind of backlash against frustration — because we feel like "cogs in a machine." We may even hate ourselves because of failure. That's when the trouble starts because: violence is a form of self-hate. Failure is not non-fulfill-ment; it is a learning opportunity.

In order to survive the changing conditions of overcrowding and diminishing resources, we can and must eliminate the negative aspects of a nature that makes us feel like cogs in a machine.

But we cannot change human nature by any traditional or orthodox means. Not by prayer, not by good works, not by psychology, education, philosophy, law, medicine, science, politics is human nature changed. Don't believe me? Ask Mao Tse-Tung, the most dedicated social engineer of the last 100 years. The Cultural Revolution in China attempted to exorcise commercialism, venality, greed, and selfishness. It failed miserably. To change our nature we must change our consciousness, which varies greatly from individual to individual.

> "Thus in life there is ever the intellectual and emotional nature — the mind that reasons and the mind that feels. Of one come the men of action — generals and statesmen; of the other, the poets and dreamers — artists all."
>
> ~ *Sister Carrie* – Theodore Dreiser

Kundalini wants to balance natural tendencies, to make the manager more poetic and the artist a better organizer. Does it always work this way? Can I predict how kundalini might affect you? Of course not, but I can show you how it affected me.

My books are about transformation. But so were the Middle Ages, about scourging the body in order to transcend it. My work isn't about scourging the body. It's about perfecting it in order to transcend it, in order to develop and maintain perfect health, cognitive awareness, and higher consciousness throughout life, and onward into future incarnations.

You see, we've moved beyond a purely religionist definition of transcendence. Transcendence can be as simple as surpassing one's early circumstances to become an artist, or as elaborate as dying on the cross. We now know — or at least we should know — that there is something beyond the physical, and we don't need prayer to invoke it. We can reach out and grab it. That is, we can take an active role in the process of connecting with the energy continuum. That is why my books are also about the biology of consciousness, about first principles, if you would, the steps to implementing a transformation of consciousness in the space of a single lifetime. We can use this process to heal and perfect our beings.

As Vivek Govekar stated so eloquently in Kundalini - The Catalyst for Evolutionary Leaps in Consciousness:

> "Unless there is a framework for scientific research that both provides support to those undergoing the trauma associated with the event and also carries out an in-depth analysis of the abilities, revelations and changes brought about post-awakening, we are missing out on valuable opportunities for using this phenomenon towards it's intended goal, the benefit of mankind."[70]

So how do we change our consciousness? That's the purpose of kundalini, the motivating catalyst behind the transformational experience. It's the key to changing our state of consciousness. How? Kundalini stimulates neuroplastic activity in the brain and, as a consequence, changes our very Being. All our behavioral aberrations vanish. We are no longer cogs in the machine.

So how do we change human nature? We don't. We run an "end run" around it; we change our state of being, our consciousness. How do we do this? By raising kundalini in a safe, permanent fashion. How does this work? My writings detail my process, but the upshot is kundalini produces an entirely new Being. It's an active process. You can't pray for it to happen; you can't do it by reading philosophy, by undergoing psychoanalysis, or becoming a scientist, lawyer or doctor. If the above were possible, it would have happened already because we've been doing these things for a long time... <u>without much</u> success.

70 http://www.kundaliniconsortium.org/
    search?q=framework+for+scientific+research+that+both+provides+support+

And you can't grasp it intellectually. Why? Because you can't see the mountaintop until you're on top of the mountain. And you can't get there without climbing!

As Bruce Lee said, "Knowing is not enough; we must apply. Willing is not enough; we must do."

You have to involve the whole being. How did I do it? I mastered three powerful meditation techniques: diaphragmatic deep breathing, control of heart rate, the backward-flowing method and, lo and behold, I was there, standing at the threshold of a new being. There are other ways, all with the same goal, namely Gopi Krishna's great hypothesis:

> "The aim of the evolutionary impulse that is active in the race is to mold the human brain and nervous system to a state of perception where the invisible world of intelligent cosmic forces can be cognizable to every human being."[71]

This is your true birthright: ever expanding consciousness — a process that has taken us "from hapless bystanders, surviving the vagaries of nature and at the mercy of circumstances, to users of tools, taking charge of our own destiny, almost immediately." A process that will take us even further in the future.

Many refuse to recognize that the process is only just underway, that in spite of the strides we've made — from caveman to modern man — there is a long way to go. They think we've reached the pinnacle of evolution, that the physical, material world is all there is. They pooh-pooh Near Death Experience and kundalini phenomena, don't think "meditation techniques, energy cultivation techniques, hallucinogens, yogic breathing practices, tantric sex" amount to much. In so doing, they deny their birthright, much the same way Esau — succumbing to his all too frail human nature — denied his.

But objective study of metaphysical states is happening. Dr. Sam Parnia, a critical care doctor and director of resuscitation research at the Stony Brook University School of Medicine, studies

---

71 Higher Consciousness and Kundalini, Gopi Krishna

what people experience in that period after their heart stops and before they're resuscitated. This includes visions such as bright lights and out-of-body experiences.

Near Death Experience (NDE) and Kundalini

Individuals who undergo a Near Death Experience (NDE) report a number of effects encountered during and after the experience. The same goes for those who undergo a kundalini experience (KE). What's interesting is that some, but not all, of the effects are the same; there's a definite overlap, even though they are different experiences.

For the moment, however, no physical science is able to attest to the certainty of the effects as reported. They lie outside what is perceivable with our five physical senses, and therefore what is perceivable with scientific instruments at this time. In other words, the effects experienced during these events take place within the metaphysical (meaning beyond the physical) dimension. In the future, who knows? Perhaps instruments will be capable of penetrating beyond the physical universe. It is not a question of belief; it's a question of technology.

Anyway, because NDE reports are so similar — in spite of the origins, locations, backgrounds of the participants — various university psychology departments and university hospitals are now saying that these anecdotal accounts are not only NOT imaginary — they are worth investigating. First among these is Doctor Sam Parnia:

> "Not just my study, but four others, all demonstrated the same thing: People have memories and recollections. Combined with anecdotal reports from all over the world, from people who see things accurately and remember them, it suggests this needs to be studied in more detail."[72]

As a corollary to this evidence, it follows that because the NDE and kundalini share effects, it is worth studying the kundalini experience <u>as well, using </u>all and every current and future method/technique.

72 Ibid

According to Sri Ramakrishna, "A man's spiritual conscious-ness is not awakened unless his kundalini is aroused." Kundalini is the motivating catalyst behind the transcendent experience. It's the key to your changing state of being. How? Kundalini stimulates neuroplastic activity in the brain, and consequently, the ability to see and experience life beyond the material, physical dimension.

How do we know this? The effects induced by kundalini are akin to those of the near death experience (the NDE). Kundalini shares a subset of effects with the NDE. NDErs frequently return from their experience with residual knowledge of the metaphysical dimension. What's striking is that these types of experiences are commonplace, and, one to another, very similar in nature, in spite of the individual's age, cultural background, geographical location, or religion. The individual returns with a greater understanding of his/her connectedness, enhanced creative impulses, the experience of being bathed in a strong white light, and the intense certainty that there is no death. According to Moshiya de Broek:

> "The common points are: traveling through a tunnel, life passing in revue and meeting loved ones. Most of them also speak of a heightened awareness in which they seem to enter an all-knowing consciousness that seems to know the answer to each question mankind has ever asked."

Moreover, the individual often returns with a feeling of no longer belonging to the physical world, or at least a feeling of the severe limitations of this world. Kundalini shares all these effects.

Cosmic Consciousness

The NDE offers a strong argument for disembodied cosmic consciousness. Again Moshiya de Broek:

> "These experiences happen during a time that the heart and brain show no activity on either the ECG or EEG scales (a flatliner). That some might argue the stop of blood flow does not mean there cannot be some weak electrical activity deep within the brain — an EEG only measures the electrical activity on the

surface of the brain — is for the moment beside the point. They should ask, according to neuroscience, is there enough brain activity to constitute being consciously aware? Decidedly, those types of brain activities appear totally absent in these patients. In fact, there is another problem which would seem to contradict present scientific insights: at a time when awareness should be reduced, if not totally absent, patients actually experience a clearer, wider awareness both in seeing and in hearing, although with a lessened brain activity. Present science says that it is improbable for someone to experience awareness with the absence of measurable brain activity."

If this is true, it means that our consciousness, or some portion our consciousness, resides outside the brain, outside the body, in a metaphysical dimension, unseen by normal people. If a person is deemed clinically dead, yet is able to observe goings-on in the physical world as well as the metaphysical, there has to be a strong case for disembodied cosmic consciousness. It would be one thing if a report of this nature came from a single individual, but that is not the case. Thousands, as cited above, have reported the same states, the same effects.

You can draw your own conclusions, nevertheless the evidence points to the patient's "consciousness" remaining intact outside the physical body during the brain dead phase, meticulously noting the activity in the room before being "reconnected" with the body at the end of the NDE. What's interesting about these types of incidents is that they only occur within the lapse of time that the patient is deemed dead. There is no overlap, eliminating the possibility that the individual witnessed the event or phenomenon before or after becoming clinically dead. And these accounts have happened more than once and have been verified as true by third party witnesses.

"Parnia's research has shown that people who survive medical death frequently report experiences that share similar themes: bright lights; benevolent guiding figures; relief from physical pain and a deeply felt sensation of peace. Because those experiences are subjective, it's possible to chalk them up to hallucinations. Where that explanation fails, though, is among the patients who have died on an operating table or crash cart and reported watching—from a corner of the room, from above—as doctors tried to save them, accounts subsequently verified by the (very perplexed) doctors themselves.

"How these patients were able to describe objective events that took place while they were dead, we're not exactly sure, just as we're not exactly sure why certain parts of us appear to withstand death even as it takes hold of everything else. But it does seem to suggest that when our brains and bodies die, our consciousness may not, or at least not right away.

"'I don't mean that people have their eyes open or that their brain's working after they die,' Parnia said. 'That petrifies people. I'm saying we have a consciousness that makes up who we are—our selves, thoughts, feelings, emotions—and that entity, it seems, does not become annihilated just because we've crossed the threshold of death; it appears to keep functioning and not dissipate. How long it lingers, we can't say.'"

How does the NDE compare with Kundalini?

People who have experienced one or the other phenomenon share many of the effects mentioned above. However, in the case of permanent kundalini, there are some effects that the NDE does not share. Kundalini triggers a superset of super-conscious effects. By stimulating neuroplastic activity, kundalini triggers autonomic self-healing mechanisms, restores health, and transforms consciousness. As opposed to the NDE, with kundalini, brain cell regeneration is a constant. Why? The kundalini process uses distilled sexual energy to refresh brain cells. Kundalini revitalizes the entire nervous system. It would seem impossible for Alzheimer's disease to exist in a permanently awakened kundalini body. This sounds like an extreme statement, obviously one in need of peer review. But if we concede to the kundalini practitioner the ability to experience metaphysical activity, especially since they, by definition, live in a permanently super-conscious state, shouldn't a brain stimulated by sexually sublimated life force energy evolve physically, or at least, degenerate much less rapidly than the brains of most seniors? And shouldn't these evolutionary characteristics be passed along to future generations?

What's more, with kundalini there is a change in the decision-making and lifestyle processes. That is what happens with a change of consciousness. The old individual is reborn in a Karmic sense. He or she is able to see and understand, sometimes for the first time, the moral and logical implications of each decision. Gone, one-by-one, are the old addictions, the old habits, the old conditioning, and the old emotional prisons. Finally, this new state of consciousness effects an overhaul of human nature. Over time our perverse and negative emotions vanish. We are no longer cogs in the machine.

There are thousands of NDE and KE accounts that reveal an energy continuum outside the present bounds perceivable to Western science. What's so special about these accounts? Why should we take them seriously? They occur irrespective of cultural, linguistic, geographic or religious influences. In other words, yes, they are anecdotal in nature, but, at the same time, asynchronous, disconnected in time and space. In fact, so disconnected it would indicate that the subjects (the individuals undergoing the experience) were in no way influenced by others undergoing similar experiences. Similar enough for any serious investigator not only to keep an open mind about the subject, but also to focus on proving/disproving the existence of this hypothesis — that the energy continuum exists.

Instead, neuroscientists tell us that the NDE is an hallucination. In a 2013 Scientific American article the author argues that Dr. Eben Alexander's book *Proof of Heaven* is not an account of consciousness existing separate from the mind, but only an hallucination.

"The reason people turn to supernatural explanations is that the mind abhors a vacuum of explanation. Because we do not yet have a fully natural explanation for mind and consciousness, people turn to supernatural explanations to fill the void. But what is more likely: That Alexander's NDE was a real trip to heaven and all these other hallucinations are the product of neural activity only? Or that all such experiences are mediated by the brain but seem real to each experiencer? To me, this evidence is proof of hallucination, not heaven."[73]

Notice how he uses the pejorative term "supernatural" as opposed metaphysical, a more respectful, scientific term. But that's what the conventional wisdom does: ridicule new hypotheses, instead of investigating them. In addition, the article was originally published under the title *Proof of Hallucination*, before it was subsequently changed to the current title, Why a Near-Death Experience Isn't Proof of Heaven. More misplaced ridicule, and very unscientific, because the article no more proves that NDEs are hallucinations than it proves that consciousness cannot exist outside the mind.

The only convincing point Shermer makes in the article is that Alexander did not see heaven. That much we agree on. But from Alexander's descriptions in his book, I do believe he "visited" the energy continuum, just like Jill Bolte Taylor did.

As for the argument that all NDEs are hallucinations, why do all NDE subjects have basically the same hallucination, despite the differences of culture, etc? If they were hallucinations, it would seem to me that they would differ. One subject would see himself in a poker game, another charging up San Juan Hill, still another making love to the Empress of China, and so on. I know my dreams are different each time. Why are all NDE accounts virtually the same?

How is the NDE related to kundalini? That the two share a set of similar effects is certain. That up to now, there is no empirical

---

73 "*Why a Near-Death Experience Isn't Proof of Heaven*" – Michael Schermer, Scientific American, April 2013 https://www.scientificamerican. com/article/why-near-death-experience-isnt-proof-heaven/

proof that either phenomenon can be scientifically observed is also accurate.

That makes it easy to discard, (even ridicule), the numerous anecdotal accounts of these phenomena. Yet, this disdain is so Western-centric, so Scientific-American, totally ignoring centuries of research that has taken place in other laboratories. Namely, the laboratory of the practitioners' bodies, those who have practiced a variety of esoteric, consciousness-expanding disciplines through the ages.

To devalue these practices is to say there is no other way of unlocking the secrets of consciousness, except through experiments performed in the labs of Western scientists, especially the cabal of neuroscientists who proclaim that consciousness does not exist outside of the brain, that the brain is like a computer motherboard, which, once it shuts down, is no longer of any use. The human body is not a computer.

Present science approaches all consciousness research with a set of foregone conclusions; they know what they are looking for and proceed to find it in their data. *Quelle surprise!*

They're as close-minded as the so-called experts who opposed Dr. Barry Marshall when he declared that ulcers were caused by bacteria. But that's the way much of science works. By resisting new ideas until they become so clearly corroborated that resistance finally topples over of its own inert dead weight.

Yes, Dr. Alexander got carried away. Better to have titled his book *One Small Step in Proving the Existence of an All-Encompassing Consciousness.*

Nevertheless, KE and NDE are real, not just it's-all-in-your-mind accusations leveled against New Age babblings. Consciousness exists outside and beyond the human brain. That we don't have the tools or methods of demonstrating this to Western scientists at this time doesn't mean we never will.

Right now, if university research focused on kundalini

activation and other energy cultivation techniques, it might shed some light on the NDE — bolstering and supporting thousands of NDE and KE accounts.

If we don't know what consciousness is how can we presume to say what it isn't? So let's keep our minds open until we can — one way or the other.

Enlightenment

"The ultimate aim of meditation is to become more and more conscious. Enlightenment, therefore, is becoming fully conscious."

~ JJ Semple

Kundalini And The Now

If your goal were enlightenment, why would you bother with kundalini? After all, even its proponents admit there are risks involved in raising kundalini. Things do go wrong: the practitioner never achieves his goal, the energy never awakens, it awakens in some halfway or frightening manner and some sort of psycho-physical damage occurs.

Besides, aren't there are other ways of achieving enlightenment? Which causes me to rework the following saying: "It is easier for a camel to go through the eye of a needle than for someone to achieve enlightenment by this or that process or method." In short, I wish people would stop talking about enlightenment as if it was like learning to drive a car.

It isn't. In the first place, no one has ever defined enlightenment. It's a condition everyone claims they'd be able to recognize should they run across someone who is enlightened. A highly subjective claim.

Secondly, designating or labeling a person as enlightened is also problematic. Is the so-called enlightened one actually enlightened or is he/she just a spellbinding talker?

Eckhart Tolle says, "The enlightened person's main focus of attention is always the Now, but they are still peripherally aware of time."

Which would seem to point out that the more you stay in the Now, the less likely you'd be to talk a lot. In fact, wouldn't someone in the Now live a fairly uncomplicated, simple life? All the better to stay focused on the Now. Simple actions = fewer distractions. Like Gandhi spinning cloth, an almost inconceivable way of life for the

Westerner.

> "So do not be concerned with the fruit of your action — just give attention to the action itself. The fruit will come of its own accord. This is a powerful spiritual practice. In the Bhagavad Gita, one of the oldest and most beautiful spiritual teachings in existence, non-attachment to the fruit of your action is called Karma Yoga. It is described as the path of 'consecrated action.'"[74]

When Tolle talks about staying in "the Now," he is repackaging "mindfulness," which itself is a rediscovery of Gurdjieff's "self-remembering" — the idea of freeing oneself from psychological time.

> "The time-bound mode of consciousness is deeply embedded in the human psyche. But what we are doing here is part of a profound transformation that is taking place in the collective consciousness of the planet and beyond: the awakening of consciousness from the dream of matter, form, and separation. The ending of time. We are breaking mind patterns that have dominated human life for eons. Mind patterns that have created unimaginable suffering on a vast scale. I am not using the word evil. It is more helpful to call it unconsciousness or insanity."[75]

How difficult it is to stay in "the Now" can once again be compared to a camel's passing through the eye of a needle. It's very difficult, and very painful.

> "If you're in an environment that is ninety-nine percent bliss and one percent pain, the pain actually represents reality to you. You need to look for it and need to find it. Most of the time, we're in so much pain that that's not an issue, but sometimes things go really, really well. In our tradition, we say that when you are in that kind of situation, you need to be aware of the whole situation and not fixate on the bliss or try to perpetuate it, but actually to relate to the pain in the bliss. It is said that there is no one-hundred percent happiness, that even in a so-called bliss state there is always a shadow. I know that anytime I've experienced something like that, that there is at least the fear of losing it

---

74 *The Power of Now: A Guide to Spiritual Enlightenment* - Tolle, Eckhart. New World Library. Kindle Edition, p. 68.

75 Ibid, p. 67.

somewhere on the periphery of that experience. In Buddhism you have to pay a lot of attention to the shadows in any situation you're in — not because you're torturing yourself, but because that represents the earth, that's the ground. In our tradition, pain is the vanguard of enlightenment. Pain is ego's response to Reality."[76]

Attaining enlightenment — whatever it may be — is so complex, yet so simple. The catch being that for most people the Simple is, and always will be, out of reach.

How does kundalini fit in with enlightenment, the Now, and non-attachment?

Very simply, it brings to bear the organic, somatic, metabolic, genetic, and hormonal resources of the body, allowing the mind and ego to rest while it does the heavy lifting of staying in the Now. Kundalini creates a new Being dedicated to returning you to your true self, or should I say your true selfless state.

Don't expect, however, that once active, you can just relax and let kundalini take over. Leaving aside the risk aspect of awakening kundalini, taming-the-ego work is never finished. Nevertheless, kundalini does jump start the process.

Staying in the Now and kundalini are complimentary partners in the great work of returning to the simple, non-attached life. Stay simple and you'll stay focused.

Finding Certainty in an Uncertain World

The most important factor in my life was not the result of a conscious decision — although aspects of the decision making process were present. Most important was my recognition at an early age that there was something out there beyond the physical, something of a more ethereal nature.

Once your psyche perceives this, you are hooked because you take on the challenge of proving it to yourself, a challenge you never

---

76 Halfway up the Mountain: The Error of Premature Claims
to Enlightenment - Caplan, Mariana, pgs. 448-454

relinquish. It may take a lifetime, but this recognition provides the basis for building a life founded on searching for certainty in an uncertain world.

This is not something derived from traditional religion; it comes from within. It happens in spite of the influence of the world around you. In fact, it is counter to everything the world teaches you, counter to all conditioning and indoctrination. For me, the a critical step in the self-realization process was listening to my body after mindlessly damaging it:

> "The mind (ego) and the body really aren't friends. The mind is a tool of the culture, an expert propagandist for fitting in. Yet, as the mind drowns out the truth, the body continues to tell it Which is your real friend? The body, you say. Do you listen to it? I didn't. And yet, at some level, I must have. I never would have made it back otherwise. Spiraling out control, there has to be some measure of omniscience, or else recovery would have been impossible. The mind is just too strong. It campaigns incessantly for all the things you think you ought to be doing, all the things you think you are missing. How can you possibly stand up to the supplications of the mind? Nevertheless, as my abilities declined, I kept a sense of awareness in spite of the things my new persona tells me about myself. Without it, I would never have found a way to restore myself."
>
> - *Deciphering the Golden Flower One Secret at a Time* - JJ Semple

At an early age, a jolt of higher consciousness inserted itself into my psyche and set me deliberating on the possibility that something greater surrounded me, that I was attached to a field of existential wisdom or consciousness (an energy continuum), which, in daily life, manifested itself through a knowledge not acknowledged by the orthodoxies of worldly life. Gopi Krishna explains it thusly:

> "The first reality we come across is consciousness. The world comes later. We know first ourselves and then the world. So the wiser course is first to understand the knower. What modern thinkers have done is to ignore or bypass the knower, forgetting that it is the knower that is doing it."

~ *The Awakening of Kundalini* - Gopi Krishna

These early murmurs of higher consciousness were almost immediately buried beneath the so-called "adjustment process" that fitting into worldly life requires us to follow. Buried, but not dead. Inert, but not extinct. All it took was an occasional murmur of the heart to awaken it.

Gee, maybe there is something out there. Perhaps...I should explore it. But where to start? Could I have missed something in the sermon? I feel it's there, just out of reach and I have no idea of how to find it. Better not wait so long the next time I feel this tremor. Maybe I'll understand it better.

And there is always a next time. Whether it's a stirring in the body, or an instance of thrall. A chord struck while reading a novel. Watching a sunset. A passionate kiss. An itch waiting to be scratched.

Eventually, I did something about the itch. I started to explore self-hypnosis, yoga, all methods of meditation, and I started to do a whole lot of reading; I was about 27 years old at the time.

At first, I didn't associate my dabbling in spiritual practices with the presentiment that there was something out there, albeit running in parallel on two separate tracks:

- The occasional presentiment that there was something behind the material world.
- My practice of yoga and meditation.

I hadn't practiced enough to realize the two would eventually meet up. Although I began to see the elemental, material world for what it was — a kind of illusory distraction — I wasn't able to connect my childhood presentiments to the yoga and meditation I was practicing. In other words, I had no coherent ontological model. That would come later...after much more practice.

What does this ontology consist of? Adi Da Samraj describes it thusly:

"Precisely what is wrong with the universal scientism of modern society — and the forms of politics that derive from that scientism

— is that the modern scientific 'world-view' and modern politics do not permit the human being his or her psyche.

"Scientism constantly forces the human being to stand face to face with nothing but elemental 'experience.' It denies all reality to the higher dimensions — which, since ancient times, have been recognized by human beings as their fundamental resource.

"Scientism denies the connection to the energies and 'creative' sources of the 'world.' Human beings are denied right 'religion' and true Spirituality by scientism.

"Scientism is simply an activity of the verbal mind. It is oriented toward the investigation of elemental phenomena without any psychic participation in the 'world.'

"Even when scientists investigate phenomena that are not merely elemental, but that belong to the realm of energies and the psyche, they do not study these things through the psyche. They study them 'objectively,' as if these invisibles were butterflies under a pin.

"However, in order to investigate such phenomena, one must enter into 'consideration' of them through the medium of the psyche — through feeling, through intuition, through all the aspects of the mind and heart that precede verbal consciousness.

"In this 'late-time' (or 'dark' epoch), people are not permitted to recognize and acknowledge the invisible dimensions of existence. Nor are they permitted any psychic connection to those dimensions, or to anything else for that matter.

"People are encouraged to watch TV and go to work and wait for science to save them. But science can never save anyone. Science is not a 'method' of salvation."

~ The Gnosticon - Adi Da Samraj

Science is supposedly value neutral, but is it? Even back then, when I started exploring, I came to realize that science was not the answer. It was always one step forward and one step back. Take the Salk vaccine and the atom bomb. Scientists ready to dedicate themselves to research, no matter how benevolent, how heinous. As in Dr. Strangelove, *I'm only a scientist; I was ordered to do it. They told me it was for the good of mankind.*

And what about kundalini? How does it fit into the above ontology?

For me, kundalini is the ultimate confirmation that existence is something more than the "scientismistic" definition we limit it to. For me, it signaled the meeting up of the two tracks that had been running in parallel. Not only did kundalini make sense of the cosmology that reaffirmed my Being's relationship to "higher dimensions," it also made sense of science. If the kundalini sub-system exists in our bodies, it must be there for a reason, and that reason boils down to the realization that human evolution is a work in progress.

Kundalini is the instrument that links human biology to higher consciousness. It is responsible for your embodiment, from embryo to fetus to infant baby to fully formed body. It drives your past, present, and future evolution — your incarnate form, your brain, your consciousness! All are related to the kundalini in you and all are still evolving. And that is what science should be studying — the biological aspects of kundalini and its connection to consciousness.

Suppose you do have an itch to explore beyond the elemental. Young or old, it makes no difference. In your heart you know there's something out there. Metaphysical, astral, causal, etheric. Whatever name you give it. No matter. Nurturing the recognition, never letting go of it leads to a series of innate revelations that no amount of propaganda can dispel. To be certain of one thing in life is an immense accomplishment.

And unlike most of the underlying assumptions of elemental life, based on sensory programming and hand-me-down opinions, you don't have to take someone else's word for what you discover along the Way. By finding out for yourself, you have emptied your memory banks of preconceived notions, zeroed the atomic clock back to its primordial beginning, stripped the psyche bare, and started over.

Finding certainty in an uncertain world takes courage. So does 'unbelieving' acquired beliefs. Yet compared to what you've been told about the world and how it functions, being certain of even one little thing, when those around you are certain of nothing, is not only a whole different paradigm, it's a manifest advantage in exploring the infinite reaches of consciousness. Finding certainty in an uncertain world helps you understand the cosmology of life and discover a "peace that passeth all understanding."

Is Ontology Real?

Word usage frequency predicts what's on people minds and what they are thinking about.

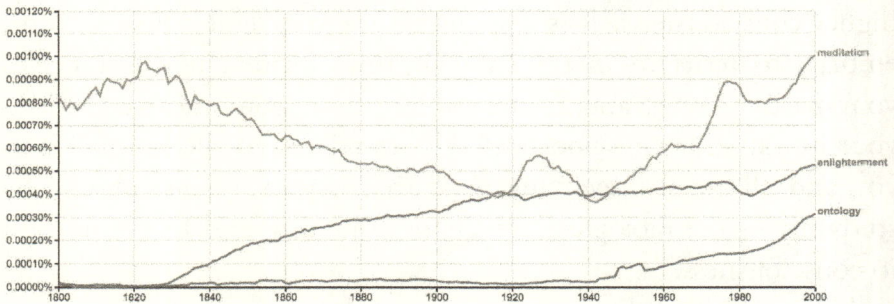

Isn't it interesting that a word like ontology — so long dormant in usage — has experienced a quantum leap in frequency over the last 60 years? Shows what people are talking and, therefore, writing about. And the more they talk, the more likely the probability that a university graduate student will focus on the enlightenment aspects that deal with the overall question of "the nature of being," as in:

on·tol·o·gy /än'täləjē/
Noun: ontology; plural noun: ontologies
The branch of metaphysics dealing with the nature of being

I'm not saying that it's going to be an overnight thing; it won't be, but there are so many researchers with PhDs that it's inevitable for some of them to become fascinated with as-of-yet scientifically unproven subjects like ontology, mindfulness, consciousness, and enlightenment — just like the researchers of the 19th Century became fascinated with biology, physics, and chemistry.

Moreover, behind the scene, Gopi Krishna's "evolutionary impulse" keeps fueling our curiosity about the scientifically unproven subjects mentioned above, keeps perfecting our Beings by favoring beneficial characteristics that can be passed on through DNA.

Keeping an open mind about the teachings is essential. But having an open mind is difficult. Why? Because an open mind means verifying everything you see, hear and feel, questioning conventional wisdom and preconceptions, and examining the opinions that control your thinking and your habits. Which actually puts you at odds with the rest of the world, a situation most people don't relish because they're so used to going along with the flow. Once you become a maverick, free to question, free to explore certain truths about your own self and about life, you live in a strange new landscape, like an explorer of old taking on the South Pole or an astronaut rocketing towards Mars. Moreover, when you start to question things, you usually don't turn away, you keep looking, eventually finding meditation and the truth that comes with meditating.

So maybe you say to yourself, *Open Mind, I have an open mind. It's my fool cousin* — fill in the blank: neighbor, supervisor, coworker, family member — *who doesn't listen. He's just stupid. Anyone who'd sit back and watch their tax money go to a bank that uses it to earn interest* — fill in the blank again. Having an open mind isn't only about listening to others, not generalizing or being judgmental, or even accepting new ideas. It's about the emotional effect that perceived slights and resentments have on you. One of the beneficial effects of meditation is recognizing when something upsets you, stops you from overreacting, helps you remain neutral and nonjudgmental. This has a soothing health effect. Not rising to the provocation, no matter how serious or how slight.

The study of "the branch of metaphysics dealing with the nature of being" begins with having an open mind. Kundalini, enlightenment, consciousness are all very well, but of very small value unless you come to them with an open heart and mind. When you do, you know ontology is real.

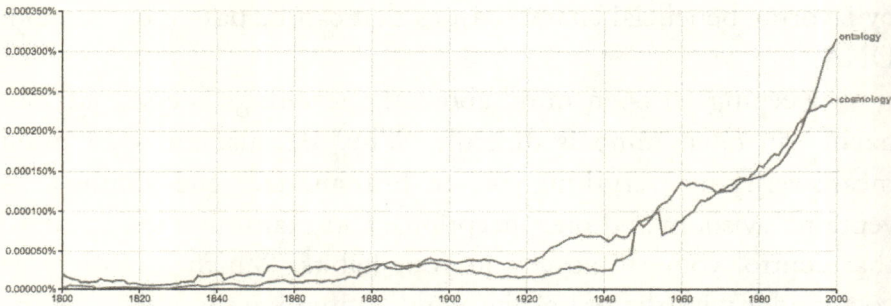

Higher Consciousness And Kundalini

This is a complicated issue, both the consciousness and the kundalini parts, separate and indivisible.

Consciousness is responsible for your embodiment — for creating a blueprint for your body before conception and then transforming that plan into your flesh and blood incarnation, which includes your brain. It works from numinous architectural drawings expressed as DNA in the physical world. Consciousness doesn't know algebra, how to do crossword puzzles, or short a stock. These are properties of the human mind, which is also an expression of consciousness.

Consciousness didn't need a book to create DNA, the universe, or human procreation. It's the non-verbal intelligence of a life force that needs no words to execute its evolutionary mandate.

The mind is a tool for creating and storing knowledge; it's good at balancing a checkbook and learning multiplication tables.

Everything the mind knows is an expression of the consciousness that created it.

Not even Darwin was able to fit consciousness into his evolutionary schema:

> "Ever since Charles Darwin published On the Origin of Species in 1859, evolution has been the grand unifying theory of biology. Yet one of our most important biological traits, consciousness, is rarely studied in the context of evolution. Theories of consciousness come from religion, from philosophy, from cognitive science, but not so much from evolutionary biology. Maybe that's why so few theories have been able to tackle basic questions such as: What is the adaptive value of consciousness? When did it evolve and what animals have it?"[77]

But don't blame Darwin; he was focused on a different line of research:

> "US-based doctor, author, entrepreneur and motivation guru Dr. Deepak Chopra recently challenged Darwin's theory of evolution, which established that all species of life descended from common ancestors, saying it is 'consciousness' and not "random mutations and natural selection" that explains where the human beings today are.
>
> "'*Charles Darwin was wrong. Consciousness is key to evolution and we will soon prove that. The human mind is an embodied and relational process that regulates the flow of energy and information in an ecosystem. All the cells in the body do not only participate in, but actually listen to the conversation anyone holds,*' he told the audience at the India Today Conclave 2015 in New Delhi.
>
> "After he read a recent exchange in the Washington Post 'Answer Sheet' blog, where Steven Newton rudely mocked Deepak Chopra's view that 'consciousness drives evolution', Stuart Hameroff, an anesthesiologist, professor, and consciousness researcher tried to re-evaluate his notions about human body and its relation with the universe to arrive at the conclusion that Chopra's view is likely to be scientifically correct.

---

77 "A New Theory Explains How Consciousness Evolved" - Michael Graziano, The Atlantic, June 6, 2016.

"Conscious feelings drive behavior which serves evolution; Darwin's theories of non-constancy of species, branching evolution, occurrence of gradual change in species, and natural selection ignores consciousness.

"The universe is more like a living organism with a conscious purpose. Modern physics sees evidence that the primal presence of consciousness is in itself the reason why, contrary to the law of entropy, the universe is not running down. In other words, consciousness or 'mind-at-large' is primal to 'human' consciousness, not the other way around. We've got it backwards."[78]

Since both biology and evolution are expressions of consciousness, there's no inherent contradiction between Darwin's avoidance of consciousness and his theory of evolution: all are derived from an all-knowing consciousness.

As for instances of higher consciousness, there are always more questions than answers:

- If there's such a state as higher consciousness, does lower consciousness also exist?
- How do higher and lower consciousness relate to each other?
- Is consciousness — higher or lower and all states in-between — relative or absolute?
- Are the various levels of consciousness definable by various manifestations?
- Is Enlightenment the highest state of consciousness?
- Is Enlightenment an absolute state or is it relative?
- Relative to what?
- How does kundalini affect consciousness?
- What if both relative consciousness and absolute consciousness exist?

To put these questions into perspective, I started a list (don't we in the West just love a list?) of the attributes and qualities that constitute higher consciousness.

Manifestations Of Higher Consciousness

---

78 "Charles Darwin Was Wrong. Consciousness IS Key To Evolution" – Vandita, ANONHQ.com, June 6, 2015

- Talents/powers/gifts — sudden acquisition of:
  - foreign languages
  - musical ability
  - art/photography abilities
  - writing ability
  - math ability
  - healing ability (oneself or others)
  - prescience
  - clairvoyance
- Realizations:
  - oneness
  - no death
  - a purposeful life
  - all violence is self-hate
  - part of an energy continuum
  - there is a preconceived blueprint for the body
  - renunciation of material objects
- Sensitivities, aversions to:
  - diet – meat, etc.
  - alcohol, cigarettes
  - drugs
  - electro-magnetic energy
  - noise
  - harsh sunlight
  - prescription medicines
- States and conditions:
  - visions
  - out of body experiences
  - revelations (as opposed to realizations: more micro than macro, for example, the imminent death of a friend)
  - invisibility, astral travel

It's a long laundry list of superhuman attributes and abilities. Whether an individual can manifest all of them, I don't know, but I would imagine it's more like a smörgåsbord — not one YOU choose from, but one that confers the requisite assortment on you, according to your genes, personality, character, karma, and level of attainment. What's more, it's gradual; you don't "acquire" these attributes in one fell swoop. You don't suddenly start hovering three feet off the ground in a blissful cloud, dispensing wisdom and healing the sick.

So if putative higher consciousness anointees manifest an assortment of the above, you can imagine the opposite end of the spectrum and the types of attributes the members of the lower consciousness group manifest. I won't elaborate; news blogs and journals are full of examples of the lowest common denominator behavior human beings are capable of.

> "In every human being, there is a desire for evolution, God, Truth — whatever name we give it. There is also the egoic mechanism whose job it is to prevent that growth process from happening. Therefore, it could be said that we both want truth and that we don't want truth."[79]

I can see my process in my mind's eye. When I look back at my life, a stranger stares back at me. This is not uncommon. In this work, life isn't a straight-line progression; it's like a stairs, a series of leaps and plateau (periods of consolidation). Whether you're a reformed prisoner or a spiritual seeker, you have probably experienced the feeling of being lost, followed by wondering if change is possible. That's the first step — searching for truth. Seeing the person you once were in the rearview mirror and wondering how you were ever that way, you not only look back at one instance of your Being, but at several, shaking your head in wonderment at the various versions — even some that appeared after kundalini's rising.

At first, I thought I had achieved something. Like the priest who graduates from the seminary, I was unable to resist the propaganda my ego fed me about being spiritually fast-tracked.

Whether or not I am any nearer to self-realization now than I was forty years ago, I do not know. Before I activated kundalini, I was a tangle of lost perspectives and jumbled thinking. And yet, back then, even as a preteen, I knew an ultimate being existed in me and that I could self-realize. My childish consciousness envisaged such

79 *Halfway up the Mountain: The Error of Premature Claims to Enlightenment* – Mariana Caplan, Hohm Press, 1999, p. 9

a transformation. The trick is not to make any premature claims to self-realization. How does one do that? By constantly telling the self that there is a lot more ground to cover.

As a child, I felt capable of doing things without my knowing I was doing them…as an instrument of consciousness. Sadly, as I grew older, I lost these insights and followed the conditioning of my social surroundings. Later, after much discomfort and failure, I came back to my early insights, thus enabling kundalini. It allowed me to step outside the mind and emotional patterns that had so long controlled me. I felt very close to the insights I'd had as a child. I began to see that even under the influence and control of the ego, I'd had moments of clairvoyance all along, spurred on, I suppose, by what Gopi Krishna called the evolutionary impulse. And I was able to learn from a series of life lessons:

Lesson One

In the hospital at age twenty-one, I had an out-of-body experience. This confirmed that I was more than my physical body.

I can see it in my mind's eye at any moment: a superior being, physically, mentally, and psychically capable of full consciousness. And when I see this being, I am enveloped in a mindfulness that puts everything into the simplest nonverbal terms. I vibrate at a higher frequency, sure in the realization that this state is attainable by me and by anyone else.

So how do you self-realize? By putting your life on hold and going after it, sampling one method or following one guru after another? Or by letting it come to you? Does thinking about self-realization in an intuitive dream state mean it exists?

Eventually I discovered GFM. I didn't practice it to raise kundalini; in fact, I had never even heard the word. I was only trying to improve my breathing to help me play a wind instrument. Kundalini found me. And once it found me, it started to act on me, first physically, then in other ways, completely overhauling my Being. Kundalini changed my physical configuration: my metabolism, my anatomy, my morphology, and my soma. It altered my spiritual essence as well — my intellect, my emotional states, my psychosomatic condition, and my consciousness. This work took place throughout my body and my brain. Kundalini did the work; I only witnessed it. And as time went on, I realized it had an evolutionary purpose: It was trying to perfect me.

Lesson Two

Kundalini has taught me that humans are perfectible. We can be transformed; we can perfect ourselves. Nevertheless, I see this perfectibility as a process and therefore it is relative, not absolute. If it were absolute, it wouldn't be a process; it would happen all at once. And maybe it does for some, but that is a different story.

Lesson Three

Having activated kundalini, I see reincarnation as an actuality. If that's true, there must exist, subsequent to this present mortality, a kind of firefly of essence that carries the accumulated energy of previous lifetimes to the next incarnation — a spark of consciousness that's never extinguished.

If you've had a near-death, an out-of-body, or a kundalini experience, you see reincarnation as a possibility, if not an actuality. At least, you see it as a hypothesis, an ontological reality. A phenomenon that will eventually be verified by science.

If you've not had an experience of this type, you probably remain not only skeptical, but hostile to these notions.

That's because, as previously stated, there's still a lot of work to do, and so-called enlightened persons are not exempt. When Jesus struggled with temptation, what was he really struggling with? Was it the devil or was it that property modern psychologists term "the ego?" Words not only change meaning over time, they actually change. What once qualified as the "devil" can now be summed up as "ego."

My colleague, Corinne Lebrun, uses a wonderful analogy to compare the attributes of average human consciousness to a piano with three octaves. Once kundalini is awakened, the deficient piano becomes an instrument of eight octaves. It's not possible for the initiate to avail himself of all eight octaves immediately, but at least — unlike in his previous limited state — he now knows those extra octaves exist. Over time, he learns to incorporate the now greater range of his instrument into the symphony of his life. Yes, life is like a symphony:

- 1st movement: Allegro
- 2nd movement: Slow
- 3rd movement: Minuet
- 4th movement: Allegro

It ends up as it starts out, unless those additional octaves are awakened, and eventually made use of.

Some manifestations of higher consciousness fall into one's lap, like when a pianist creates an improvisation never before attempted; some demand further practice.

Does the realized pianist end up with a potpourri of talents, powers, gifts, realizations, sensitivities, conditions heretofore un-imaginable, allowing him to attain his predestined level on the pyramid of consciousness? I'll leave it to you, the reader, to make the final determination.

What Is Enlightenment?

"Most people live at the bottom of the mountain. They make nice little villages there, even cities sometimes. They have families — and they love their families or they don't — they find work and friends, they're happy or they aren't, and they go to church or temple or they don't. And they die there."[80]

Enlightenment is also an expression of consciousness and that's why it's so hard to define. Like consciousness, it cannot be perceived by the mind. So we attempt to define it by seemingly contradictory statements and approximations: Zen-like koans that tend to confuse

---

80 Ibid, p. 5

the beginner who's attracted to the subject, but doesn't know where to start:

"You can find it if you don't try."

"You can achieve it if you don't want to."

"If you try to define it, you'll fail."

"If you're following someone else, you'll never find it."

"If you claim to be enlightened, you are not."

Which raises the question: How do we know who is and who isn't enlightened? Is there a committee for voting an individual In or Out? Sort of like enshrining someone in the Baseball Hall of Fame? Perhaps, it's a sure thing for people who've had a lot of books written about them. The Bible, anyone?

"Readers will also find themselves faced with differences in the way various teachers language their teachings and the discrepancies in the way that each approaches this subject. In some case it is merely a question of terminology (e.g., one teacher uses 'enlightenment,' another 'liberation'; one talks about the 'self' as being the ultimate, while another talks about the 'self' as the ego)."[81]

Is declaring an individual enlightened an objective or subjective process? Are there standards? Wouldn't the whole notion of standards risk ridicule and scorn? Wouldn't the standards be fraught with exceptions, in fact, wouldn't there be double standards? Yet, there seems to be certain qualities that people mention when they talk or write about enlightenment.

First, is there such a state as enlightenment? Second, if there is, is enlightenment absolute or is it relative? That is, can a person be more or less enlightened or is there nothing in between the state of complete enlightenment and the state of being completely unenlightened, i.e., an individual that spiritual teachers describe as being under the control of dualistic mind/emotion paradigm?

According to Osho, enlightenment does exist, but because of the variance among individuals, people not only come at it

---

81 Ibid, p. xxiii

from different starting points, they also exhibit different states of attainment, a statement that gives credence to the notion that higher consciousness is relative, not absolute.

I see it as a process. Whether the result is full or partial enlightenment — because we inhabit bodies — there is always work to do. And that's why it is not a battle between information on consciousness and consciousness itself. Labels don't matter; polemics don't matter. What matters is how you manage the process on a daily basis.

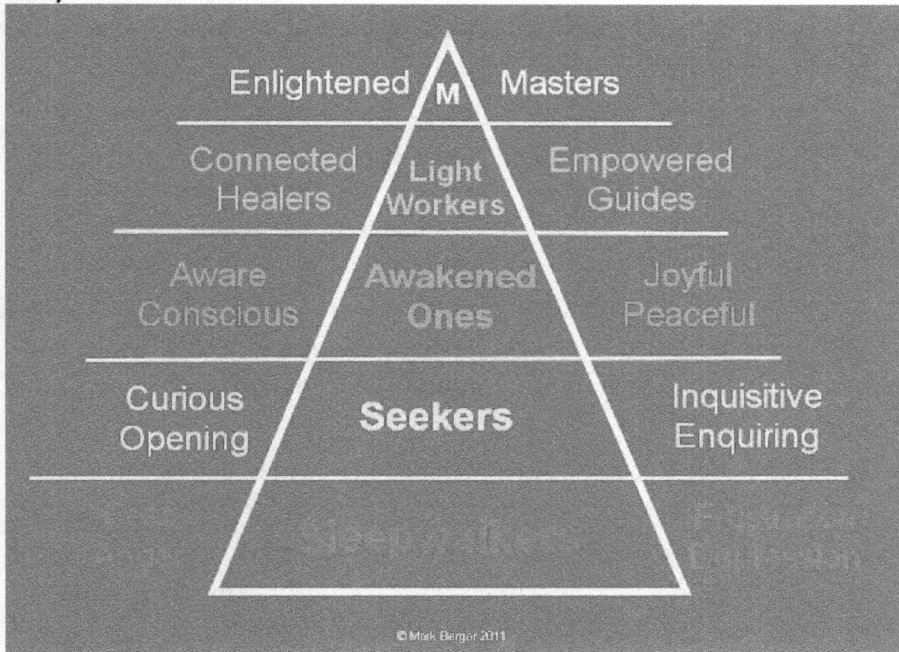

Maslow Squared

Want to know if someone's enlightened? Move in with the person for three weeks. Nothing beats living with someone in proximity; it's the best way to feel a person's magnetism/charisma or realize he's a self-appointed pretender. Of course, the person you label as exalted and noble, someone else might deem a lowlife. And what about candidates who are dead? That's tricky; spin-doctors have been around for a long time. So you see, it's not that easy to tell. Formulae don't work; neither does proximity. So you say, "Maybe I can't explain it, but if I met someone who was enlightened, I'd know it in an instant." Ah ha, the old gut feeling gambit.

Bravo, because that may just be the way.

There are many books dedicated to enlightenment. I have not read all of them, not even many of them. I don't know if they offer a complete understanding of the subject; I don't know if that's possible. Why? Because the many aspects of enlightenment that would have to be lived and experienced would also have to be classified and reduced into some kind of definition for everyday consumption. What's more, even if we could define what enlightenment is, would any "normal" person be able to relate to it?

> Whenever anything becomes as popular as enlightenment has
> become today, it must lose the essence of it's meaning, because
> true spiritual principles cannot be communicated in mass form.[82]

From birth, we'd need to capture biological markers of large numbers of individuals in order to test various hypotheses that some were genetically, somatically, and metabolically predisposed to enlightenment.

Okay, you probably saw it coming; I have a hypothesis. I'll state it at the outset: to wit, that because there is such a staggering leap from the ordinary dualistic state of mind/emotion to the uncluttered, free-wheeling condition of enlightenment, it must be driven by a powerful release of energy. It doesn't matter if this energy is induced through meditation or similar practice or if it's the result of a spontaneous release: the energy is always present. What else could account for such changes in Being, such evolutionary leaps of consciousness? Higher consciousness needs energy; kundalini supplies it. What is the most powerful energy source in the human body? The energy of reproduction, the energy that creates new life from tiny eggs and sperm cells — the same energy that, once

---

82 Ibid, p. 13

sublimated, triggers kundalini.

If the energy in semen can create embryo, fetus, and full-grown offspring, it must also be an evolutionary driver as well as the power behind great creative genius. What else could be responsible for the bursts of creativity, whether it be artists like Michelangelo or Renoir, musicians like John Coltrane or Beethoven, writers like Shakespeare or Tolstoy, or filmmakers/performers like Bruce Lee or Steven Spielberg?

In genius, the energy flows freely; that's one of the karmic mysteries of human ontology. Why and how geniuses are endowed with it. Ordinary folk need to sublimate it through some sort of energy cultivation practice, send up the spine to the brain to stir kundalini, expand consciousness, and induce a complete change of Being.

"A man's spiritual consciousness is not awakened unless his kundalini is aroused."

~ Sri Ramakrishna

Is an aroused kundalini a prerequisite for enlightenment? I raise this question because many spiritual investigators say that a biological phenomenon (kundalini) triggers the metaphysical condition (enlightenment). If so, it would appear that an active kundalini has a cause and effect relationship with enlightenment. If this is accurate, it means an aroused kundalini acts as the biological foundation for preparing and optimizing the nervous system and the brain for full consciousness. And so meditation has a two-fold purpose: activating permanent kundalini and inducing higher consciousness, indeed, the type of higher consciousness that leads to enlightenment…that is, if such a state actually exists.

Like-Minded People

"Groups don't think, act, or have motivations, only individuals do. Each individual is different from every other. How can we fit in one world? There isn't much in common when you extend the relationship beyond the one of mutual self-interest, so someone will have to sacrifice. Any relationship should last only as long as it is beneficial for each party. Intimacy needs to be cultivated and nourished."[83]

Like-minded people are the basis of groups, but finding and maintaining like-mindedness over a period of time is an illusion, bolstered by the urge to fulfill certain needs. Don't think so? Look at the divorce rates. What starts out as a testament to like-mindedness ends up in a lawyer's office because like-minded people are needy people, and needs diverge over time. How do I know this? I was conditioned to be needy; we all are. Our cultural markers direct us to identify with the needs of others, and, by extension, subsume their needs as our own — as if what others have is somehow more desirable than what we have.

To see this mechanism in action, look at popular culture. For example, the highly-regarded HBO television series, "The Newsroom."

> "In 'The Newsroom,' Emmy-winning executive producer, Aaron Sorkin, uses the operation of a fictional cable news network as the heart of the story, with Jeff Daniels portraying the network's lead anchor and leading an ensemble cast. Episodes are written around actual recent news events, reported by a staff that takes its collective responsibilities seriously, but corporate and commercial obstacles — plus entangled personal relationships — fly in the face of their public mission."[84]

While the show venerates the news gathering process, it revels in the vicarious interplay of the characters' compatible and incompatible needs, leaving the viewer with a field guide to neediness. In fact, "the entangled personal relationships" segments occupy more screen time than the news-gathering segments do, and are so entangled it's amazing that these hard-charging producers and reporters get any work at all done.

It's not that those segments are less interesting or less well

---

83 *How I Found Freedom in an Unfree World* - Harry Browne
84 "The Newsroom" – HBO, http://www.spectrumondemand.
     com/tv/hbo/9181989/the-newsroom

constructed. It's that any personal neediness the viewer might have is amplified by a parade of familiar tropes in each of the character's relationships. At one point, there's a play within a play in which one of the neediest characters encounters a "Sex And The City" tour bus that's hosting a guided tour of Manhattan locations featured in that show. Need on top of need on top of need.

In this sequence, that character, Maggie, who lives with co-worker Don, who she doesn't love, is given notice after a YouTube video in which she confesses her love for co-worker Jim, who she does love, goes live and is viewed by Don who tells her their relationship is over. Maggie locates the woman who posted the video and beseeches her to remove it. At the same time, Lisa, Maggie's roommate, dates Jim, much to his chagrin because he loves Maggie.

Maggie discovers that Lisa has also seen the video and now wants to end their friendship. As the downtrodden Maggie ponders her next move, the double-decker tour bus, with Sex and the City plastered all over it, appears on the roadway alongside her. Frustrated by Jim's reluctance to commit to a relationship with her and anguished at his persistence in remaining quasi-faithful to Lisa, Maggie rails against the injustice of her plight to the tour bus passengers on the open-air, double-decker bus, only to have Jim emerge from among the amazed passengers, aghast at the melodramatic nature of her indelicacies. Jim, it turns out, is on the bus because a colleague had suggested he get in touch with his feminine side.

So...for starters, Maggie needs: Jim's love, Lisa's friendship, and Don's respect. She also wants to move up the ladder professionally, is frustrated that she's been unable to pull off her Don-to-Jim switcheroo in classic Sex and the City fashion.

Were you able to follow all this? I hope so. I don't know if I could. Anyway...

How does this sort of intrigue affect the viewer? Without being aware of it, the viewer is sucked into a cesspool of neediness.

Why can't I have job like that? Be chasing a guy while another guy is chasing me? Vent my frustrations on the street from time to time? I deserve better; I NEED better!

Groups are unproductive because everyone goes full-speed ahead; everyone wants to impress, to prioritize their particular laundry list of needs.

In life, needs compete. And the more ardent the competition, the less likely the individual is to slow down and take stock. Who has time to be mindful of his or her situation when 15,000 new Hillary emails are made public? Who has the time or the inclination to be mindful?

Mindfulness is being aware that you are You in the present moment, in spite of what else may be happening around you. It's not something that comes naturally; you have to learn and practice it. You have to acquire the ability to slow down, much as you do when you meditate.

> "Lama Thubten Yeshe says that Westerners, although they are very intelligent and strong in their desire for "perfect wisdom," have a difficult time with spiritual sadhana (practice) because they simply don't have the foundation for it. 'When difficult circumstances arise, the negative energy overpowers the positive because they have never built up within themselves the force of good habits and because they lack deep, internal understanding of the nature of karma, or cause and effect.'"[85]

Mindfulness is an extension of meditation, a practice you can call upon to recreate the meditative state at the first sign of provocation, turmoil, or stress...if only you can remember to do it. That's the hard part: remembering yourself! Nevertheless, once you're adept at remembering yourself in the present moment, you can extend your practice of mindfulness to include being mindful of superfluous needs that may be controlling your thoughts and actions. You can bring them to the fore, turn them around, examine them in all their

---

85 *Halfway up the Mountain: The Error of Premature Claims to Enlightenment* – Mariana Caplan, Hohm Press, 1999, p. 20

aspects, and then dismiss them forever.

Being mindful is being present in the Now, and still getting your work done! Your actions are, in a sense, purified. You become unattached to the outcome, more aware of how you are doing at a given instant and less attached to the goals of your actions.

Woody Allen is a past master at using his characters to portray neediness, right up there with Anton Chekhov. In Allen's *Crimes and Misdemeanors* (1989) his leading character's needs lead him into the murkier regions of the soul including murder-for-hire and the need to rationalize it.

In *The Seagull*, Chekhov's Boris, a successful writer, taunts the beautiful young aspiring writer/actress, Nina. In this passage he uses the seagull as a metaphor for her:

Boris: This is a beautiful place to live. [He catches sight of the dead seagull] What is that?

Nina: A gull. Constantine shot it.

Boris: What a lovely bird! Really, I can't bear to go away. Can't you persuade Irina to stay? [He writes something in his notebook.]

Nina: What are you writing?

Boris: Nothing much, only an idea that occurred to me. [He puts the book back in his pocket] An idea for a short story. A young girl grows up on the shores of a lake, as you have. She loves the lake as the gulls do, and is as happy and free as they. But a man sees her who chances to come that way, and he destroys her out of idleness, as this gull here has been destroyed.

And so, over the course of the play, he does exactly that — destroys Nina with Iago-like "motiveless malignancy."

Both Allen and Chekhov introduce us to the fact that because art comes to the artist intact — as a result of their talent — artists tend to become heedless of the strivings of others. Witness Boris's wanton destruction of Nina and Irina's belittling of her son's writing. Thanks to an innate talent, the artist's needs of self-expression are taken care of, so they must manufacture new needs, exemplified in

The Seagull by the self-fulfilled characters unconscious destruction of the weaker characters.

What does this have to do with kundalini? Kundalini not only opens you to mindfulness, it overhauls human nature, allowing you to become less attached to real or perceived needs. Moreover, it puts "like-mindedness" in perspective, that the urge-to-merge is largely an illusion, that you don't have to run alongside a tour bus blurting out your despair. That being yourself with yourself in the moment is satisfaction enough.

The Polemics Surrounding Kundalini

"Fools gold exists because there is real gold." ~ Rumi

Drugs and Kundalini

"Our meditations are nothing but drugs — perfect drugs, without any chemicals in them. A man who can meditate will not be able to enjoy the drug, any drug. Because, his meditation gives him so much peace and the drug will disturb it."

~Osho

People explore drugs for the same reasons they explore kundalini and other spiritual pursuits and energy cultivation methods. I use kundalini as a stand in for all awakening experiences. So why do we take drugs? Why do we pursue the awakening experience?

Simply put, to reach for something out of reach. Call it higher consciousness. Awakening. Self-realization. Whatever. Some impulse drives us to know more about what lies beyond the boundaries of our material world. Intuitively, we know we cannot accomplish this without stopping the mind. And that's why we turn to drugs — because they stop the mind. They put the day on hold. Our frustrations, our disappointments, our shames, our guilts, our regrets stopped by a puff of smoke, by swallowing a tablet, by sniffing a line, pumping a liquid into a vein.

Drugs provide us with a blank canvas. They let our alter ego run wild. Most of the time we don't know where it will lead us; we just go forward, confident there is something out there and we will find it. So what's the difference between drugs and kundalini? Do they somehow lead to the same place?

"Many people start their journey towards God, truth, samadhi, because they have had a certain glimpse somewhere. Maybe through drugs, maybe through sexual orgasm, maybe through music, or sometimes accidentally. Sometimes a person falls from a train, is hit on the head and he has a glimpse. I'm not saying make a method of that! But I know this has happened. A certain centre in the head is hit by accident and the person has a glimpse, an explosion of light. Never again will he be the same; now he will start searching for it. This is possible. The probable is no longer probable, it has become possible. Now he has some inkling, some contact. He cannot rest now."

~ Osho

That's a big picture description of my explorations. In the 60s and 70s when I was young, I experimented. I didn't know Spiritual from Wonder Bread. I sat in church, listening to the minister drone on, eager for the sermons and the strictures and the admonishments to end. Yet, I dug the Bible on an allegorical level. I could identify with Jesus and the challenges in his life. But there was nothing to shake me or open me up. And I needed something — a means of turning my mind off, a platform for my curiosity, a way to harness my energies:

"We spend a lot of time learning the poses and practicing them. It gets so it doesn't feel right unless we start the day with yoga. At no time, however, do Margo and I discuss its spiritual aspects. The pure physicality preoccupies us. Years before the appearance of the yoga mat, Margo sews together some padded quilting to cushion our bodies against the hardwood floors. We lie on our 'mats,' watching and learning from each other, until our movements are synchronized. Sometimes, yoga practice leads to sex. It seems like a natural extension. Frequently, I am stoned during practice. To me, there is no separation. If I think about the spiritual aspect of my life, it is from the Timothy Leary point of view. According to him, the sacred mushrooms, yoga, mescaline, pot, Buddhism and LSD open a spiritual connection. I accept the notion that certain drugs stimulate clarity; it happened to me. Once with the cat, once in the GWU Hospital, once on acid in the mountains of West Virginia, lying under a tree with Margo, Roper and friends. Looking up at leaves swaying in the breeze, the flora and fauna come alive. I find myself observing the cellular structure of nature. Or so it seems. I don't realize until much later that I am not even scratching the surface. At the time, however, it's all very meaningful. In my wayward fashion, I'm looking for empirical

knowledge. And to be honest, drugs are an instrument..."
~ *Deciphering the Golden Flower One Secret at a Time* — JJ
Semple

Drugs were the instrument; they opened me up. I was able to say to myself, there is something out there. And I proceeded to explore. Not having an addictive personality, I accepted the insights of my drug experiences and moved on. Not as in, "Wow, drugs are bad for me. Better find something else." I didn't approach it that way. I didn't condemn drugs and step away from them. I got to a point in my practice where they became superfluous. It came about organically, in the natural order of things. Had I waited longer or experimented with more dangerous drugs, a good part of my life might have been wasted. Understanding the recovery process is no easy task; it takes courage and commitment. Had I to do it all over again I would avoid drugs altogether.

Nevertheless, as I got deeper into yoga and meditation before long drugs faded away of their own accord. Here were disciplines, unlike religion, that actually gave something back, something I could witness in my body. It was a beginning, yet I knew this practice could take me farther than any religion.

I had given up on orthodox religion; I had exhausted it. Why? I didn't feel comfortable with the one-way, take-it-on-faith approach. I wanted to play an active role in my spiritual development. If there was something out there, I knew I could find it on my own. Orthodox religion doesn't allow that. They want you to take everything on faith. They are the go-betweens. You on one side; God on the other. The Church in the middle.

That wasn't me. And by the look of things nowadays it doesn't suit the majority of people. They want to take responsibility for their own development — up to a point. Remember Jonestown. Keep it in the back of your mind. Every time someone offers you the Keys to the Kingdom think of Jonestown. And remember how you got into this work. Remember it's up to you — not some surrogate. No one knows more about you than YOU!

And while you know there's something out there, don't stop being skeptical or suspicious. You will get to the point where drugs don't matter. And that's important because addiction is always a danger when you play with drugs. In spite of all the claims and counter claims about gateway drugs, if there's such a thing as or not, I know from personal experience that one tends to sample. What follows next is purely a function of one's psychological makeup. If you have an addictive personality, if shutting off the mind at all costs is of paramount importance, you go deeper into sampling. You get hooked.

Or you become motor impaired, as per this Australian study:

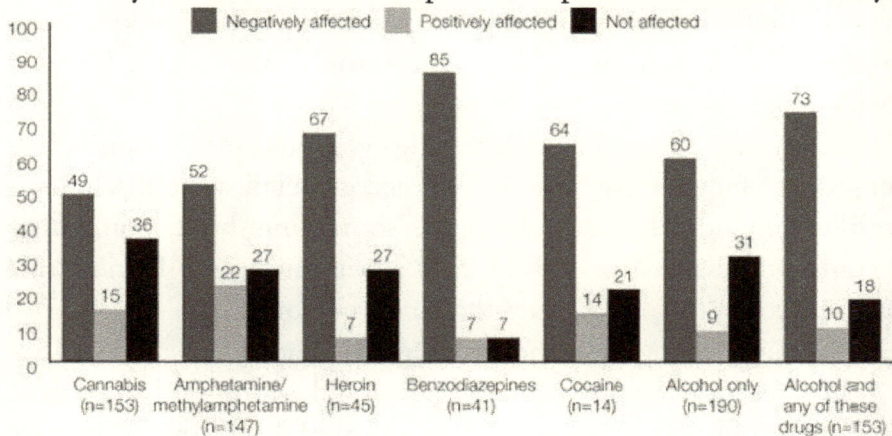

You don't need drugs, in fact, once you get into meditation, you unleash the true energies in the body, and they are more powerful than any drug, including prescription medicines. All drugs, whether prescribed or surreptitiously consumed, are addictive. They are a crutch to fall back on, and, in the act of falling back, these chemical elements act on the natural processes of the brain, inhibiting the production of endorphins and other useful, beneficial neurotransmitters and hormones. What's more, drugs turn you into a different person, one you were NOT meant to be. Although at first you may believe drugs make you a cooler you, you soon realize it's not about cool; it's about addiction and scoring your next high. And you're on a treadmill to misery: physical, emotional, and spiritual.

> "The really religious person is one who has become aware of the futility of desiring, of the impossibility of having anything here in this world or thereafter in the other world. You can only possess yourself. You can only be the master of your own being. If you are not trying for that... It is hard work, there is no shortcut to it; notwithstanding what Timothy Leary says, there is no shortcut to it. Acid, drugs, are not going to help you there. That is very cheap, it is very cunning. It is a chemical deception. You want to get into the world of your innermost being without any effort. It is a dishonesty. Without earning it you want to possess it."
> ~Osho

I know there are people who meditate and still use drugs. I can't imagine what this does because I can't imagine it for myself. I also realize there are those who don't accept that meditation is more powerful than drugs. They don't accept it because they haven't experienced it. Meditation eliminated my interest in and use of drugs, including prescribed medications. I take none.

When Kundalini Isn't Wanted

I receive many inquiries asking how to activate Kundalini. Before answering I always ask the person why he or she wants to. More than likely, the answer is, "Because..." followed a pause and much hemming and hawing. Which shows me that little serious reflection has been given the matter. As a follow up, I ask the person what prompted his/her interest. Often I'm told the person was inspired by my, or by some other writer's, Kundalini books. Gratifying as that might be if the book is one of mine, the reader's admission makes me realize that I am now, in some sense, responsible for what happens.

Stepping back to analyze the situation objectively, I understand how writing books on Kundalini can appear to typecast writers as cheerleaders for the phenomenon — without any of us wanting or attempting to be one. That's not why I write about the kundalini, nor is it the way I view my role, which is more educator than evangelist.

To be a cheerleader for something, you must want to elevate it above other rivals. Kundalini is not competing with anything; it is the Life Force.

Nevertheless, I'm probably guilty of cheerleading to some degree; just because kundalini and its physical power have played such an important role in my life. Even after forty years of living with it…something new happens every day.

To feel the Life Force active inside yourself and to watch it work is humbling and, at the same time, hard to keep still about.

I kept still for many years, but finally after more than thirty years with an active kundalini, I felt it was time to add my experiences to the expanding canon of kundalini research literature.

As time goes on, however, and I encounter an increasing number of heartbreaking stories like the following comment submitted to The Kundalini Consortium blog in January 2017; the need to educate, if not to warn, becomes more urgent as you will see after reading the following comment from someone who definitely did not ask for or want kundalini:

> "Why does any of this have to happen? Why can't this kundalini bull shit just bother the people that seek it, why cant they have it??! Their the ones that want it. I don't want this. I hate this!!!! I just want to be normal, I just want to go back. I'm just so tired and freaked out all the time. It's like I take tiny doses of acid every day. I can feel my brain has physically changed, I can feel it, I can feel everything… :("

The comment ends with an emoticon frowning face, hardly adequate in assuaging the person's pain — his desperation. Unfortunately, it's not uncommon. The following is all I could muster as a reply, not very comforting, but I believe it's better to be honest and factual than to make empty promises:

> "Kundalini is an evolutionary driver; in and of itself, it is not

malevolent. Trying to stop, or mitigate it, is not possible. It appears that some spontaneous cases like yours are difficult to bear in one way or another. There is no why or wherefore. Upon activation, kundalini takes inventory of the body and nervous system, relays this information back to the brain, then begins sending healing energy to the various parts of the body that need it. Its purpose is to jump start your evolution during a single lifetime. There is a regulating mechanism that normally adjusts the energy so that only the right amount is released. Unfortunately in spontaneous cases, this mechanism sometimes releases more energy than the person can support."

So how safe is kundalini:

"There is no gentle way of easing into this experience. People who prepare all their lives to receive this blessing, through a regimented set of practices, breathing exercises, yoga, a diet of fruits and vegetables, cleansing rituals may never receive the blessing, and people that are totally unprepared and clueless about it stumble into it as I did, through a spontaneous awakening as a byproduct of drug use, meditation, tantric sex, while delivering a baby — only to wander through life looking for answers. The rare individual that prepares for this through yogic practices and receives it under the auspices of a true guru maybe one of the few that can ease into the subsequent process with minimal trauma, but most aren't that lucky. The disoriented, terror-filled stage which makes the person look and sound 'crazy' is almost a given.

"Any guru that does not warn you about this is doing you a huge disservice. It is better to read true accounts of people that have undergone a real awakening, people in the modern era, not ancient sages. It will save a lot of time and may even provide simple, common sense answers like my previous description of terms like hell, heaven and purgatory as seen from a 21st century perspective, but with the aid of mystical experience. Stay away from the hucksters."[86]

Almost every negative account I've listened to is about discomfort. <u>Sometimes extre</u>me discomfort, and even pain. I remember when

86 ~ "No pain, no gain… don't let anyone tell you otherwise" – Vivek Govekar, The Kundalini Consortium, January 7, 2013

my kundalini first awakened, wondering how I was going to support this energy streaming into my head, a force that intensified each time I lay down. The answer came quickly: no matter how intense the energy, each time I got up, the energy went into a kind of holding pattern until the next time I lay down. At night, it was there, but didn't conflict with my sleep. At certain times, it almost tore my head off, but was never painful and always went into neutral when I worked, slept, cooked, drove a car. Whatever activity I was into, it released the correct amount of energy.

And this is where my case differs from those who feel even the least bit of discomfort. Practiced correctly, GFM and other meditation methods activate a kundalini that's not only an invigorating charge of life force, but also one with its own governor or control mechanism that calculates, measures, and releases just the right amount of energy for a given activity. It knows how much is needed, always releases the correct dose.

What do all these cases of discomfort have in common? They all report either some sort of neural discomfort that manifests itself as tingling, itching, burning, prickling, buzzing, stinging or a constant overdose of energy that cannot be controlled, one the body cannot support. These symptoms are not imaginary; they are real and they allow hardly any respite. It's like the governor is not working properly.

Why are these cases so different from mine? I believe it has to do with one of three factors or a combination of all three:
- The activation trigger (the method, or lack thereof)
- Physiological, psychological, or emotional blockages
- Karma

I can't prove it, but I just don't see the same factors operating in cases with persons who've used a method like GFM. Many negative accounts are the result of involuntary or spontaneous activations.

What's more, not everyone agrees on what triggers kundalini, what its effects are, or how to live with it. What is happening inside a given individual is not only difficult to express; interpretation is left to the listener's ability to extract the details correctly and to confirm that the speaker's terminology is understood. So I often wonder: m I interpreting correctly what he/she is telling me? And that's why I believe in keeping the terminology simple, free from doctrinal or scriptural influences.

Kundalini accounts vary greatly, not only because triggers and effects vary greatly, but also because adepts and newcomers alike do not use the same terminology. There is no authoritative kundalini lexicon or dictionary.

However, blaming kundalini is senseless; it's like blaming evolution for enabling us to walk on two legs instead of crawling on our bellies. Kundalini isn't the culprit. It's an evolutionary force that's always present. In and of itself it's not malevolent; it's that the intensity or the dose of energy that certain people have to support is just too much to bear, especially in spontaneous cases.

So what can you do if kundalini should ignite spontaneously? Not much. In fact, the only suggestions I have come up with are:

Something I chose not to do, and that is: see a doctor. Perhaps, medical science will accept, understand, and even be able to treat kundalini symptoms some day, but at the time of my activation, not only did medical science refuse to acknowledge the existence of kundalini, it assigned kundalini stories to mental illness, I didn't need that; I found it better to "Go It Alone" than to rely on dubious advice or wrongful diagnosis. Fortunately, in my case, it was the right thing to do. Given my assessment of what had happened, my only option was surrender, and I did.

Stop all energy cultivation practices. Wait a while to see if the symptoms lessen.

Sure, there are times when I wish I could lead a "normal" life instead of being a guinea pig for esoteric science. But that's not possible, not for me or for any person in whom kundalini is active. Problem is: some suffer more discomfort than others, which, with our American sense of fair play, does not seem fair at all.

It bothers me to not be able to help. But I have not met anyone who can. Unfair as it might appear, it falls on the individual to wait it out: that's all you can do. Because It is doing you. There is no turning the clock back.

Kundalini is what it is — the energy behind the evolutionary impulse which seeks to improve yours as well as my Being. Would your purpose in writing books about evolution be to cheer for evolution or would you write to clarify how it works? I write about kundalini not to cheer, but to educate and communicate the surprise and wonder it provoked when it awakened — What triggered it, its effects, what it did for/to me, how I worked to integrate it into my life, and how I live with it.

One thing I can do is: not glorify or embellish kundalini, neither its purpose nor the challenges in awakening and/or living with it.

One thing you should do is: don't pay someone who claims to be able to help you redirect kundalini energy without first checking references! If, by any chance you know of someone or some process who CAN clear and/or redirect the energy, let me know and I'll do my best to get the word out.

The Journey or the Destination

"Self-realization begins at birth; it is the journey as much as it is the destination."

My book, *Deciphering the Golden Flower One Secret at a Time* is sometimes criticized as *not* being a comprehensive breakdown of secrets in *The Secret of the Golden Flower*.[87]

---

87 This controversy is now moot. My new book, *The Secret of the Golden Flower: A Kundalini Meditation Method* explains the teachings and the meaning of *The Secret of the Golden Flower* (SGF) and is now on sale at Amazon. "Since the publication of *Deciphering the Golden Flower One Secret at a Time* in 2008, readers have asked for an in-depth guidebook on using the SGF to awaken kundalini in the manner, and with the same results, as those described in my memoir." https://amzn.to/2JMhMGQ

This is not only inaccurate; it contradicts the book descriptions on all retail and other Internet sites:

Amazon description

"Choosing to focus on my journey from birth to maturity has sparked a wholesale discussion on genres — How-To books vs. memoirs. This is not a How-To book; it's a memoir of my journey. I don't leave anything out."

Life Force Books description

"*Deciphering the Golden Flower One Secret at a Time* is a definitive tell-all journal of obstacles met and overcome on the path to activating Kundalini. It is not a How-To book; it's a narrative of my journey. I don't leave anything out."

The Internet is a public forum where off-the-wall meets cogent interpretation. Nonsense meets sense. And it's up to the reader, should he or she be so inclined, to evaluate the various positions, separate the wheat from the chaff. Yet, no matter how misguided or off the mark a criticism might be, there's always some worthy element.

In this case, because I decided not to separate the journey from the destination — I never intended to — it sparked a wholesale evaluation of my approach. Should the journey be considered part of the experience — in this case a kundalini awakening? Does the effort to attain something count in the end result? Should the means enjoy the same weight as the ends? Beyond the fact that the journey is usually a humanizing experience, there's the ultimate question of: What is the destination? Miracles, super powers, bragging rights? Gopi Krishna had this to say:

"A question was asked of Ramana Maharshi, 'Do you see spirits?' He said, 'Yes, in my dreams.' I would like to tell you something which is probably not known in the West, I mean especially to the younger generation. There is not a single mention of miracles in the Upanishads, which are the fountainhead of all metaphysical and spiritual thought in India. There is not a word in favor of miracles in the dialogs of Buddha; in fact he condemns them. Not a word about miracles in the Bhagavad Gita. Krishna condemns those who practice meditation to harm others or gain some worldly object for themselves, or in other words miracles. Not a word about miracles in the sayings of Ramakrishna, Raman, Sri Aurobindo, nor Swami Sivananda."

So if it isn't miracles or superpowers, we can surmise it isn't bragging rights because there'd be nothing to brag about. So what is it? What is the destination? Is it greater consciousness, better decisions, better health, longevity, better self-control, knowledge of life and death, a connection with the energy continuum. Do all these come with a kundalini awakening, the moment it occurs? Thanks to my struggles, I believe I have an inkling and that is: you're better off not wanting. No expectations, no longings, no yearnings.

Whatever the destination it takes time. It has for me anyway. For Gopi Krishna, too — if you read his books. And guess what? Understanding is acquired along the way, during the journey! Through focus, through travail, through trial and error. Through getting knocked down and bouncing back up. Through becoming single-minded.

I could continue to evangelize my personal experience with the solitary path, the challenges I faced, the ways I stumbled, and the hurdles I overcame, but if we in the West are to develop a Western spiritual tradition, we need to become more self-reliant — better spiritual detectives and better evaluators of everything we see, hear, and feel.

So what if I did not attempt a line-by-line interpretation of *The Secret of the Golden Flower* at the time. That was never my intention. Why? Because there happens to be a lot of them out there already. From Carl Gustav Jung to Osho. I preferred dealing with the really important secrets in the context of how I discovered they were important and how I ultimately came to practice the teachings and master them. Namely, Diaphragmatic Deep Breathing and the Backward Flowing Method. Why take a narrative approach?

People identify with the struggle of the journey. If the struggle isn't real — doesn't lead the seeker through a series of dark night of the soul crises — can the process be authentic? Not if it isn't lived in its entirety. Not if it produces a cloying mess that obfuscates the vital elements of the struggle.

There was another reason I took this approach: I wanted to document the difficulties the Westerner faces in even getting to the starting point of the self-realization journey, especially in 1956 when I began my quest. I have Indian and Chinese friends who grew up with meditation and yoga practices all around them. I never heard these words until I was in my late twenties. Even when I did, there was very little information extant. As for kundalini, I didn't hear the word until after I had activated it.

My journey took me from HS graduation to college to the USMC to college again to work to travel to work, 18 to 35, all before I'd found anything substantial, before I even had a clue that a phenomenon such as kundalini existed.

And that was just the materialistic aspect of my life; there were many other aspects: relationships, family, health, addictions, pursuits and dreams. Like everyone, I was juggling a whole medley of issues, but unlike most of my friends, not doing a very good job of it. I needed to document the choices I made in getting from a point far behind the starting line to where I ultimately ended up: a kundalini practitioner and writer. Even today, I still look back and wonder how I got to where I am today. The least I could do was to retrace my steps so that other Westerners, be they more or less apt or predisposed than I was, can nevertheless use my odyssey as a roadmap for finding a way forward and for choices to avoid.

Awakening kundalini is akin to a crash landing on an unknown planet. There is no way to be fully prepared, no guidebook. The greatest preparation, in fact, is the ability to improvise.

Imagine crashing a plane in unfamiliar territory. Right away, you have to find food, shelter and repair your equipment with only a limited toolkit and a manual written in an unknown language. A rush job with life and death stakes — the kind of desperate mission that requires a task-oriented personality. Take stock and get on with the job. And don't neglect intuition. It may save your life.

Enough about theory, already. About idealizing the destination! It never works out the way you think it will. There are years of coming to terms with an active kundalini at work in your body. Better to learn the practical aspects of living with it and not yearn for ecstatic states of bliss. That's escape. Kundalini is not escape...

Hopefully, as living empirical science proliferates, raising kundalini will become a safe, everyday occurrence. Our race will make the next incremental leap in consciousness. Perhaps the spiritual pioneering by disparate groups and individuals currently underway will prepare the groundwork for safe, permanent awakenings.

No, your journey won't be the same as mine. Nor will its outcome. But the more journeys that are documented, the more understanding brought to the endeavor. In acquiring the tools for the soul's long journey as it shape-shifts its way along the energy continuum, there's much work to be done, so many discoveries to be made.

Once again Gopi Krishna's farsighted assessment:

"A few more confessions such as Alan Watts', and a probe directed to the avowals of thousands of human beings who have had the unmistakable experiences of the kundalini force are perhaps necessary to put open-minded and enterprising men and women of science on the trail of what is the greatest mystery of creation still lying unsolved and even unattended before us."

It's not an either - or. The two go together: the Journey and the Destination.

No Practical Advice Whatsoever

This exchange occurred on FB. It's not the first time I've heard this, and it probably won't be the last.

Reader: I've purchased your book, I've read, but I didn't understand the purpose of your book, there is no practical advise whatsoever [sic] ...

JJ: Like Gopi Krishna's Kundalini: The Evolutionary Energy in Man, *Deciphering the Golden Flower One Secret at a Time* is a narrative memoir. These types of books offer practical advice in limited quantities. Why?

In the case of kundalini, each experience is so different, both as to how the experience is triggered and how it affects the individual in whom it is triggered. How can one offer substantive practical advice without knowing the circumstances of a case? Would you want a lawyer to offer generalities in a divorce case? Or a hitting coach to say, "Get up there and swing away."?

That's why most books on kundalini triggers and effects, that are not memoirs, offer information laced with "received wisdom." In fact, offering specific advice can be dangerous and misleading for neophytes who are completely in the dark. It's much safer to generalize. Yet, generalities don't satisfy the reader who's looking for more.

On the other hand, in order to offer "practical advice" in each case, a separate book would have to be custom-written for each individual. And that's not about to happen. In your case, without knowing anything about you or your situation, even to the point of whether you've had a kundalini experience, how it was triggered or how it affected you, I'm not qualified to comment or advise, in a book or in person. It would be presumptuous.

So why do authors write memoirs, or narrative stories? What purpose do they serve? In a word, their purpose is "Identification," a universally accepted literary device. The reader, or viewer in the case of a play or movie, identifies with the protagonist's struggle. If it weren't for the identification factor, many works of art would not exist — works like, *The Iliad, Beowulf, Don Quixote, The Graduate, Portrait of a Lady, Rocky, Hamlet, A Moveable Feast, Anna Karenina.* The fact that they have existed for such a long time means they must be an respected literary form, in which the creator is saying, "This is the way it happened to me, or to him or her. Do you see something in this story that resonates for you?" Even the Christian Bible is based on identification: for millions, Jesus is the ultimate object of identification.

Memoirs stimulate readers to feel good about themselves: either by looking down on the protagonist (there but for the grace of God go I) or looking up to him/her (when I grow up, I'm going to pattern my life on hers). Some people cannot relate to characters in a book, no matter how noble or how degraded; their brains are not wired that way. They objectify situations. Memoirs put you in the moment; how-to books place you at 20,000 feet. If you aren't moved by great stories and great characters — if you don't relate to their struggle — you'd better stick to how-to books.

Many readers of *Deciphering the Golden Flower One Secret at a Time*, who enjoyed the narrative (see Amazon reviews), tell me they were also able to "read between the lines" and extract useful information that they then applied to their own search for self-knowledge, namely:

- Meditation is the best way to permanently activate kundalini
- Kundalini is a biological phenomenon, not a religious one
- Kundalini repurposes sexual energy, into "psychic fuel"
- The kundalini activation experience takes place in a moment, learning to live with its effects takes many years
- Kundalini has autonomic self-healing properties
- Kundalini rejuvenates the body, retards the aging process
- Kundalini curbs addictive tendencies
- Kundalini removes self-destructive tendencies
- Kundalini is not for everyone

As for specific practical advice, judging from its positive reviews, readers tell me that *The Biology of Consciousness: Case Studies in Kundalini* offers an objective, topical survey of the issues surrounding kundalini. *The Secret of the Golden Flower: A Kundalini Meditation Method* is even more specific.[88] Whether these books are

---

88 Visit: https://amzn.to/2tgGDHA

more to your liking is for you to decide.

In the end, most seekers discover that the road to self-knowledge is quite lonely. No matter how many books read, ashrams visited, retreats attended, questions asked and answered, the bulk of the work — like that of a scientist — is accomplished under laborious conditions by the solitary seeker him or herself.

Sacred Cow Terminology Obscures Real Meaning

"Names can be designated, but they are not fixed terms."

~ Introduction to *The Secret of the Golden Flower* – Thomas Cleary translation

No one dares speak out against word casing sacred cow terms like "enlightenment," yet few understand them, empirically at least. It is better to use simpler language, metaphysical in place of spiritual, for instance, because metaphysical is a term most people can agree on. It means "beyond the physical" while spiritual connotes more subjective meanings.

Since most people's understanding of terms like "enlightenment" and "duality' are based on their experiences in the physical world, it is only normal that their "definitions" reflect their material perceptions and experiences — in other words, the boundaries of their material concepts and their entrapment therein.

After a kundalini awakening, one begins to experience beyond-the-physical, meta effects, perhaps for the first time. This provides the subject with kind of "grokking" insight into the beyond-the-physical realm. All of a sudden he/she knows there is no death, no duality. This is both a revelation and a realization, metaphysical and empirical at the same time, a product of a kundalini awakening. Over time, one moves gradually from the physical to a greater understanding of the metaphysical, but it takes time, lots of time.

It's like climbing a mountain. Can you describe the mountaintop before you've seen it? Not likely; the climb takes time.

You can waste a lot of energy wondering about what the top of the mountain is like. Better to spend the energy on getting there.

Once you are there — at the figurative mountaintop — you can apply the same observational, scientific principles to your metaphysical experiences as a scientist applies to a laboratory experiment. You may even add a dash of poetic expression, elaborate on its mystical aspects. You are transformed.

Nevertheless, one term that does need a new casing is kundalini. Not that it's a bad or inadequate term; it's connotations are too varied. Is it a cult, some people wonder? An ancient religion? An Indian anatomical term? A biological actuality? Something I don't need to know about? Something I should avoid because it's scary? An imaginary force? An actual energy center in the body? A chakra? A nerve? A spiritual practice? An esoteric teaching? A holy scripture? Or all of the above?

Unlike terms such as meditation, enlightenment, consciousness, kundalini cannot be easily visualized. Mention meditation and you get an across-the-board instant mental picture of its meaning and context. Mention kundalini and you get all sorts of vague connotations.

Until we come up with a -tion, -ment, or -ness term for kundalini, the confusion will continue. Problem is, there just doesn't seem to be a better term at the moment — a situation epitomized by a book like *The Secret of the Golden Flower*, which is all about raising kundalini, but never mentions the word.

It's all about spiritual transformation. And yet, the labels keep us apart. We share this goal of transformation — and yet the labels separate us, classify us, make us suspicious of one another.

The new-age spiritual marketplace can't keep up with itself. A new teaching appears; the author tweaks the labels; cobbles together terms from several traditions; adds a few new terms of his own, et voilà, a new sensation is born. Three weeks to enlightenment! New and improved! Tell your friends!

"Readers will also find themselves faced with differences in the way various teachers language their teachings and discrepancies in the way that each approaches this subject. In some cases, it is simply a matter of terminology (e.g., one teacher uses 'enlightenment,' another 'liberation'; one talks about the 'self' being the ultimate, while another talks about the 'self' as the ego)."
- *Halfway Up the Mountain* - Mariana Caplan, Hohm Press, 1999.

There are many teachings out there. It's hard to keep score in this new-agey environment. The only thing that matters — besides the labels — are the teachings that work and the teachings that don't work. And the teachings that work for one individual, but not for another, and so on...

If we were material scientists, we'd be using the scientific method to verify each and every teaching that comes along. The ones that didn't work wouldn't last long. I can't verify any teachings other than the ones I've tried myself, namely Raw Foods and Golden Flower Meditation.

But who says the scientific method can't be used to verify the workability, the feasibility, the viability of a metaphysical system? Who says the scientific method doesn't apply to the metaphysical world in the same manner it apples to the physical world?

Can I verify all the teachings out there? No, I can only verify the ones I've worked with in the laboratory of my own body. That's where the verification process takes place. Did you think it took place in a university? That you could learn it out of book, take an exam, and get extra credit? You have to do! As Bruce Lee said, "Knowing is not enough; we must apply. Willing is not enough; we must do." Of course, before I found Golden Flower Meditation, I tried various systems. I gave them a chance, and when they didn't work for me, I moved on.

If you're truly interested in exploring the metaphysical, forget about Terminology and Labels and just practice.

"Keep away from people who try to belittle your ambitions. Small people always do that, but the really great make you feel that you, too, can become great."
~Mark Twain

Open Letter To Dr. Oz

This letter was sent Tuesday, January 29, 2013. To this day, no response has been received:

Lisa & Mehmet Oz,

I'm sure you've heard of kundalini. But do you understand its purpose? I ask because my kundalini experience has deep, biological healing implications. I've written about it in *Deciphering the Golden Flower One Secret at a Time.*

I realize you get a lot of submissions, don't have time to pursue all of them. I understand that you take a lot of heat for offering alternative healing strategies, related to unproven supernatural beliefs. Kundalini is not a belief system; it's biological fact. Google kundalini and you will be submerged by a tidal wave of accounts, anecdotal, yes, but alike in so many ways, it's impossible to discount them.

This energy (kundalini) has been active 24/7 since that day over forty years ago. What's more, from that day to this time, it has labored to restore my body to its state before my accident. Not the gone-awry body of a seven-year-old; the symmetrical body I would have grown into had the accident never taken place.

When I talk to doctors about this, their eyes glaze over, but I bring the story to your attention, however, because this week's The New Yorker article leads me to believe there might be just enough interest for your organization to pursue it.

So why is this important for medical science? Suppose you accept my account, that the kundalini energy has been able to reconstruct my body, to restore it to its planned original, perfect state, with all its talents, as if the accident never occurred. If this is true, where did the plans/blueprints for my perfect body reside from the age of seven (my accident) to thirty (started meditation)? In some ethereal computer memory-like storage? In DNA? In some metaphysical compartment associated with my being?

Shouldn't science explore this, wonder if there are blueprints for our incarnation? That these plans remain associated with us despite deformation or illness? That kundalini energy can access these blueprints and then use the nervous system to convey healing energy to affected areas? That this work continues until completed? That our bodies hold extraordinary energies, little known, little appreciated by science because we only have anecdotal accounts like mine that cannot be verified by scientific methods at this time?

That's my story. As soon as the kundalini became active, it started to restore my body according to its blueprint. Anecdotal or not, I know this to be true because I've lived it. At first I couldn't believe it, but after 40 years of observing it at work in the laboratory of my own body, I now do.

Is Kundalini Worth It?

The Kundalini Consortium blog and hundreds like it, many books, websites, symposiums, and gatherings focus on the topic of kundalini. To what avail? What sort of impact is the discussion and buzz around this topic having on society at large, if any?

What does "worth it" mean in relation to a topic like kundalini? What kind of value can be placed on it? A monetary value? Another kind of value? Religious? Spiritual? Educational? Ontological? Philosophical? Biological? Esoteric? Evolutionary? Sociological? Medical? Metaphysical?

What if there was no such thing as kundalini? What if there was no such thing as Major League Baseball or the National Football League? No such thing as banks? Life insurance? Museums? Libraries? Could we do without them?

Could we do without gardens? I don't think so. Food to perpetuate life is an essential, not only for the present population, but for the future of humanity.

And what about the others? Are any of them necessities?

Tomorrow is Sunday. Suppose there were no NFL games? Could we survive? No NFL, no banks, no insurance, no TV, no museums or libraries — we'd still be here on Monday.

No kundalini, however, and come Monday, life on earth would start grinding to a halt? Why you ask would something that I've never heard of have such a profound impact? An impact similar to the disappearance of food, say.

Quite simply, although kundalini works behind the scene, so to speak, and is not yet widely known by most of the world's population, it is not only the driving force behind evolution, it is responsible for each and every person's — whether alive today or in the future — unique incarnation. What does the term incarnation mean exactly? In this context, it means the formation of your body from the moment of insemination to the moment of your birth. It's why no two people look alike, why they don't behave the same way — eat or dress alike.

It is not a belief system; it's biological fact: do away with kundalini and you do away with humanity. In one fell swoop we're back to the dawn of evolution. How can this be true? Well, as our bodies take shape in the womb from one day to the next, something has to be responsible for the embodiment — from embryo to fetus to full-grown individual — process. And while scientists don't know what it is, people who have succeeded in raising kundalini do. They understand that evolution, as well as the formation of living organisms, is powered by kundalini energy. Kundalini exists for a purpose.

If it didn't serve a purpose, evolution would have eliminated it. That's how evolution works; it gets rid of unnecessary traits or functions.

"The Indian mystic Osho said, when the quantum physicists, with their new methods, went from the world of matter to the subatomic world, they went - without knowing it — from the physical to the etheric plane. According to Osho, if you go deep in the physical body to the microcosmic level, there is a more subtle electrical body called the etheric body. The etheric body is sort of a blueprint of the physical body. In the etheric body, also called the emotional body, feelings, sensations and thoughts exist as waves while they exist as particles in the physical body. At a certain level of attention, the waves and wave packets at the etheric level collapse into particles at the physical level. This is, of course, a quantum mechanical process."[89]

Like food, kundalini is one of the essentials in the biological chain. So, yes, kundalini has an underlying, essential evolutionary purpose. But, that said, do people have to know about it? Can't we prosper and lead a merry 'ole life, just by having it run in the background like an App on your smart phone that counts the number of steps you take everyday?

That may have been true in the past. Kundalini (as *Prana Shakti*) could just toil away in the background maintaining autonomic functions, but today our survival is in doubt. Faced with so many threats (environmental, mass migrations, war, terrorism, racism, hunger, disease, economic collapse, corporate greed) our continued existence is imperiled. We must take an active role in evolution. And that, perhaps, is why so many books and blogs on spiritual topics are being written today...because biological processes like *Kundalini Shakti*, that were formerly unknown or ignored, are beginning to be recognized as essential to our survival: the evolutionary impulse is serving them up to us on a conscious, elemental level.

"Unfortunately, most human beings are not plugged in. They are trying to generate their own power. So they eat five times a day, but still they are tired most of the time. It is a struggle to keep life going. Energy is not just in terms of physical energy or activity, energy is in terms of life. Existence is energy, isn't it? The basis of <u>existence</u> is energy. If you know that basis, it is like knowing the

89 ~ Quantum Mechanics and the Etheric Body

foundations of life. If you understand the ways of the energy, you know the whole mechanics of creation. So if you are plugged in, you know what the power is, what it can do and what you can make out of it. You are plugged into an endless source of power – that is what is Kundalini."

- SADHGURU

So, while kundalini has worked behind the scenes throughout human history, because of its importance in the energetics revolution (yoga, meditation, mindfulness, energy cultivation, etc.) now taking place on earth, it is coming to the fore. Its intrinsic value has not changed, but what we know about it and the way we approach it has.

Converging Paths

"How to create intelligence? First become more and more alert in small things. Walking along the road, become more alert, try to be more alert. For such a simple process as walking along the road — you need not have any alertness. You can remain stupid and walk well. That's what everyone is doing. The stupidity does not hinder you at all. Start from small things. Taking your bath, be alert; standing under the shower, become very alert. That cold water falling on you, the body enjoying it... become alert, become conscious to what is happening, be relaxed yet conscious.

"And this moment of consciousness has to be brought in again and again, in a thousand and one ways: eating, talking, meeting a friend, listening to me, meditating, making love. In all situations try to become more and more alert. It is hard, it is certainly difficult, but it is not impossible. Slowly, slowly, the dust will disappear and your mirror-like consciousness will reveal itself; you will become more intelligent."

~ Osho

Self-Remembering and Kundalini

I've witnessed the varying effects of kundalini awakenings on many subjects, including myself. Each experience is unique — from the way kundalini is triggered to the way each individual lives with it. Usually, the most stable experiences are those triggered by meditation. The ones caused by random events or stimuli are often discomforting, and sometimes unstable, in that they come and go. However temporary or unstable, every experience poses challenges because of the variety of psychological, spiritual, and emotional states and conditions the subject find himself in as a result of a kundalini awakening.

I receive many inquiries from people who think that, once awakened, Kundalini will solve all their problems. This is as unrealistic as it is untrue, especially since most of these inquiries come from people who have not yet activated their kundalini. Kundalini, in and of itself, changes the being, but does not necessarily hold forth the prospect of a better design for living. Neither as concerns the purpose of life or the ways and means of living it to the fullest.

First of all, what does living life to the fullest mean? Is it a winning formula for material comfort? A means to spiritual transcendence? A life of contemplation and retreat? Is it a catch phrase for feelings of entitlement, that because the subject has activated kundalini, he or she is suddenly exempt from the stress and strain of everyday existence? Or is it merely the prospect of escape?

In the aftermath of a kundalini awakening, everything seems to converge at once. Yet, although you must come to terms with kundalini in your own way, at the beginning, you will not know what to expect, you will not understand the challenges or the various effects of kundalini. Your first challenge is to become an observer of this newly activated energy in your being, an occupation that takes time. Your mind will attempt to structure and classify, to understand what's going on, how to benefit from it, and how to control it. Over time you will understand it as well as benefit from it, but you must learn to be an astute observer. Second, you can't control it, so don't try. Accept it.

As you observe the effects of kundalini on your being, you will spend a lot of time coping with the physical and emotional changes you observe. Meanwhile, life outside goes on. And as it does, you may not realize that your perspective on material life is actually changing, that the way you've seen things up to the moment of your kundalini awakening — your work, your relationships, your morphology, your feelings, your world view, your priorities, your take on cosmology — has also changed. What used to be important may be less so, and things you never thought about are suddenly foremost in your mind. There is a psychic restructuring as the kundalini prepares you for the future, including modifying your DNA. You are likely to experience a number of new impulses, notions that you could be doing more, that you should be doing more. Feelings of panic, feelings of being overcome, feelings of being possessed, feelings of being misunderstood or abandoned, feelings of isolation.

Frequently, subjects become lost in trying to elaborate some great cosmological design. That's all well and good. Meanwhile, as noted above, life goes on. Not all impulses are meaningful. No matter how lofty your sentiments might be, you aren't obliged to follow up on them. For reasons of character or personality, it simply may not be possible. In spite of kundalini, you are who you are.

> "Master Lü-Tsu said, 'When there is a gradual success in producing the circulation of the light, a man must not give up his ordinary occupation in doing so. The ancients said, When occupations come to us, we must accept them; when things come to us, we must understand them from the ground up.'"
> ~ *The Secret of the Golden Flower* - Lu Yen, Richard Wilhelm, Translator

If you find yourself wanting to heal the sick or run for Congress on an anti-nuclear platform, in spite of the fact that you've never done anything like this before, chalk it up to the over-stimulation kundalini induces. Take your time; don't act impulsively. I'm not saying that if you have a real proclivity or talent for something new that you shouldn't pursue it, you should.

Don't try to do everything at once. It takes time to come to terms with a kundalini condition; it takes time to learn to live with kundalini. So take the time; don't be impatient. One of the secrets of life in the material world is self-control. Because of the on-rushing, all-at-once convergence of new energies, random impulses, and changing perspectives, you may actually become impatient and prone to lose control. Yes, in spite of the tremendous energy flow into your life, you may become impatient with the world and its imperfections.

That's part of living with kundalini, and at the same time, inhabiting a body. If we didn't inhabit bodies, there would be no need for material attachments, negative emotions, war, greed, pride, fear, pain, etc. However, if we live in our bodies with this newly awakened kundalini energy, the world outside may overwhelm us with its pettiness, its selfishness, its foolishness. SO, how do we manage the situation? How do we cohabit with kundalini?

That's where self-remembering comes in. Once you learn to practice it, it works alongside kundalini to temper your frustrations with the world.

> "There are moments when you become aware not only of what you are doing but also of yourself doing it. You see both 'I' and the 'here' of 'I am here'- both the anger and the 'I' that is angry. Call this self-remembering if you like."

~ *Views From the Real World* - G. I. Gurdjieff

How does self-remembering work? In moments of stress or negative emotion, you need to become the silent observer, both an actor in the play of life and an observer who watches how the actor behaves. Gurdjieff called this quality self-remembering; it has since been renamed mindfulness.

Self-remembering brings you back to yourself. What do I mean by "back to yourself?" You've probably heard idiomatic folk sayings like, *He was beside himself* or *She's out of her mind*. There are many sayings like this that denote an altered state of consciousness, a state in which the subject is so totally caught up in negative emotion, over-excitement, or stress that he/she loses control.

Next time you feel caught up, try this simple technique. Tell yourself: I am here now. I am [Bill Jones]. I'm standing here in a line at the bank. There's an argument at the counter. I am here in my body. I do not react to what's happening around me; I simply observe. My name is [Bill]. I am observing myself standing here. As I stand here watching myself, I am in my body, unaffected by the angry exchange taking place.

Immediately, you will feel a warming sensation, just by repeating the words: *I am here now*. I promise you it will feel it — something akin to refocusing a telescope or a camera lens, as you focus from wide to narrow, then from narrow to wide. As you come back to yourself, your focus is both narrow and wide at the same time. Even when it's you at the center of a dispute, you'll learn to step back and observe your behavior in the moment.

This technique controls impulsiveness. There's a lot more to it, of course, but for now try the exercise on pg. 86 of *The Backward-Flowing Method: The Secret of Life and Death*. It consists of exerting control while dreaming — the point being that, if you can control your dreams, how much more control will you be able to exert while awake.

Self-Remembering And Mindfulness

Mindfulness is to Self-Remembering as *The Secret* is to *The Power of Positive Thinking*. Now, what does that mean exactly?

It means that systems of knowledge and their associated practices keep getting updated every so many years, but the denominations (the names they are called by) have to be changed to create enough buzz for the latest iteration to make the top-40, hashtag hit parade.

Take self-remembering, for example. It was mindfulness before the term "mindfulness" passed into the new age lexicon. George Gurdjieff pioneered self-remembering back in the 1930s and 40s. It was a useful system then and it's still useful, even if the mindfulness craze has supplanted it. Both acknowledge a Buddhist influence; both share pretty much the same approach and practice — even if the ends and the means vary. No matter! It's still the same basic concept under a catchy new name:

> "And herein lies my great help; this is the first step in the teaching that Gurdjieff brought from his extensive travels and seekings throughout the Middle East and Asia. He taught that to be mindful, or as he would put it, to 'remember myself' one needs to bring these two parts of myself, the mind and the body, together. The mind watches over the body and observes its functionings and the body is rooted in this present moment, in this present life. Then instead of these two parts going their separate unconnected ways, they can combine and have a relationship, working together towards a common good."

~ Lunatic Outpost Forum

That's what happens in our "Fifteen minutes of fame" culture. Buzz terms attain hit parade levels of notoriety for a brief period. Someone comes along with a slight variation; the current buzz fades with the setting sun to be reborn with the rising sun as its latest iteration.

It happened that way with one of the biggest fads of the 1950s, Dr. Norman Vincent Peale's *The Power of Positive Thinking*, which became *The Secret*, as the same idea was repackaged and sold once again to a new generation...and will probably be sold in some form or other to a another generation at a later date.

Mental Chatter and How to Identify It:

1. Thoughts that repeat themselves like a tape that keeps playing the same tune.
2. Reliving negative past situations or visualizing fears over and over again.
3. Dwelling on the past or fearing the future. This prevents us from enjoying the present. The past is gone, and the future is the product of our present thinking and actions. The only time that exists is now, the present moment.
4. Compulsive inner monologue that disturbs our peace and makes the mind busy.
5. Never being here. Always thinking on something else, instead of what we are doing now. If we always think on something else we never enjoy the moment.
6. Constant analysis of our and other people's situations, reactions and behavior. Analyzing the past, the future, things we need or want to do, our day, yesterday and the distant past.
7. Almost all involuntary thinking and daydreaming are some sort of mental noise. This is often a constant background noise, which often intrudes into foreground in the middle of everything we do.

So what does Mindfulness have to do with kundalini? How are they related? Once kundalini awakens, there's a gradual expansion of consciousness. I'm not referring to ecstatic, visionary experiences, which, although they certainly do occur, act only as mile markers on the long road to a more developed higher consciousness. In most cases, they are not the "real thing," merely indicators of a greater awareness to come. As kundalini slowly expands consciousness, it also overhauls the rational capabilities of the mind — two separate operations, two different types of consciousness:

"Knowledge proceeds through what Buddha called the five skandhas or Aggregates, which includes sensual perceptions and conditioned experience by way of the psyche or personal consciousness. To know is to comprehend noologically, through intellect-based thought.

"Gnowledge is to understand through metasensory awareness and unconditioned experience through the thymos or impersonal consciousness. To gnow is to understand by way of gnosis or Right Discernment, the gnowledge that Siddhartha Gautama, the 'Sage of the Shakyas,' implied when he said, 'Be a Lamp unto Thyself.'"

~ Science and Spirituality – Ve Marco, Science & Spirituality FB Group Post

As "gnowledge" (the gnostic approach to human ontology/cosmology) expands, mindfulness becomes an autonomic by-product. Our attention turns inward; we are able to recognize our programming and we begin to resist it. It doesn't happen overnight. Some of our programs — the most tenacious and unshakable — are those passed down to us by our parents. Tics, habits, idiosyncrasies — these are the hardest to recognize because they're part of our genes. We may recognize them, but we have trouble overwriting them until our awakened kundalini induces an anatomical, somatic, and metabolic shift. Gradually, we become aware of the programs that "run us" and, with a mindful attention, we overwrite them. When kundalini awakens properly, mindfulness is an autonomic offshoot.

Unfortunately, terminology prevents the various strains of mindfulness or self-remembering from joining forces and cooperating. Each tendency or path is so possessive of their own little piece of the pie. Too bad. Mindfulness has been around in various avatars or incarnations for a very long while, appreciated by many traditional as well as gnostic faiths. Witness these thoughts, borrowed from an Orthodox Christian website:

"Watchfulness is the action to guard us from our automatic reactions to thoughts stimulated by our senses. It is being attentive to your inner self. The Greek word that is translated as watchfulness is 'Nepsis'. It comes from 'nepho,' which means to guard, inspect, examine, watch over and keep under surveillance. Watchfulness has been described by Elder Ephriam of Philotheou as 'the ax which shatters the large trees, hitting their roots. When the root is struck, it doesn't spring up again.'

"Saint Hesychios sees watchfulness as follows: 'Watchfulness is a continual fixing and halting of thought at the entrance to the heart... If we are conscientious in this, we can gain much experience and knowledge of spiritual warfare.'

"He shows us that this involves an effort to intercede on our thoughts, forcing them to be examined, to shine the commandments of our Lord on them. He emphasizes the importance of this by calling it warfare. We know in warfare we need to have effective weapons that are stronger than those of the enemy."

‑ "Ten Point Program For Orthodox Life: Being Watchful"

Does Mindfulness need kundalini? Must an individual activate kundalini in order to practice Mindfulness? No, but in most cases, kundalini effects a shortcut to a meaningful practice of mindfulness. Whether the term applied is mindfulness, watchfulness, self-remembering, or some past or future avatar, mindfulness and kundalini work together, albeit from different angles, to shape and influence the awakening process.

The coupling of mindfulness and kundalini is a nice way to end this book because it foreshadows the fact that the work is never finished. Kundalini awakened? Fine…but there's more to do, much more, and if there's a practice with more relevance to living a fruitful, empathetic life than mindfulness, I can't think of one.

OTHER LIFE FORCE BOOKS TITLES

Deciphering the Golden Flower One Secret at a Time
JJ Semple - Life Force Books, 2007

Curiosity and circumstance often propel individuals beyond the confines of their upbringing, dumping them into unfamiliar, unexpected life situations. Thus was JJ Semple transported into a trial-and-error process of self-discovery along a path that took him from the Eastern Brahmin establishment, to France, to a meeting with Gopi Krishna in India, and back to the USA. What he found along the way was Kundalini, the biological basis of both science and religion. This memoir describes how the author used *The Secret of the Golden Flower* to activate his Kundalini and reverse the effects of a childhood accident.

The Secret of the Golden Flower: A Kundalini Meditation Method
JJ Semple - Life Force Books, 2018

Since the publication of *Deciphering the Golden Flower One Secret at a Time* in 2008, readers have asked for an in-depth guidebook on using *The Secret of the Golden Flower* (SGF) to awaken kundalini in the manner, and with the same results, as those described in JJ Semple's memoir. *The Secret of the Golden Flower: A Kundalini Meditation Method* is that book, a much-anticipated companion guide to the SGF as well as a sequel to Semple's autobiographical kundalini memoir.

The Backward-Flowing Method
JJ Semple - Life Force Books, 2008

For the first time ever, a book dares to reveal the secrets of the world's most influential meditation method – a series of techniques originally compiled in the 9th. Century masterpiece of Chinese alchemy, *The Secret of the Golden Flower*. One-by-one, the author reveals the techniques behind these meditation secrets, providing clear instructions on how to use them.

The Biology of Consciousness: Case Studies in Kundalini

JJ Semple - Life Force Books, 2014

An evidence-based examination on whether consciousness "ex_sts" after death. JJ Semple explores a revolutionary hypothesis: that an active Kundalini is capable of modifying an individual's DNA and then passing the beneficial mutations on to future generations. Not only are these helpful mutations passed along to future generations, the individual retains these Kundalini-induced characteristics and incorporates them into his/her next worldly incarnation.

Female Kundalini

Margaret Miranda Dempsey - Life Force Books, 2014

"When I was first told to let my experience go – to not allow myself to become absorbed by it or to let it disturb my everyday, normal life – I was reluctant to do this. I felt that something special had happened and I didn't want to forget about it or let it go. It is only now, so many years later, that I understand why it is essential to let this kind of experience go."

Seminal Retention and Higher Consciousness: The Sexology of Kundalini

JJ Semple - Life Force Books, 2014

In the East, semen conservation is recognized as a prerequisite for success in practices that lead to activating Kundalini. The thought is that sooner or later, as one matures, an individual might want to practice energy cultivation techniques such as meditation, mindfulness, yoga, and Tai Chi in order to expand consciousness.

Available at online stores and at bookshops
throughout the world, in Print and eBook formats.

www.ingramcontent.com/pod-product-compliance
Lightning Source LLC
Chambersburg PA
CBHW021042090426
42738CB00006B/150